Monsters From The Id

Monsters From The Id

A Study of Emotional Deprivation and Its Impact On Society

John L. Cooper

Authors Choice Press

San Jose New York Lincoln Shanghai

Monsters From The Id
A Study of Emotional Deprivation and Its Impact On Society

Authors Choice Press
an imprint of iUniverse.com, Inc.

For information address:
iUniverse.com, Inc.
5220 S 16th, Ste. 200
Lincoln, NE 68512
www.iuniverse.com

ISBN: 0-595-18044-2

Printed in the United States of America

CONTENTS

PREFACE

"Morbius was too close to the problem.
The Krell had completed the project.
Big machine, no instrumentalities, true creation.
But the Krell forgot one thing.
Monsters, John…
MONSTERS FROM THE ID!"

Wilcox, F.M. (Director). (1956).
Forbidden Planet (Film)
Hollywood: Metro-Goldwyn-Mayer Motion Pictures

INTRODUCTION

Look about you, and what do you see? You see an American society that has become a self-destructive social system. No, I am not kidding, and if you have any doubts, the evidence can be seen in the general behavior of the people. They are filled with anger and frustration, which causes them to express a great deal of aggression and violence towards one another. It can even be said that Americans are insensitive to their own humanity; and for many of them, murder has become just another blood sport. But, what is most shocking, and even frightening, is the fact that our children are becoming an endangered species.

What has caused the American social system to become so vile? No society was supposed to function this way; and in humanistic terms, it is not normal. To be sure, this situation has created massive psychological and emotional problems for the people, and the problems cut across all segments of society and class lines. The rich and the poor are suffering similarly. Cloudiness fills the minds of them all. The people are confused. What has brought this social enigma down on their heads? What is behind this mystery?

To answer the question from above, I must first say that it should never have been asked because there really is no mystery here to be solved. To speak of a mystery is to speak of something unknown. But are we unknowns? Do *you* feel like a mystery? I think not. Nevertheless, there is a definite answer that can be given to the question, and it is the following. Behind the mystery is the maker of monsters: emotional deprivation. Therefore, it is the purpose of this book to discuss and explain the phenomenon of emotional deprivation and its impact on society.

In detail, the phenomenon will be traced from its beginning in the family with its effect upon the male and female child, and its ultimate influence on the adult relationships of men and women as parents and romantic lovers. In particular, attention will be given to two very important, recent social events, Women's Liberation and the sexual revolution that began in the 1960s. These events are important because the modern feminists tried to use both these social forces to overcome the suffering they experienced from emotional deprivation.

In studying our phenomenon, we want to specifically know how it causes us to become filled with anger and frustration? And, it should come as no surprise that we can get our first clue from Sigmund Freud. In his book, *Civilization and Its Discontents*, he said that society by its very nature generates frustrations in people since it suppresses basic impulses and restricts individual freedoms. He was referring to the need of society to socialize its members, and thereby force them to repress their innate selves in favor of playing social roles. This is done because society wants all its members to conform to its traditional norms. But, the innate self is the possessor of the true individual character of every human being. It is what we were born to be, and it sets each one of us apart from every other person on earth. But most importantly, by its own nature, it will resist conformity.

When the innate self is repressed, it is forced into the unconsciousness of the mind, or into the id. Freud believed we were born with the id, and it drives us to seek immediate gratification, pleasure over pain, and the expression of our uniqueness as a distinct individual. Because of the power of the id, the innate self will oppose that which represses it. In this case, society is responsible with its socialization and conformity. As a consequence, the innate self becomes embroiled in a struggle for survival, in which society can be perceived as an adversary, if not an enemy; and with the support of the psyche, the innate self sends forth monsters from the id to do battle with the social system in effort to save itself.

Throughout this book, the term *monsters from the id* is used as a metaphor to depict the variety of struggles that are going on between individuals and society as the self tries to prevent being displaced, gobbled up, or eliminated by conformity. These struggles range from battles between minds to outright murder. And to be sure, the use of the metaphor is not to imply that there are no real monsters afoot in America. They are here: the Charles Mansons, the Theordore Bundys, and the Jeffrey Dahmers. Over the years, social scientists have not given much consideration to Freud's comment on the nature of society, but it may well be one of the most insightful, if not prophetic, observations he ever made. For one thing, it implies that there is something nefarious going on with society; and we may wonder, what might that be? We have been taught that the social system serves our needs; and it gives us, as individuals and as a group, a better chance to survive from one generation to the next. But, Freud's admonition suggests that something else might be happening. There is even a hint that society maybe working against our best interest; and if so, then society would be a threat to our long-term survival.

What a brash conclusion, and is it an exaggeration? Perhaps. But I would not be so quick to make that judgment. A brief survey of the dysfunctional nature of American society certainly tells us that the system is beset by some very serious social problems. There is our ongoing struggle with racism and sexism. We have a political system that purports to be democratic, but a closer examination indicates that it operates more like a corporate oligarchy that serves a privileged elite at the top of a social hierarchy. And, America has a capitalist economy that is based on profit making which requires the exploitation of workers and consumers. Moreover, Americans love guns, and they like to use them on each other. And, if we add to the situation the self-destructive behaviors of drug and alcohol abuse, and promiscuous sex during a time of the AIDS crisis, we then have an American society that seems, in the overall, to be less than positive and wholesome.

If our society abides by all these negative forces, can we say that it is functioning in the best interest of its people? I think not. For instance, there is just too much violence at all levels of the system, and such widespread violence certainly tells us that we are an aggressive group of people. Where does all of this aggression come from? Psychologists know that when people are frustrated they become angry, and anger often leads to aggressive behavior. Therefore, if Freud is correct about society generating frustration, then society may also be a primary source for causing us to exhibit aggression, aggression that maybe the basis for much of the violence that is being committed.

Frustration may also be the basis for most of the social problems in our society; and it leads me to ask: specifically how is this society causing its people to feel frustrated? Obviously, whatever the cause, it must be fundamental to the social system. In fact, all indicators suggest that it begins in the most important institution of our society: the family, and this should come as no surprise because the family is the alpha of all things social.

In America, we have an entire population of people who suffer from emotional deprivation. Consequently, we have a society of frustrated, angry, aggressive people with a potential, if not penchant, for violence. This potential has created a reservoir of free-floating aggression, as expressed by John Dollard,[1] which is available for the individual to tap into at any time. Violence is even likeable in our society.

Free-floating aggression refers to a society that nurtures and sustains an atmosphere of aggression. This atmosphere exists because Americans use aggression as a standard means for solving problems. Verbal assaults, physical abuse, and various types of weaponry are commonly used to settle differences. Through television and motion pictures, the entertainment industry and law enforcement, we are constantly exposed to images of aggressive behavior and the justification for its use. There is an air of social legitimacy about it, and anyone can rationalize the use of aggression to solve his problems because it is normative behavior in our society. Aggressive behavior is also suitable to our social credo of individualism, and it is consistent with the notion of competitiveness that is exampled by our capitalist economy and our sports industries in particular. Again, I am speaking metaphorically when I say there is a reservoir of free-floating aggression in society. The point must be made that it is not a physical thing, but an attitude, a belief that is in our heads. The belief says that it is all right to be aggressive towards others. It's a natural, American trait.

Unfortunately, aggressive behavior among members of society produces a destabilizing element. Violent behavior between societal members can become a force that could destroy the system, and some social scientists believe that such a threat is already at hand. So, let us stop kidding ourselves. The American society is in deep, deep trouble, and we know it. Indeed, matters are quite desperate, but the social cheer leaders, the politicians, the pundits, the capitalists, the sycophantic entertainers and sports figures, are not about to admit that there is something quite disturbing at the cultural core of our society. However, it cannot be denied that there is a malaise that is spewing over the social landscape like water over Niagara Falls, and as Americans look with great anticipation to the new millennium, it is becoming clearer that we live in a socially sick society.

What is the basis for this sickness? If we listen to the explainers, those who would rationalize the situation, and the people who understand nothing but their own taken-for-granted attitudes, they give us ready made diagnoses for all our social ills. They do not speak of emotional deprivation because they are in the business of reassuring the public, and their efforts amount to little more than politically expedient commentaries. But when we do look closer at their diagnoses, it does not tell us much. It seems we have been given prognosis without first knowing the definition of the social disease.

However, there is no mystery here, either. The disease that is chewing up American society is violence, and it has its roots in emotional deprivation. We need to understand this dynamic if we are going to have any chance of coming up with a realistic, meaningful solution to our problems. In any case, reaching some answers will not be easy. Consider this, if the disease is social, then we are both victim and purveyor of it. Moreover, to further exacerbate the problem, we live in a bureaucratic world today, and we are training ourselves to think more and more like computers. We now categorize our social ills by code names and deviant traits. This allows us to give a measured focus to them, and then we can put them away in our brain files. That is very much what we use our minds for today. They are simply filing cabinets to store useless data from the worldwide net. The more information we store in our filing cabinets, the less common sense we seem to have. As a result, our society has become a conundrum that we cannot understand.

Because our filing cabinet brains have too much useless information stored in them, most Americans are not consciously aware of the scenario of frustration leading to aggression that gives way to violence. Nevertheless, it was violence that gave birth to America, and the activeness of violence has sustained this society for the last four hundred years. When the Europeans first came to America they used violence to crush the Native Americans, and later they used it to enslave African people. Then the colonialists fought the Revolutionary War that gave them independence from England, and we as a people have glorified the violence of war ever since.

As well, we have a gun culture in America that guarantees that the murder rate in the United States will remain the highest among all the countries in the industrialized world, and one of the most unsettling things about this is the fact that the supreme law of the land gives sanction to the right of private citizens to own guns in a fashion of the old Wild West. The Second Amendment to U.S. Constitution says that individuals have the right to keep and bear arms. That clause was written to support a militia, and there is no need for it today. But Americans still want the right to own and carry guns. Presently, what the Second Amendment does is legitimize gun violence; and in turn, the existence of the gun culture gives support to the reservoir of free-floating aggression.

Violence is easily recognizable in war, as criminal behavior, and certainly when it comes to murder. But the malaise of our society bespeaks of more subtle forms of violence, forms that are up close and personal to us all. Violence, as I use it here, can be acts of commission and omission. It can be of a physical, psychological, or emotional nature, but the commonality is in the violation of another person's rights, sensibilities, and humanity. To dehumanize another person is one of the worse acts of violence anyone can commit; and remember, we are both the victim and the purveyor in this situation. Therefore, we are also prone to commit these acts of violence against ourselves, and this causes us to function collectively very much as a self-defeating, self-destructive force. At the same time, violence is indicative of a feeling of alienation and spiritual emptiness that is an outgrowth of emotional deprivation.

As we end the twentieth century, spiritual emptiness seems to be the cultural signature of the young people of this generation. They seem to be suffering more severely from emotional deprivation than any other Americans in the past. What could be the reason for this? The average American youth today lives in a middle-class community, and he probably has the highest standard of living for a nonproductive person in the history of western society. Yet, he is very emotionally troubled. Why?

In a very interesting book, *Understanding Media: The Extensions of Man,*[2] Marshall McLuhan said that in the modern world, people would return to a tribal society, and for informational purposes they would stop depending upon the written word. The children of this era, raised in an electronic age, would have a new kind of social consciousness that would be different than the minds of previous generations. Astonishingly, McLuhan's commentary seems to be more prophetic than Freud's. His prediction has come to past. The young people of the nineties are of a vastly altered consciousness than their parents and grandparents. They have grown up psychologically wired to machines. Most of their social stimulation and nurturing has come from electronic devices, and the importance of direct human contact in their lives has been greatly diminished.

The average American youth grows up watching television for entertainment and information purposes. He probably communicates as much, if not more so, with his peers over telephone lines, cellular phones, and with E-mail. He is sure to have a CD Walkman, audio and videotape recorders. And, he is very likely to be familiar with computer generated, electronic games. He will also be a big fan of Hollywood action movies;

and as to sports, most youngsters watch more of it on TV than they actually play themselves. This suggests that all too many young people today
are living vicarious lifestyles, in the shadow of media heroes. Such an attitude and proclivities lends itself to imitating, copycatting, hero-worshipping, and probably delusions of grandeur. To be sure, a young person of
the electronic age can feel that he is psychologically and emotionally wired
up to the characters on the motion picture, TV screens, and virtual reality
people in his electronic games. These are his role models, and the status of
the screen hero is thought to be transferable to him. If a child grows up
with a weak sense of self; that is, low sense self-esteem, then he will be
more susceptible to a vicarious type of lifestyle.

It was Confucius who said that a picture is worth a thousand words. I
wonder how many western thinkers have actually tried to understand
what that really means in terms of how human beings take in information.
It means that the information is presented to the person in pictorial or col-
lage form as bursts of imagery and energy. Taking information in pictorially has quite a different effect upon the brain and consciousness than if
one were reading words. The letters of the alphabet are arbitrary symbols
that a reader must learn to interpret in a certain pattern in order to get
them to make words. There is no certain pattern to pictorial information.
It just comes at you in one full swipe, and the eyes have to take it in whole.
Reading can then give the consciousness an orderly process for taking in
information. By its very nature, the intake of pictorial information can
bring confusion, if not chaos, to the consciousness.

Given our reliance upon television for the gathering, communicating, and
the sharing of information, there is little doubt that the intake of pictorial
information has overtaken the written word, and this is what Marshall
McLuhan was talking about when he said that the "Medium is the message."
All Americans, young and old, have been affected by this phenomenon, but
we see it more clearly in the present generation because they really have
known no alternative. Electronics have been a major feature of their lives
since they first started walking and talking. The dolls and action figures they

played with came right off of the movie and television screens. Using these action figures was a subtle form of interactive video play.

When we talk about pictures today, we are talking about motion pictures, action pictures. Hollywood studios brought motion pictures to the theaters, but it was television that brought it into the home and institutionalized it as a part of every American's daily life. Hollywood gave us fictional story lines and dramas, but TV gave us real life action in the hard news and documentaries. And the information wasn't coming to us in the somewhat stilted form of the written word in newspapers, magazines, or books. It was coming at us in living form and as action. Even if it was just Walter Cronkite or Dan Rather reading the news off of a teleprompter, there was always a human face and voice giving life to the written word through articulation.

We have been told that we now live in the Information Age, and I would stress that the information is largely coming to us in the form of action. Our reception of all this pictorial information can only serve to rev up our emotional engines. For the young people who have been impacted by this Age all of their lives, they probably feel as though they are wired into a perpetual action mode. Add to this the fact that our society is a highly mobile system. Our people are constantly on the go crisscrossing the continent, and indeed the world, in cars, buses, recreation vehicles, trains, airplanes, and ships. And we live in a culture that praises youthfulness and beauty. If you want to fit in, then you must stay active. Join a health club, become a runner, diet and take the weight off. You must be doing something to keep yourself young and healthy, even if it is just running in place. Personal actions of this type also help to keep our emotional engines revved up, and the forces of our electronic, machine oriented society keeps the pressure on us to stay active.

Generally speaking, the action mode that pervades the collective consciousness of Americans is indicative of a vicarious lifestyle that lends itself to copycatting and delusions of grandeur. This is a prescription for aggressive behavior; and as such, it can lead to violence. Hollywood motion pictures have always been an action medium, and violence is a staple of motion pictures. On TV, violence is used constantly in present-ing both news and dramatic shows. Since motion pictures and TV are the chief dispensers of entertainment and information today, violence has become one of the major forces of communications for the American people, and to some extent, for all the people around the globe who participate in the entertainment media of the western world.

Violence is institutionalized in American society, and it is embedded in the basic structure of the social system. This is clearly indicated by two major negative forces in this country. They are racism and sexism. Notwithstanding all the civil rights and sexual harassment laws that have been passed by the government in the last forty years, social inequality between the races, men and women, is still very much with us. As the modern feminist would say, this is the white male's world, and blacks, women, and other minorities are allowed to live in it by their sufferance. White males, by and large, make the laws, and they more than anyone else dominate and control almost all of our major institutions. There can be no social dialogue without their imprint on it.

There is one thing in particular that is significant about racism and sexism. Both embody all the aspects of violence that attempts to dehu-manize a person. It is the express purpose of racism and sexism to deny individuals their rights, their normal sensibilities, and their humanity. This kind of violent communications is so common and flagrant in our society; it has come to be called institutional racism and institutional sexism. And society has adopted soft, everyday words to mask their true purposes. We speak of prejudice, discrimination, and bigotry, but these are just cover words for the commission of violence.

Capitalism involves us in yet another masquerade. Social inequity is blatant in a capitalist economy, and there is no misunderstanding about the dedicated purposes of such an economic system. It exists for profit making, and as Karl Marx pointed out more than a century ago, you can-not have profit making without exploitation. This truth hides behind a bogus idea of free competition in an open market system. However, the system encourages a dog eat dog economy where the law of the jungle prevails. This is social Darwinism, the survival of the fittest.

To the archcapitalist, profit making is the most meaningful thing in the entire world, and making money is the sole purpose of his productive life. He will strive mightily for it, and he can feel compelled to do almost anything to accumulate it, slight of hand, lie, cheat, and steal. To this extent, money is absolutely more important to him than the people who generate it: his workers and the consumers. By exploiting them, the capitalist is dehumanizing them. This too, is a form of violence. Our society gives strong support to capitalistic beliefs and behaviors, and we are encouraged to use capitalism to overcome our spiritual emptiness. In profit making, the individual can gain wealth, power, and status that can lead to hedonistic, material rewards. Such pleasures, we are told, will take away our feelings of emotional deprivation. But in the end, the old axiom holds. Money cannot buy happiness, and it can't buy you love.

Nevertheless, the capitalist, economic philosophy pervades every aspect of our social system, and because that philosophy is based on the law of the jungle, it encourages the use of violence. Every institution has been effected and debased by it, and we can see this in a particularly gross fashion in the sports and entertainment industries. In these two industries, the focus is on the individual player or actor, and we see the violence exploding as raw human emotions. Another point is that these industries are also very compatible with our present vicarious lifestyles. And, because the players and actors are media figures, we can feel electronically connected to them. They seem to communicate directly to us as role models, and this enhances our desire to worship them as heroes. As a consequence, these thespians and sports personalities, on screen, stage, and ball field are defining the character of the world we live in, the quality of it, and the morality of it. They are the true teachers of America's values today. It is no longer art imitating reality, but reality is imitating art. And our top sports personalities have assumed the lofty position of demigods. Today, TV sports have become a mania. It is primetime, living room, mass entertainment, and it helps to keep our action mode in hyper gear.

The debilitating process of emotional deprivation has been accelerating in the last two to three decades. This seems to be a function of the Electronic Age. Young people, who have been nurtured by electronic devices, seem to have trouble establishing a true sense of self, and they are being influenced by a developing collective consciousness that is dependent upon free-floating aggression. This aggression is invigorated by their vicarious lifestyles, and it constitutes the basis for random acts of violence. There are still gang fights, turf wars, and drive-by shootings that occur frequently in the inner cities. But, in the suburbs and Middle American towns, there are also skinheads and the black-coat mafia groups that threaten and terrorize young and old people alike. And recently, schools have become killing grounds as angry students, with pistols, rifles and bombs, have turned on their peers.

To be sure, our society has become weighted down with generalized, everyday violence, and some of these acts have become so common and tolerable, we no longer recognize them as forms of violence. Racism and sexism have been mentioned, but there is also exploitation of the masses by profit making corporations and government policies that favor the rich elite and by contrast punish poor people. There is the disregard of the needs of the mentally ill and homeless people, and the overall perpetuation of unemployment and poverty in minority neighborhoods due to de facto segregation. These actions are taken for granted, and it is only the most outrageous, egregious forms of violence that get our attention. This tells us that there is a new social attitude that is undercutting the moral fabric of society, and this present generation seems to be in the vanguard that is bringing about this change. The presences of free-floating aggression is producing a large group of individuals who seem to function without a moral compass.

What could this possibly mean? Emotional deprivation, and its violent outcome, maybe leading us down a devastating social path. Like sheep, we are being led to the slaughter, and the leader of the pack is each one of us. We are the victim and the perpetrator. We are in control of this out of controlled society, and there are no surprises for us. Examples of where this devastating social path might be leading us are right before our eyes. All we have to do is look at it, analyze it, and try to understand it. Following McLuhan's premonition, there are primarily two American institutions that are laying out the agenda for our future generalize, social behavior. They are the motion picture and sports industries. Study the present course of these two industries and it will become perfectly clear where emotional deprivation is leading us. Therefore, in coming chapters, we will take a long, hard look at the two of them.

Consider this: why is so much of the violence today focused on women? And, why are women so distrustful of, and violent towards, themselves? Maybe there is no one answer to these questions, but whatever is the cause for all the violence in society, women seem to be at the center of it. Is this coincidental or something else? This is not to say that women are the perpetrators of most of the violence. No, they are not. They are more often the victims of it, but it still begs the question, why is so much of the violence focused on them?

Think about the following. A boyfriend or husband beats a woman every 12 seconds a day. Approximately 2 1/2 million women are battered each year. Over a dozen women face a rapist every hour. America has the highest rate of rape in the western world, and 3 out of every 4 women will be a victim of a violent crime during their lifetime. And, one of the most dangerous things any American woman can do is get married. What are we to make of all of this? There is one thing that can be said about it. Women in this society are in desperate straights, and matters are getting worse.

Women are the core element of any society because they are our human progenitors. Without them, there can be no society now or especially in the future. They must produce the babies that become the people that populate the system. No people. No society. This is axiomatic. Therefore, women should be held in the highest regard within any society, and they should be given the support and respect due to them as the social forbear-ers of us all. Society was inaugurated for the purpose of maximizing our species survival chances. That means, above all else, society should provide for the well being of women and their offspring. The best societies will do this because that is how social systems better their chances for survival from one generation to the next.

However, given the violence that confronts them, American women are not being treated with the respect and dignity they deserve; and since women are the bedrock of any society, ill treatment of them has negative ramifications through the entire social structure. To be sure, this is exactly what we see, violence from the bedroom to the board room, from the ghetto to the suburbs; among the rich and poor, the black and the white, the sane and the uptight. Everyone is getting into the act.

Yes, violence is used to hurt people, but in America it has other purposes as well. We do use it as a major form of communications, and that is why it is so prevalent in the motion pictures and sports industries. This being the case, it means that these two institutions will become ever more influential in our society. Moreover, they can give us some specific ideas as to where emotional deprivation is leading us; and if my analysis is correct, emotional deprivation is leading us back to a more primal state of consciousness. The evidence of this will be shown in both real and symbolic terms.

We have spoken of the id. It is the bases for all our instinctual drives, our need for food, clothing, shelter, sex, and pleasures of all kinds. But most importantly, it is the repository of aggression. These are all primal forces that support our desire to survive and be our unique individual self, but we are confronted by society, which requires us to play roles and func-tion as a false person. As Freud said, this all develops out of society restraining our basic impulses and restricting our individual freedoms.

We grow up then feeling suppressed in some way or another. Suppressed by the designation of color, ethnicity, religion, racism, sex, sexism, wealth, poverty, rank, status, class, pretty, ugly, fat, skinny and any of the many social categories that seek to socially define and classify us. From the time our mothers initiated primary socialization, we have been under pressure to conform, to fit in, to belong, but from the depths of our unconscious mind we know that this conformity is a threat to our psychical, spiritual survival; and in a religious sense, it is a threat to our soul. Conformity, which is not of our own choosing, denies us the right to be our innate self. As a member of a category or classification, we cannot know true self-realization. As such, we are just actors playing social roles.

Yes, we are all being suppressed by society, but our human spirit is not broken. It continues to struggle against socialization from the level of the unconscious mind. This is where the innate self has been repressed to during the very early years of childhood, and it is from this level that every individual fights the restraints that society has placed on him. The character of the fight is determined by the id and the distinct individuality of each one of us, or the X-factor; but the purpose is all the same: oppose society and defend the innate self against conformity. As an individual, we are being threatened with destruction, and the battle must be joined with that in mind.

Modern America is a high-tech, materialistic, hedonistic society. We have more bodily comforts than we know what to do with, and our religious leaders might tell us that we have paid for it with our souls. That's a very damning assessment because it is the soul that makes us human. Without it, what would we be? Think of Dr. Frankenstein's creation. It had no soul, and it became a monster, a vicious, psychotic, violent killer. The creature was a symbolic throwback to the primordial days of human history, and it reined terror on the community. Does this sound familiar?

The primordial world was one filled with monsters and violence, and back then human kind lived a very tenuous existence. Daily life was a struggle for survival. People lived under a siege mentality, and much of their behavior was motivate by fear. Those primal instincts of the id were the governing force of the individual's emotions. But as time past, humans evolved, progressed and society was developed, and the primordial world was left behind. However, over the centuries, society has instituted a socialization process that has increasingly forced our innate selves to retreat back into our unconsciousness, back to the state of being when humans were without a moral compass. It was the time of the conscience-less primitive.

We thought we had left our primitive nature behind us, but it has returned. In our unconscious mind, in the land of the id, we find ourselves in a world of monsters and violence again, and that is the world we have now projected on to society. As a result, our past has become our future. The monsters from the id have become real monsters in fact. The violence that we see occurring throughout our social system can be thought of as a self-fulfilling prophecy. Once again, we must recognize that we are both the perpetrator and the victim in this situation. In all ways, we are the monsters from the id.

So then, ultimately where is emotional deprivation leading us? Like armies of the night, it is leading us against ourselves. It is a debilitating, self-defeating, self-destructive force that threatens our long-term species survival. That is why women are specifically targets. Since they are the progenitors, this puts them directly in harms way. As a consequence, women are under attack symbolically and actually. They are being stalked in motion pictures by serial killers and monsters, and they experience the reality of it in their everyday, daily lives.

And what of the general violence in movies and professional sports? Undoubtedly, it is but a reflection of the violence that is prevalent throughout our society and the turmoil that is going on inside of us, the struggle between the id and the superego. As innate beings, we are losing the struggle. The story lines in the Hollywood motion pictures tell us this over and over again. Motion pictures used to imitate real life, but now they represent it. And, like motion pictures, professional sports, is sure to become more primal and violent in nature.

The French philosopher Rousseau is reported to have said that human beings are born free, but everywhere they are in chains. That succinctly states the case I have tried to present here. However, as a matter of survival, the human spirit will always fight to break the chains. The generalized violence that has engulfed our society speaks to this effort, and it is a rebellion of sorts. At the same time, what it means is that individual Americans are trying to reclaim their souls; and if necessary, they are willing to turn monsters loose on society in order to accomplish it.

THE FAMILY

If there is a social rebellion going on because people are trying to reclaim their souls, we need to try to understand this process? Where should we begin? How do we get a grip on it? Well, we should begin at the beginning, once again, with the family. It is the most basic institution of society, and if there has been any tampering with our souls, it is likely to have begun there. Of course, we Americans do not think of the family as having anything to do with our souls. In fact, most rational, western people do not believe that they even have a soul. That is a lot of spiritual, religious, New Age, mumbo jumbo. Given this reality, let us put our thoughts of the soul on hold for the moment, and we will concentrate on how society uses the family. It used to be our most respected and revered institution. But today, the family is just another service institution of the social system, and as such it has been co-opted and used primarily to teach the young to be conformists.[3] As a consequence, the traditional role of family has become less important. In this context, before we can study what the family has become today, we need to recall what it is about the family that makes it so important to society and to each one of us as individuals. Moreover, it is very likely that such a review will have much to say about the origins of emotional deprivation.

To begin with, make no mistake about it, society has always rest on the institution of the family, and the role of the family has always been three-fold: procreation, the nurturing and rearing of the child, and socialization. The first two functions derived from biology and the emotional bonds that exist between a mother and her child. The third is cultural and varies from society to society. All three functions coalesce in that extraordinary period of life when a child is in a state of non-consciousness. Which is to

1

say, the child has no conscious awareness of self. This occurs approximately during the years 0-3. Of course, this is a generalized time frame that can be longer or shorter for some children.

At the same time, just as society rests on the institution of the family, the primary purpose of the family is to nurture and rear children. Obviously then, the nurturing function is critically important during those early years of the child's life, the years 0-3. This is the time when the child's basic emotional makeup is being formed, and the impact of it will influence his behavior for the rest of his life. In particular, it will set the tone for his participation in personal relationships.

Now, I have just made some very broad and general statements about a period that is enormously important in all of our lives, and I can say that the conclusions stated here are supported by many years of social research on the subject. Indeed, it is well established, based on medical and social data, that the most important stage of social development for any child is during the very first few years of his life.

There is a fundamental reason why the period 0-3 is so critical to a child's social development and the status of the family. At that time, there is a unique relationship between mother and child. To fully understand it, we should recall that the relationship begins when the baby is still in the womb. For nine months, the mother and the fetus form the most intimate physical, spiritual, and emotional connection that can exist between two persons, and it is the only time when two human beings can be individually conjoined as one. During pregnancy, the umbilical cord of the baby is connected to the placenta in order for the baby to receive oxygen and other nutrients. This allows the fetus to become emotionally and physically in tune with its mother's body and spirit during the gestation period.

At the end of nine months, the baby is born, and it is discharged from a warm, comfortable environment that had been totally his own. Even if there were a multiple baby situation in the womb, with all the babies conjoined to the mother, each fetus would still experience the environment as his own. The important point here is that the infant passes from the known to the unknown, from a secure womb-bound home to an alien world. To be sure, birth, in and of itself, is a process of dissolution, and that maybe one of the reasons for the trauma of birth that women experience. Similarly, birth has to be a shock to an infant.

A newborn child immediately becomes a part of a family. However, he is truly a stranger in a strange land, and the situation is exacerbated by the fact that human babies are born without any conscious, survival instincts and the physical ability to look after themselves. Newborns are totally dependent upon someone else to take care of them. Nature provides that that person should be the baby's mother foremost and always. Circumstances may arise that causes the mother to be separated from her child: death, illness, or the child maybe given up for adoption. But, in any case, no surrogate mother can replace the infant's inherent need and dependency on its birth mother.

This is an interesting term that has arisen recently in our society, "the birth mother." It suggests that there are other kinds of mothers besides a woman who gives birth to her own child. But, by implication, this is a very illegitimate term. It is one of those verbal quirks or ruses of modern society that attempts to replace biological fact with social rationalization. It is an attempt to deny the fundamental importance of natural maternity. We all know that the basis for any social group begins with the birth of a child and motherhood, but if we can convince ourselves that motherhood does not begin with biology, then as a society we can pretend that we do not have to be beholding to this truth. Society can then make up its own rules about motherhood as it goes along, for the better or worse of it. Unfortunately, the evolving notions of motherhood have had a negative impact upon the character of the family today.

Nevertheless, whatever is the character of the family, the maternal parent-child relationship is still tremendously important to a newborn baby for a very significant reason. In our modern times, we revel in the belief that we have subdued nature, that we are in control of our worldly environment, and that humans are masters of all they survey. But in the process, we have forgotten what is the essential responsibility that any parent has to her offspring. She must teach the little one how to survive in his environment. This is no less true for human mothers and their babies. We may masquerade this fact with more sophisticated language and involvements in complex organizations, but the truth of it remains the same.

Remember that the child is born into an alien environment and he is bereft of survival instincts. Therefore, he must be taught everything he needs to know to survive in the strange, unknown environment he finds himself in. Unlike most animal species, human babies may be born into any of the world's many different geographical locations, from the North Pole to the South Pole. This requires them to learn many different cultural strategies if they are to survive in the particular alien environment of their birth. Initially, and for optimum results, who is best suited to teach the offspring what he needs to know to survive in his new surroundings? Nature provides his mother, and the resources and other members of the family support her.

Because the child forms a unique bond with his mother when gestating in the womb, he is born with a sensory awareness of whom she is. The infant knows her touch, the smell of her body, and the sound of her voice. In the alien world he is born into, she is the only familiar thing to him. Being close to her body, feeling her arms around him, hearing her identify him as her one and only child is what gives him a sense of comfort and security. It is a bit of the feeling of being back in the womb. And because birth, by its very nature, is a process of dissolution, it is most important that an infant should feel as secure as humanly possible after being discharged from his mother's body. A sense of comfort and security can be quite helpful in easing the shock of suddenly becoming a newborn child.

Learning begins for the infant right after birth. A secure and stable family would be very helpful in this regard. The more secure the child feels, the more open and willing he will be to learning, and this is quite significant because of the kind of delicate learning that takes place during this non-consciousness stage of human life. The consciousness of self-realization that we come to know as we grow up, normally establishes itself in most people around the age of three. To understand this once in a lifetime situation, we need only to think about our past, back to the age of 0-3 years old. It is very rare for the average human being to have any memory of this period of his life, and there is a very specific reason for it. At that time, we have no sense of *I*; and for all practical purposes, we have no awareness of being a distinct, separate, individual entity. In this context, there can be nothing for us to remember. Remember what, about whom?

For most Americans, it is a mystery why a child has no consciousness at the beginning of its life. But if Westerners truly believed in human spirituality and the transmigration of the soul like the people of the Far East, there is an explanation that is readily available. One begins with the notion that all human beings have a soul, and the soul is eternal. It resides on earth for the purpose of spiritual development, and this is something that can not be accomplish in a single lifetime because the soul must experience all facets of human living. So, the soul goes through a series of bodily incarnations until it completes its process of spiritual development. But, during the way, after each rebirth, there is this period of mental inactivity, a lack of consciousness, which gives the reincarnated soul the chance to forget the previous life and prepare for the new one.

With a cleansed mind, the learning for the infant child can begin. In the first instance, the learning is sensual, and it occurs because of stimuli from the surrounding environment, from both people and things, that arouse basic, primal feelings of being accepted or rejected, of experiencing pleasure and pain, and of knowing hunger and satiation. What all this learning does is impact on, and shape, the developing emotions of the child. It will be these emotions that will give him the sensory feelings of who he is as an individual person once his consciousness has emerged. Or, to put it more accurately, this learning forms the basis for the development of the child's sense of *I*. Now it should be clear why this is the most critical and important time for the social development of any human being. If a person has a questionable sense of who he is, then he will have difficulties relating to other people.

The most important thing for the child, during his first few years of life, is the developments of a strong sense self or *I*, but without consciousness, he is unable to do this on his own. We can also presume that nature was very purposeful in denying the newborn this ability. Since an infant must begin to learn his necessary survival techniques soon after birth, it is important for him to have some means to interact with the alien environment he finds himself in. There is a natural sensory bond that exists between a mother and her child at birth. She can act as the infant's consciousness and sense of *I* in the larger world beyond his innate awareness. As her child is familiar with her touch, her smell, and her voice, she can use all of these faculties to bring the new world to him; and by doing so, she defines and explains the alien environment. No substitute mother would be able to do this as well as a child's maternal parent.

Therefore, mothers who adopt a child, and any other kind of surrogate mother, can never be the first best option for a newborn child. Of course, this does not mean that women should not adopt babies they did not give birth to. Infants need interaction with adults whether they are the maternal parent or not. An infant child cannot survive in this world without adult support. I am just trying to make it clear that we have been playing down the importance of the individual, maternal parent raising her own child with the mistaken societal belief that any adult can do it, male or female, if the desire is there. It is this kind of deadly thinking that has given rise to nannies, au pairs, baby sitters and day care centers raising other women's infant children. Obviously, the use of surrogate parents in the home will inevitably weaken the family structure.

Therefore, any mother who turns her child over to others to rear during the first stage of his life, even if it's to relatives like grandparents, is doing an emotional disservice to the child. The worse thing the parent can do is to put her child in a day care center. This robs him of the individual attention he needs from his own mother for the development of his singular sense of *I*. In day care, he is just one child among many. He will not be treated any differently than the other children. Day care centers may have the unintended effect of slowing down or inhibiting the development of the child's sense of subjective consciousness. It is the social skills of the group that will be emphasized in day care and not the distinctiveness of the child's individual self. This is directly opposite to the kind of stimulus the child needs at this stage of his life. And it is an indication of society unnecessarily intervening into the natural process of childhood development.

But, there is an even more sacrosanct reason why a maternal parent should not turn her child over to others to rear. In the immediate sense, the newborn needs to feel safe and "taken care of" after his birth from the womb. Of course, this is done, in part, by providing the child with food, clothing, and shelter. But more importantly, the mother transmits a personal and emotional sense of security to the baby through touch and other kinds of stimuli, hugs, kisses, cuddling, face rubbing, pinching, breast-feeding, gently biting the little ones body, especially his behind, smiling in the baby's face, talking and singing to the infant, and so on. In a word, the baby is made to feel wanted, safe and protected through the giving of love, affection and nurturing by the mother. The family setting gives additional meaning to this effort. No surrogate can do this as well, and least of all caretakers in day care centers.

A further comment needs to be made about breast-feeding. American women generally do not breast-feed their babies. While there is clinical evidence that tells us breast feeding infants has very good health rewards for the child and the mother; by reducing the general risk of infections to the baby and helping the mother's uterus to return to normal size after birth, for societal reasons the biological good of it is ignored. Too many women want to, or have to, go back to work soon after birth, so they are inclined not to breast-feed. Then, there is the more supercilious reason that some women have given for not breast-feeding. They want to get the baby's father in on the exercise. He can wield a bottle as easily she can. Modern feminist philosophy supports this idea of men trying to be female nurturers, but this is all very shortsighted and does not serve the best interest of the baby. And lastly, for the most superficial and inane reason of all, many women, if not most of them, do not want to breast-feed because they have been sold on the idea that it will deform the shape of their breast, and this will take away from their appearance, making them look less attractive in cleavage-displaying dresses or bikini-type bathing suits. Imagine not doing the best for your baby because you want to make a fashion statement.

The nurturing is also the chief means by which the mother conducts sensory learning with her child, and because the nurturing makes the child feel wanted, safe, and loved, he is much more willing to learn what she wants to teach him. Essentially, mother's nurturing gives the child a broad base of emotional support, and this is something all children need if they are to develop a consciousness that reflects a strong sense of *I*. To underscore this point, let me make following observation.

Americans have long held the belief that parents should not spoil their children by giving them too much attention. This notion tends to manifest itself all too readily during this period 0-3 years old. Many parents believe that the child must be weaned away from his mother as soon as possible. Parents are told not to let their baby sleep in the same bed with them, put the child in a crib at the earliest possible moment, and ideally even put the little newborn in another room. If he cries because of the separation, don't go and pick him up if he is not hungry or wet. Parents are made to think they are doing this in the best interest of the child. The baby is pushed away so that he will not become overly dependent on his parents. This is thought to be particularly true for male babies. A boy child might become fixated on his mother and become tied to her apron strings.

However, it is a strange societal notion that a mother can do emotional harm to her child by giving him all the love and affection she can during his infancy. This is precisely what the infant child needs, as much love and affection, and overall nurturing, as he can get, which will give him a feeling of a broad base of emotional support. Therefore, a child should sleep with his mother, and he should do so until he feels comfortable enough to do otherwise. The more secure and wanted he feels initially, the sooner he will be able to leave her bed. The important thing is, that soon after birth, the newborn child should not have to suffer yet another shock by being forced away from his mother. Being close to her is how he will develop a strong, subjective sense of self, and that can be the basis for later life feelings of self-esteem, self-assurance, and self-respect. The stronger the child's sense of *I*, the more confidence he will have in himself totally, and in his individual abilities.

By the same token, if the child does not get the sufficient, broad based emotional support that he needs to develop his distinct sense of subjective self, then he will suffer emotional deprivation. This is to say, that if he is denied the emotional ingredients needed to develop a healthy, supportive consciousness, the child will grow up unable to recognize himself as the unique, innate person he was born to be. Emotional deprivation will inhibit, to a lesser or greater degree, recognition of the self, and it will block feelings of self-realization.

In short, the emotionally deprived person will grow up feeling inadequate, unfulfilled, and spiritually empty, which is indicative of a lack of self-esteem. He will have doubts about who and what he thinks he is, and he will suffer alienation. However, as we will see shortly, the child is socialized to believe that the way he can overcome his spiritual emptiness is by conforming to society's edicts and its plan of success for all social members. In America, that means seeking power, wealth, status, hedonistic, material rewards, and being sexually promiscuous.

But, there is a problem with this scenario. Intrinsically, how can there be categories of success for individuals? As well, it is a generalization to say that all children in the non-consciousness stage of life must receive sufficient, broad based emotional support or they will suffer emotional deprivation. How much is sufficient for any given child? No one can really say. If we accept the notion that each person is a distinct human being, one of a kind, then the necessary emotional support each child might need would be particular to him or her and no other. Only the child's mother might have a clue as to what that might be, and this is another reason why a substitute parent can never serve the child as well as the real one.

But here is the most important point to this matter. In the relationship between a mother and her child, there is always an X-factor that cannot be generalized. The X-factor refers to every child's distinct individuality. Consequently, there are no strict, tidy rules for how a mother should give her child sufficient emotional support. There are only parameters to work in, and each mother and child has to work out the dynamics for themselves, the character and quality of the nurturing involved. Each individual mother should keep in mind that when her child was in her womb, he experienced everything she did in the physical, psychological, and emotional sense. At birth, she and her infant are spiritually in tune. To determine her child's emotional needs, she should let her maternal intuition guide her.

It can be said, without equivocation, that any person, anywhere in the world, who is a member of a society, has suffered emotional deprivation, and this is an absolute truth for two basic reasons. One, all societies socialize their members; and two the non-consciousness stage of human life is definite and occurs only once. Taking the second point first, the maternal parent will have only that one time frame, the first years of life, to help or inhibit the basic development of a strong sense of *I* in her child. If the opportunity is missed, there is no way to go back and do it over. Once the consciousness evolves, the sensory links between the mother and the child are changed forever. Psychically, a child, or an adult for that matter, who has a full sense of consciousness, would be unable to emotionally receive the nurturing his mother would have given to him during the non-consciousness stage of life. And, notwithstanding the calls by Women Liberationists for equality and social justice, and contrary to the self-serving, anti-Freudian philosophy of the modern feminist, essentially the problem of emotional deprivation does began with the maternal parent. The father's role in this unfortunate situation is something less in the first instance. I will explain that role later in the book.

It is truly shameful the way Women Liberationists and the modern feminist have attacked those of their own sex who find being a mother and homemaker a rewarding way of life. It shows how confused they are about their own worth as progenitors, and that they have fallen victim to the social tyranny they railed against. If they really understood how important their role is in shaping the consciousness of all human life, I don't think they would denigrate motherhood. However, Women Liberationists are right to question the role of motherhood in society, but they do so being totally unaware of the part they play in the suppression of a child's basic impulses and the restriction of his individual freedoms. Women have allowed themselves to become the chief instrument of socialization for society, and it is primary socialization that generates the frustration that Freud referred to. Now it is time to detail just what this means.

To understand the situation we are in, we must challenge some taken-for-granted attitudes. Human beings are social animals, and it is therefore assumed that society, as we have come to know it, is necessary for our survival. But, how often have any of us stopped to really think about what society is and what it asks of us? Society is constituted by a large group of people who have a common heritage and who live together in relative autonomy. These people function together in organized patterns of behavior that we identify as institutions. There are many institutions in society like the family, the economy, the educational system, and the political system. All these institutions operate together to form a social structure. There is no doubt that this social structure today has come to dominate our lives, if for no other reason than the fact that we have become so dependent upon it; and as we will come to see, we have become more dependent upon the social structure than the family.

No one is certain as to when society, as we know it, began, but there was a time when this society, and western societies overall, did not exist. To be sure, there are many different kinds of societies around the world even now, but there is one thing they all have in common. They are all products of human effort and enterprise, and all have family units. This is to say that people make societies. Societies don't make people. However, there has been a great deal of myth, fantasy, and shibboleths that purports to tell us that it is society that makes us human. What nonsense. But, it is true that social scientists believe that we do not become fully human until we become socialized. This is a ridiculous notion because being human refers to being Homo sapiens, the species we were born into. It is not a social category. We are human because of our biology and not because society deems it so.

Because of our Judeo-Christian heritage, with its belief in original sin, we are taught that without societal institutions, values, morals, mores, and codes of conduct, we would be nothing but an anarchist rabble living by the law of the jungle, trying to destroy one another like the lower forms of animal life on this planet. But it is said that we are fortunate, and we should be thankful to society for allowing us to live with civility; that is, by our brains and not our brawn. We are reminded in many ways that because we were born into a society, we have tacitly agreed to the social contract, and we must give up certain individual freedoms if we want to be a member of the group. It is posited to us that all individuals must work for the greater good. Individual wants and needs must always give way to the interest of the many and not the few. That is the only way, we are led to believe, that we can survive from one generation to the next.

If this is our understanding of society, than something is terribly wrong. Things are turned upside down. If individual people create society, how can society be considered of greater importance than the individual? Why are society's values, morals, mores, and codes of conduct generally directing my life? No one ever asked me, at anytime, if I wanted to live by the same beliefs, standards, and rules of my parents. It was just taken-for-granted that what was right for them, must be right for me. The truth is, we are all socialized to believe the propaganda about society being more important than the individual, and for all practical purposes, by the time we become fully mature, we believe it. But, let us take this assumption apart.

We have spoken of the fact that it is the maternal parent who initially has the responsibility for teaching the child how to survive in the alien environment he is born into. The days have past when she would have to teach the child about the dangers of the jungle or forest. The environment she has to teach him about is the modern social reality, and one of the first things she will do is to prepare the child to accept the power of "legitimate authority" over him and the rules and regulations of the social games he will have to play. As the instrument of primary socialization, she will began the process of diminishing his sense of individual self-worth in favor of the importance of the group over him. It is she who will begin to turn him inside out.

To be sure, a mother does not socialize her child because she intentionally wants to weaken his sense of self and individuality. She is motivated by her maternal instincts to have her offspring survive. What she teaches him she thinks will be used toward that end. However, the centuries of social evolution have now duped her into performing a task that is opposite to her intentions. Oh yes, what she teaches the child may very well allow him to survive in his society, but ultimately that survival may be against his own individual best interest. In any case, a mother wants her child to belong to the same society as she does because she is not likely to believe that there is an alternative for him. As a rule, for children everywhere, they must become members of the society they are born into or they will be ostracized. In modern society today, as in the past, ostracism will threaten the child's chances for survival in his social group.

Essentially, what is this process of socialization? From the point of view of the collective, the group, it is how the individual person becomes an active member of the society. It is how the individual learns and internalizes the attitudes, values, and behaviors he needs to know to interact with other participants in the social system. Socialization wants to ensure that every child born within the society will develop the identity and the motivations required to perform social roles. All members are assigned roles based on sex, class, wealth, education, political standing, religious beliefs, ethnicity, and much more. It is clear that socialization is all about the individual serving society. Today, the family is expected to give strong support to this notion.

Because the child is born with its special relationship to his mother, and because the mother functions as the child's *I* during his non-consciousness stage, she has an open track straight to his emotional core. The child looks to his mother for nurturing in the form of love and affection. He will probably get it, but it may be given at a price. His mother wants him to learn the rules and values of the society. In effect, she wants him to conform to society's norms. Therefore, starting with the mother, and later the father, the child may be given the nurturing he needs on the bases of reward and punishment. As he is taught, and accepts, the behaviors his mother wants to teach him, he will be rewarded with love and affection. The situation becomes more complex as the child grows older and he has to learn etiquette, mannerisms, and social roles. But, it is still all about conformity.

To be sure, the child is being coerced into conforming. In the non-consciousness state, the child seems to be guided by some kind of unconscious motive to seek out the love and affection he needs for self-development. In the first instance, he knows his mother and he is drawn to her body for nurturing. But his mother may play with his emotions. Her nurturing can ebb and flow with the child's submission or resistance to conformity. For instance, if child allows himself to be isolated in a crib, baby carriage, play pen, walker or a nursery room without crying too much, then he is being a good baby and the level of nurturing may go up. Unknowingly, the child is submitting to his mother's authority. But if he cries in defiance of these "normal" conventions, then nurturing maybe moderated or withheld until he behaves in a more acceptable manner. The child's mother can rationalize that getting him to conform is for his own good, but conformity maybe robbing the child of his individuality even before he has had a genuine opportunity to express it.

Love and affection, the nurturing the child needs, should be given to him unconditionally and solely because he is loved for himself. It should never be used as a form of reward, but because of the role of mother and the family unit's involvement in primary socialization, it is almost impossible to stop this from happening. If children could learn about their social world without the pressures to conform, we would see an entirely different kind of social person emerge. But societal propaganda tells us that without conformist behavior, there would be social chaos and anarchy.

When love and affection is withheld from the child, for an extended period of time, for whatever the reason, it will produce emotional deprivation. Because of the reward and punishment nature in the process of primary socialization, it is inevitable that emotional deprivation will occur. All who pass this way will suffer with it to a lesser or greater degree. The character and quality of difference is a function of the X-factor and each family as a distinct social unit.

Let us take another view of how socialization substantiates emotional deprivation. We are all distinct human beings, and we are all born with our own innate sense of self. We can assume that we were born with our innate self because we are supposed to use it as the basis from which we should operate in the larger world. That is to say, it would seem that we were provided with our differences to distinguish ourselves as individuals. We are not given our differences to become minions in a herd. But socialization is allowed to invade our inner selves and coerce us into conforming to some general categories of behavior that society requires. However, as individuals, there can be no category that can cover the innateness of everyone. We are then forced to behave in social roles that society ascribes to us, and the roles will not allow us to be our innate selves. And it should be noted that role by definition is false. Therefore, if society wants us to play roles, than society is asking us to function as a false being.

This is a form of alienation, and alienation is definitely an expression of emotional deprivation. To be sure, if we cannot function as the person we were born to be, it is frustrating because our basic impulses are being suppressed and our individual freedoms are being restricted. Since frustration can also mean that we are blocked from satisfying and fulfilling our basic impulses, then frustration is also an operative of emotional deprivation.

It is very interesting why role-playing has become so very important to socialization, and it is not solely because society requires it. Its importance mirrors the relationship that exists between the mother and her child during his non-consciousness period. It was pointed out that the mother plays the role of the child's *I* during this time frame. As the child develops, he learns social behavior by mimicking his mother, and later the child will play his mother's role in respect to himself. George Herbert Mead said that the child first takes the attitude of others, and then he learns how to play the role of others. From this, he learns how to assume roles generally in society.[4]

Mead was very specific about the fact that in the beginning the child learns his role-playing from the significant others in his household during the first few years of his life. They are his mother, father, and other family members. The significant others are persons the child has an emotional relationship with and whom he interacts with most often. By this standard, the mother is definitely the chief significant other in his life far and above any other person. This is true for all the reasons I have already mentioned about the unique bond that exist between a child and his maternal parent.

The significant others of a child constitute a very specific social world for him. It is a social world that is like no other, and he will experience it only once as an individual without consciousness. This special little social world will leave its imprint on him throughout his lifetime. It should therefore be a world that gives him unconditional love, broad based emotional support, and an overall sense of comfort and security. The family environment should be a sanctuary for the child until he develops his own sense of consciousness. But because the mother and family unit are used in primary socialization, the child must struggle against conformity at a time when he should be learning about himself. Unfortunately, the world of the significant others are used to prepare the child to bend to the will of generalized other; which are the rules and regulations, the norms, of social conduct that go on outside the home. Eventually, all the rules of the generalized other are internalized.

Internalization is obviously very important to socialization. Indeed, without this process there could be no socialization. Think about all the propaganda, the rules, norms, values, and edicts that we are first introduced to outside our person, but later we come to experience them inside of us as restraint, guilt, and control. Internalizing social norms helps to suppress our basic impulses and restricts our individual freedoms. Given this development, it seems we would be better off if this process did not happen. That it does occur, gives credence to the strength and influence our mothers have over us during the early years of our lives. We internalize her teachings, and our emotions are shaped by it.

Social scientists have led us to believe that internalization, as a function of the socialization process, is benign, but this is not the case. Internalization, by its very nature, creates emotional conflict within us. Mead pointed out that socialization produces a particular social self for the child that is different than the innate self. He called the social self the *Me*, and the innate self is the *I*. As well, *Me* represents role-playing, seeks recognition from the group, and wants the child to conform. The *I* stand for our distinct individuality. It wants the child to be independent, please the self, and seek aesthetic rewards. The *Me* evaluates the self materially. The *I* evaluates the self spiritually. And finally, the *Me* is at all times perceived as being objective and outside the person. It is always me in respect to someone or something else. The *I* is always perceived as being subjective and inside the person. We can speak of the *I* in terms of itself, and not necessarily in relationship to something else. The *I* is experienced as who we are. The *Me* is experienced as who we are in comparison to others.

Conflict occurs in us because socialization causes us to internalize the *Me*, and the *Me* then tries to put restrains upon the *I* in favor of conformity. This frustrates the *I* and causes the person to feel alienated and without the freedom of mind, spirit, and body to be himself. Or, to strike that familiar bell again, basic impulses are suppressed and our innate freedoms are restricted. In the overall, Freudian theory suggests that this phenome-non leads to repression, and there is a battle going on at the unconscious level of our being. If the *I-Me* conflict is occurring, as I have described it, then society is definitely responsible for most of our psychological and emotional problems, and we can surely understand why socialization in the family would also have an active part to play in this process.

The earliest years of a child's life are taken up entirely with family. The nature of the interactions between child and family members are unique, and that uniqueness will forever identify him with his family group. No other experience will be so deeply ingrained in him. He will change in a thousand different ways as he matures and grows old, but the imprint of family will be with him until he dies. All of this is to say, as an institution, the family is the most powerful, the most influential social force we will encounter in our lifetime. It is no wonder then that it affects us at the unconscious level of our minds. How can we come to understand the con-nection between the family and our unconscious mind? Let us follow the trail that was open to us by Freud.

Dr. Stanford Lyman states in his book, *The Black American in Sociological Thought*,[5] a psychoanalytic movement began in America in the 1920's, and American social institutions soon came under psychoanalytic study. These studies attempted to link frustration to the social structure as expressed by Freud in his book *Civilization and Its Discontents*. Lyman takes note of the movement because he is interested in the basis for preju-dice against black Americans, and in his evaluation he studies the etiology of prejudice as it may have its origins in the family. In doing so, he exposes how the structure and functioning of the American family gives support to the process of emotional deprivation.

To speak of the child here is to go beyond that period 0-3 years old. The child now has consciousness, and he is a prime subject for primary socialization that will continue throughout his pre-pubescent years.

Mother, father, siblings, and perhaps other relatives are the child's sig-nificant others. They are the constellation that defines his family. This being the case, Gordon Allport, a Harvard psychologist, prior to the Women's Liberation movement, pointed out the following. The atmosphere of the American family was suppressive, harsh, authoritarian and critical.[6] It was an environment where the parents' word was law. His description may seem a bit odd because we don't usually think of the family in such objective terms, and taking note of the American family at the close of the twentieth century, especially middle class families, most people would probably say it is hardly suppressive and harsh. Indeed, the opposite is thought to be true, but if we consider Allport's atmospheric description of the family as causing the denial of the innate self, then we could agree that the family is indeed still quite suppressive and harsh.

It might also be said that the days of authoritarian parents are a thing of the past. We now accept the fact that children have fundamental rights. And as such, the American family is thought to be more democratic today than ever before, and children are given their say on many family issues. But, obviously this does not involve the child during his non-consciousness period of life. That is a time when the parents' word is absolute and law, and the minor person must accept the attention as given to him, for the good or the bad of it.

The true nature of the family today is not all that different than when Allport evaluated the institution, and if there is any doubt that his analysis is still applicable, think about this. He said that parents give or withhold love in an arbitrary manner, and it causes the child to become very sensitive to the possibility that they will disapprove of his behavior. Essentially, love, which is the embodiment of nurturing in the overall sense, is given on the basis of parental approval, the conforming to norms, and the overall acceptance of socialization. As the child develops consciousness and grows older, he may wonder, "Do my parents love me for myself? Or, do they love me because I am the social person they programmed me to be?" The child is uncertain about what he must do to receive unconditional love. As a consequence, he can grow up feeling that he did not get the love and approval he needed when he was the ultimate dependent.

Of course, Allport is describing the elemental process of emotional deprivation. We first spoke of it beginning with the chief significant other, the mother, and if there were a good family structure, the father would be the next most important person in a young child's life. The father's earliest role is likely to constitute the very first true social relationship the child will have. Initially, a newborn's relationship with his mother is biologically based. It is the mother who uses her relationship with the child to begin primary socialization, but it is usually the father who comes to represent the "legitimate authority" of the larger society. Fathers today may not be the traditional authoritarian personality, but they are still acknowledged as the titular head of the family's hierarchy. To be sure, even if they work, most women are comfortable with this kind of spousal relationship.

Within the household, parents can hold absolute dominance over their child, and this has the effect of teaching him to respect and covet authority and power. This attitude works very well in a hierarchical, capitalistic society like our own that encourages the acquisition of power and wealth. And, like the family, the American political system is non-democratic, as it primarily serves a privileged elite. The family experience of the child prepares him to accept his place in this type of functioning polity. Mentally and emotionally he is taught to accept someone else having power and authority over him, and it seems all very natural because the process begins with his parents.

In the hierarchy of the American family, the child is at the bottom. Lip service is paid to the notion that he is important, but since the family has become just another service institution, nonproductive persons in a capitalist society are scorned and looked down upon, if not ostracized. Because small children are neither workers nor consumers, their needs are not considered to be a top priority. Parents today, especially the so-called baby boomers, would surely argue vociferously to the contrary. They can point to the fact that currently, in many families, both parents are working hard to provide their children with a middle class, materialistic way of life. But it is just this kind of thinking that makes my argument. Children need their parents to give them more personal attention and not more material-istic goods that can be bought in a store. The truth is when you find both parents working, frequently it is because they are trying to maintain a bourgeois lifestyle, or the two are engaged in their individual career paths. This is to say that their working is more for themselves, their community image, and not for the sake of their children. Of course, because of the high cost of living in a capitalist society, in many families both parents have to work to make ends meet; but, by definition, this is not the case for the middle and upper classes.

A middle class couple may work very hard, to earn money, because they want to give their child material things. They can think that this is one of the best ways to show their child that they love him. More importantly, as the child grows up, material things can be given as rewards. This is not the case during the period 0-3 years old. The reward that needs to be given at that time is love, affection, and overall nurturing. If the nurturing is used to entice the child to conform, socialization can have a very Pavlovian impact on him.

This is to say that the child tends to be socialized on the basis of reward and punishment. Punishment here is not meant to mean physical abuse specifically, although that is still very much an option for parents. In fact, rather than physical discipline, most of the punishment the child experi-ences occurs when his parents withhold the unconditional, unrequited love he needs; and to be sure, this is more emotionally harmful to the child than spanking. Think of the situation that the child is in. In the first instance, he finds himself in an alien world where he is totally dependent upon others for survival. He especially needs love and overall nurturing. When it is being withheld because he is being punished, he can come to think that his parents do not love him, and this can cause him to lose respect for himself. This is especially true when the mother is the principal person behind the child's deprivation.

Under these conditions, a child will grow up, as Allport says, being fearful and distrustful of his own impulses because when he tries to be his innate, socially unmodified self, his significant others will tend to punish him. And when the child enters the larger social world, he may project his fears and distrust onto others. Allport adds that this is one of the causes of white prejudice against blacks. I would also state that this is a basis for sexism, homophobia, and many other kinds of bigotry. Moreover, when you distrust and fear others, it is easier to rationalize using violence against them.

What we learn in the family is played out in the larger system of society. While each person's family experience is unique to him, that experience is no longer uniquely individual as it once was. With television becoming the single most important force that is teaching morals, such as they are in our time, and values, and influencing behavior, the family experience is more generalized than ever. This situation has been exacerbated by the character and needs of the middle class, suburban communities and the capitalist notion of what constitutes a materialistic, bourgeois lifestyle. What this demonstrates is how deeply the process of socialization has penetrated the family, as a private institution. Take a look at the younger generation, and you see very little social variety among them. TV and other forms of mass media keep them well informed as to what they are suppose to wear and how they are suppose look and act.

The general conformist behavior of young people today tell us that the family unit has changed considerably since Allport evaluated it, but unfortunately it does not seem to have changed for the better. As a psychologist, he looked at the personal relationships in the family, but a fellow social scientist, Talcott Parsons, looked at the structure of the American family, and he, too, reached some rather distressing conclusions. Parsons saw that there was a direct correlation between the family structure and the role it plays in shaping a child's behavior. The society wants certain types of behavior from its members, and the structure of the family helps to deliver it.

Parsons goes on to say that the child rearing practices of the American family is likely to produce anxieties and insecurities that lead to frustration. As such, the family will cause the child to suffer emotional difficulties.[7] To begin with, the American family is by and large a nuclear family. A nuclear family refers to one that consists of a mother, father, and their immediate children. Gone are the days when there are large, extended families, sometimes known as farm families that were made up of more than three generations. Families are smaller today because society requires it. The nuclear family is more compatible with an urban, highly mobile, white-collar society.

The nuclear family tends to be isolated from a larger kin group. In an extended family, there would be many more significant others. And, at the time Parson's made this statement, his idea of a nuclear family was one where the father was out working and the mother was home looking after the child. In this situation, the child becomes too dependent upon the mother for the love and nurturing he or she needs. As a consequence, the child will become overly anxious about his mother's emotional state. This is particularly true for a boy child who will also be dealing with Oedipal issues. He is likely to feel jealous about the affections his mother shows his father.

Parsons is correct in asserting that the structure of the American family sets the stage for the child to be dependent primarily upon his mother for most of his emotional support. But this is not such bad thing when his mother is functioning as his I. Indeed, this would seem to serve the child well. However, because his mother initiates primary socialization, she is not likely to be giving the child unconditional love, but rather she will be socializing him on a reward and punishment basis. It is a mother's responsibility to help her child develop a strong sense of I, but if she does not do this, in a nuclear family, with the father away most of the time, there may be no other significant others to pick up the slack. In an extended family, there would be many more adults available to the child to give him some emotional support.

Of course, more mothers' work today and for this reason, the nuclear family is less of a family than it used to be. As a result, many children during the crucial, early developmental period of their lives have neither parent at home to nurture them. They may have spent more time with babysitters or at the day care center rather than with their parents. And, because this is the era of home and personal electronics, in a significant other sense, children may feel a closer connection to their electronic machines than to their mothers and fathers. The nuclear family structure has furthered this occurrence. In particular, an entire class of young people find themselves lonely and isolated in the suburbs. With their parents less available, they turn to their friends and their electronic machines for nurturing and support.

The nuclear family structure puts additional pressure on the mother to provide the child with all the love, affection, and nurturing he needs. She obviously has a biological urge to do so, but she has also been saddled with the responsibility for primary socialization. The biological then confronts the sociological and the mother can find herself beset with emotional conflict. She must try to serve two masters. The alternative is to reduce the pressure by not facing up to the conflict. The easier path to follow is the sociological one because the mother can judge the impact of socialization on the child by his behavior, social adaptation, and conformity. Under these circumstances, the child is not given unconditional love, and he can never know specifically what his performance will bring. Parsons says that love, therefore, becomes very precarious in the child's life.

Both Allport and Parsons spoke of the modern American family as being unable to give the child the overall unconditional love he needs to develop a strong sense of self-esteem. In other words, they are talking once again about the process of emotional deprivation. But more importantly, the two of them are stressing the fact that the modern American family is failing to perform its fundamental human function. Argue as one will, this fact cannot be altered. The primary purpose of the family is to raise children. Indeed, a family is not a family without children. But, by and large, Americans have lost sight of this elementary fact.

Family is no longer defined by its members, but rather by economic and cultural designations. Most Americans think of their families in terms of status, acquisitions and lifestyle, and the basis for all this is money, which is very consistent with the power of the almighty dollar in a capitalist society.

Today, most people relate to their families as a function of an economic class, and the class is largely based on income. This has helped to de-individualize the family as being unique to the person who was raised in it. Now we talk more broadly about families of the poor, the lower, middle, and upper classes. But these are not real, human categories. It is all statistical make believe. To force us to try and comprehend them as encompassing the reality of our lives is surreal, and it brings forth a phenomenon of alienation by designation.

Given our designee status, it is no wonder that most Americans no longer believe that a unique family background is important, but then why should they? Most of them did not grow up in one, and this is especially true of the present generation. But if we could only focus our thoughts for a moment and remember, we would recall that there was a good reason for each one of us to have our own special family experience. The family used to be a safe haven for the individual. It was a place where he could withdraw from the larger social world to regroup, recuperate, and refurbish himself psychologically and emotionally. But because society has so deeply penetrated the home through television, most of our families are a reflection of the larger social ethos we see on the tube.

Indeed, the home is no longer the place of the heart, and the family is not a comfortable place of refuge. The family is more like a place of uneasiness, frustration, and very likely discomfort. It carries the psychic reminders of a non-consciousness experience that has committed all of us to the ravages of emotional deprivation. And who do we feel is responsible for this? Largely our parents, with our mothers taking most of the blame, but we also throw aspersions on the family unit as a hold. We will tend to find fault with siblings because it is likely that if we didn't get the love affection we needed in the past, and then it might have been because a brother or a sister got it instead. Casting blame is so typical of human behavior, especially when a person has a low sense of self-esteem.

What once made the family a place of sanctuary for an individual was the understanding that it was, in the final analysis, a very personal and private institution. That notion has literally flown away. Today, the family is much less private than it used to be. Starting with government mandated school and health programs, most of the private functions of the family have been slowly stripped away. At the same time, changing economics and demographics have also played a role; and more recently, technology has helped to make the family more accessible from a distance. There is the telephone and the wireless cell phone that allows an individual to get in touch with family members anytime of the day or night. And now, even more astonishingly, there is the computer and the Internet that allows a person all kinds of verbal, written, and visual communications with his family from practically any place in the world.

The family was also thrown open for public review and criticism by attacks from the activists in the Women's Liberation movement. Riding on the wave of the disenchantment that Betty Friedan spoke of in her book, *The Feminine Mystique*,[8] the Libbers chided, derided, and defame homemakers until housewifery was given a bad name. Many young women were persuaded that traditional marriage, motherhood, and housekeeping were little more than a life of servitude and martyrdom. And once they came to such a realization, they used this attitude to decrease their commitment to the family. Of course, they did not speak of it that way. Their public and political line was that they were fighting male chauvinism and dominance; or, as some married women said, they were leaving their families to find themselves. But these were nothing more than convenient rationalizations because the reasoning behind it was strange and flaky. It was much like the complaints of thousands of men during the Second World War. They made a public show of not wanting to go to battle, but secretly they welcomed the adventure. Even with its dangers, for some of them, going to war seemed better than the humdrum routines of work and home life. They were happy to get away from the pressures of family responsibilities.

In the 1960s, American women in general were very conflicted about their status in the family, and the Libbers were particularly affected this way. They were mostly middle class suburban women who found themselves trapped between biological need and the demands of society. The liberation movement offered them a way out. They could put all the blame for their internal dilemma onto men. But to accuse men of being totally responsible for their emotional unhappiness was more fabrication than fact. For example, the married women who turned away from their families to find themselves were not indentured slaves, but in many ways that is how they described their roles as wives and mothers. As well, these women got married, by and large, on their own volition. Oh yes, there may have been family and other social pressures on them to do so, but in the final analysis, no one put a gun to their heads to make them get married. They did it because they wanted to fit into the mold society prescribed for women at that time. And it was not men alone who put forth this prescription. It was women, too. There was a time, when there was no technology and no urban society, and women wanted to stay home, to take care of the children and to be protected from the wilds of nature beyond the front door. And society complied by practically mandating that they become homemakers. With the dawning of the Women's Liberation movement, women were saying this old arrangement had long been out of date and no longer acceptable.

The women Libbers were also demanding that men become better househusbands, and thereby relieve them of some of their family duties. This would allow them to become more involved in activities outside the home, and this has happened. The number of women attending college, graduate, and professional schools have increased tremendously. They are active in politics, business, the medical professions and all occupational fields across the boards. And based on individual choice, women should have all the work opportunities and options the same as men. But it cannot be denied that with so many more women leaving the home, the effect on the stability and viability of the family in respect to the child was deleterious. Just the fact that so many more women rely upon day care is an indication of this.

The notion of men becoming better househusbands is also based on somewhat of a false premise. The Libbers have fostered the idea that nurturing is totally a matter of socialization. Anyone, male or female, can be taught to be a good nurturer for a child. We have been informed that there is nothing innate or biological about it. Given what has been said about the unique relationship between the maternal parent and her child, this seems to be a strange form of female logic. If men could be as good nurturers as women, then they would have been born with the capacity to bear children. If nothing else, they certainly would have the capacity to breast feed an infant.

With women pushing for their spouses to become more like mothers than the traditional fathers, disarray has developed in the family. Some husbands have fallen into line and acquiesce to the demands of their wives. Others have resisted. They say they are being "pussified;" and as a result, the child gets caught in the middle of this feud. However, fathers should be more involved in the upbringing of their children. They should give love, respect, and overall support to them, but they should do so from the male perspective without trying to be like the mother. That kind of male performance would even be emotionally confusing to the child. It is only his mother who can function as the child's I. No matter how hard he would try, a father trying to play a mother's role would not be successful at it. Nevertheless, fathers should develop good, solid relationships with their children. A child has a need for both a mother and father. If both of them are playing the mother's role, then the child will be denied the significant other that should be his father.

Inadvertently, the Women's Liberation movement has caused many women to be in competition with their children. The Libbers hawked the notion that marriage and motherhood, essentially family life, forced them into a kind of martyrdom, where their lives were no longer their own. They became chattel to their husbands and children, but with the women's movement they had now come to see the light. Women were ready to reclaim themselves from the life-stealers. The issue was time, and the new woman of the twentieth century would decide how to use it. And however that was to be done, it would benefit her in the first instance. She would no longer put her needs second or third to her children and husband.

This kind of thinking inevitably plays down the fundamental relationship between a mother and her child. For example, it is a justification for putting the child in day care, having babysitters, and other kinds of surrogates, and it will test their relationship dearly in a nuclear family. The child will need motherly attention, but his mother may be more interested in herself. The mother will compete with her child for the time she has available. It is the child who is at a disadvantage, and the mother will likely allocate the time so that it serves her interest first. It is an obvious fact that many mothers are spending fewer hours today with their small children, and at a time when the need for their presence is critical. As women withdraw more and more from their children and families, they rationalize that it is not the amount of time they spend with the family that is important, but it is the quality of the time. In this case, the women are absolutely wrong. Time does matter when you are talking about that critical period of 0-3 years old in a child's life.

In the past, one of the best family times of the day was the dinner hour. Generally, all meal times were good for bringing family members together. The entire family would sit down at a dining table and eat a meal that had been prepared by a person in the household, most often the mother. The food would have been cooked as only she could do it, and whatever the meal was, all would share and partake of it. Blessings might even be said at the table, and there was always the communal feeling of family together-ness. Dinner times used to be special, but not anymore. The liberated woman doesn't have the time, the inclination, or the ability to cook as before. Children eat more prepared and fast foods then they eat home cooked meals. It used to be a matter of pride for the adults in a family to prepare a good home cooked meal for their children. But today, the adults would rather buy their children McDonald's hamburgers and fries, or a Domino's Pizza instead.

When we used to accept the family as being the most important institution in our lives, it was also at the heart of our social system. Just a few centuries ago, the majority of American people were involved with agrarian pursuits. Large families were quite common, but more importantly, these families performed the bulk of the required productive work for the society. Then along came industrialization and increased technology, and the family was pushed out of the arena of productive work. Family members began to work away from the home, and this help to undercut the standing of the institution in society. As a consequence, society has lessened its support for the family in favor of other institutions like the economy and politics.

Sociologists have pointed out that advances in medicine have also had its impact on the family. Infant mortality has gone way down, and the birth rate has also dropped. Primarily, there are fewer births because the family is not used as a productive unit. And, in our agrarian past children worked on the farms, and they were economically important. Today they are considered to be dependent, nonproductive members of society. It comes as no surprise that as the family has become less dependent upon the child for productive output, the family overall has come to give much less emotional support to the child than previously had been the case.

There is no doubt that the family as a social institution is much weaker than it used to be. As such, the family has lost much of its ability to influence and control its members, especially the young people. This has caused the family to fail at a very needed function society requires. Society has always been confronted with a basic problem that is indigenous to its existence. With so many millions of different people in the system, there must be a certain measure of self-control exhibited by its members toward one another. Indeed, this societal need has helped to give rise to socialization. We usually learn this self-control at home, but since the family is no longer held in high esteem, its members, in particular the young people, have little desire to follow its behavioral prescriptions.

The family's significant others would seem to be well suited for the purpose of teaching the child self-control. However, there is a new significant other in the home. It is the TV as mass media, and the child is getting much of his primary socialization directly from the tube. In the past, this kind of input was filtered through the family's significant others. Now the child learns many lessons and anecdotes of life that he may use to develop his own sense of self, straight from the outside world. The message he gets from the TV is consistent with the action nature of our time, and he is tuned into an active, free-spirited, libertine approach to life and living. With this type of influence nurturing him, there is little or no desire for the child to exhibit self-control as he grows up.

The development of self-control is the way society gets us to inhibit our own basic impulses. Family members used to be the guides and role models for the child to follow, and because they were his significant others, he had a very personal incentive to mimic their behaviors. But with a weak family institution, with possibly both parents frequently away from home, and the child being looked after in a day care center, there is much less desire to develop the self-control society expects of him. To be sure, this situation will work to alienate the child, and very likely cause him to develop a rebellious attitude towards the family and other social institutions. Rebellion is a form of aggression that can be directly attributed to frustration that is brought on by emotional deprivation.

To be sure, I have been talking about the American family in the broadest sense as a social institution, but the American family unit does have certain variances. Class placement and socio-economic standing help to establish our system of hierarchical, social stratification. There are upper class, middle class, and lower class families. They do not all function the same because of family size, income, education, religion, and ethnicity. Nevertheless, the family as a social institution has been weakened at all socio-economic levels. To put it simply, the family name is not what it used to be. Even the Rockefeller name doesn't ring elitist, family bells anymore.

One cause for a more weakened family, at all socio-economic levels, has been the sexual revolution. It began back in the sixties, and the dust from its impact has not settled yet. Society has always attempted to regulate and/or control sexual behavior. Starting in the last century, with revelations by Freud, the sexual mores in western society have been in a continuous process of change. The change has been towards decreased societal control, and here at the beginning of the twentieth-first century, practically all restrains have been removed from private, consenting adult sexual behavior. Premarital sex and fornication is encouraged for both males and females. Only the lamest person today would object to someone having sex outside of marriage.

The implications of promiscuous sexual behavior for the family are obvious. It has made marriage seem less inviting at a time when marriage has been given somewhat of a bad name by Women's Liberation. Fewer marriages mean fewer families. However, if we listen to the social sycophants, marriage is thriving as always. But that is not quite true. Yes, the majority of Americans will get married, but the actual number of people getting married is not as important as the number of people who stay married. About fifty percent of the present day marriages end in divorce, and all too frequently, there are children involved who must bear the emotional burden of seeing their families torn apart.

There is no doubt the promiscuous sexual behavior has had an effect upon the divorce rate. Nevertheless, many divorcees remarry, but very often the second marriage involves children from two different original families and this causes problems. Or, you have a situation where the child's household is made up by an old and new parent during the most formidable years of the young person's life. These types of situations underscore the instability of the American family today. Moreover, new no-fault divorce laws encourages couples to seek divorce much more readily than they might have done so in the past, and with women having careers outside of the home, this also puts a strain upon marriages. As well, women are getting married later and having children at an older age. All of this is having an impact on the nature and stability of the family.

Surprisingly, the sexual revolution has brought into question the biological basis for the family. The male and female of the human species must have sex to reproduce. Or in some way, the egg of the female must be brought together with the sperm of the male. Traditionally, this was done through intercourse. The two slept together, as we say. Human beings are unique in the animal kingdom. They can have a desire to mate all year around. This fact has always been an inducement for members of the opposite sex to form some kind partnership or union, which ultimately leads to a family. In America, that union has been marriage, but now that promiscuous sex is encouraged for both males and females, long term unions are not sort after as readily as before. It is the era of the one nightstand.

As well, promiscuity has brought forth the contraceptive pill, and other pregnant preventing options for women; and of course, there is the abortion for "unwanted babies." All of this has reduced the number babies being born, and it underscores how children, the most important element of a family, have been socially reduced to an option rather than a necessity. Also, beginning with the beatniks and hippies of the 1960s, new forms of the family have arisen, and they are testing the traditional waters seeking, with varying degrees of success, a legitimate place in the social structure. There are now communal families, gay families, religious cult families, spiritual occult families, Mafia families and the most bizarre new form of all, the childless family.

This last point is a strong indicator of just how much the idea of family has changed in society today. The institution of the family was essentially created for children. It takes nine months for a pregnant woman to give birth, and once the child is born he must be totally supported for many years. A family was used to ensure the well being of pregnant women and to shore up support for the child in its early life. But today, the purpose of the family has been rationalized to suit any group's purpose and lifestyle. It shows how the idea of family has shifted away from the personal and private to the larger, more public community.

The new notions of the family disregard the fundamental fact that it is primarily a nurturing institution. Of course, the family is there to give support and comfort to each one of its members, but when young children are involved, the family focus is to be on them. It is the mother who is the chief dispenser of the nurturing, and it points up the fact that there are two basic relationships that a woman must maintain in the family: the mother-child and the wife-husband. The mother-child relationship is biological. The wife-husband relationship is social. The family has been weakened in recent years because women are giving more attention to the wife-husband relationship. It is a consequence of Women's Liberation, and the battle women have engaged in with the chauvinist pig.

In seeking social equality, women have, of necessity, turned the traditional family structure upside down. They want the family to be more elastic and accommodate their desires to be out of the home, but if the women were to be honest, the main issue for them, in this respect, was not the chauvinist pig. Women did not want to entirely give up their place in the family. They have a nesting instinct that matches up with their maternal drive. Nurturing is not only a need of the receiver, but it is also a need of the giver. The family is as much about nesting as it is about anything else, and women cannot change what nature has provided for. But the Libbers are in full swing trying to deny that there is such a thing as a maternal instinct. They say the idea is a culturally generated myth used by men to get them married and into a family situation. It is difficult for me to understand how women can say this with a straight face. Who is the person who teaches primary socialization, the mother or the father? And, is the basis for it biological or societal? Their cultural gambit makes for a weak argument.

The family unit has never been a perfect one for all concerned, but for centuries it has been a viable institution because in a subtle way, the biological and psychic needs of both men and women were allowed to complement one another. As women have a nesting instinct, men have a natural roaming instinct. Consequently, for centuries women were quite comfortable staying at home, and men were uninhibited in fulfilling their desire to test their muscles in the wider world. Now women want to reverse these positions, but this is putting a strain on the natural, complementary relationship that has always existed between men and women. In striving for a reorganization of the family, women may be tampering with a fundamental force of nature, and whenever we challenge nature, there are always unanticipated consequences.

Mating is certainly a basic force of nature, and the family, as an institution, came into being to serve this very necessary human function. This emphasizes the fact that the nesting instinct and the maternal drive are innate, and so is the male ego. It is the male ego that supports the roaming instinct, and it makes a man want to prove himself in the larger world. Men have a burning need to compete with each other and leave their mark on the natural environment. Women are not ego-driven like men, and this makes nesting and being homemakers more satisfactory to them. Clearly, the male's ego makes him more suitable for activities in the outside world, and contrary to what feminists' thinkers have said, the male domination of society may be due more to his ego needs than any specific desire he may have to suppress the female.

This question of ego has much to say about the relationship and duties of men and women in the home. Men do things frequently for ego rewards. They crave an audience, and they relish a challenge. They like to show off and posture themselves, especially before women. Men find great joy in impressing others with their abilities. They are constantly looking for a platform to perform on because for them the whole world is a stage. This is one of the reasons why men love to play sports and admire sports figures in a vicarious way. Home life per se does not offer the male the opportunities to get the ego rewards he desires, and nature meant it to be that way. It is the male's ego that makes him want to protect his family, and to try to make a better life for them by confronting the unknown and conquering it.

But, women are playing down the male's ego. As it relates to the family women want men to become better househusbands, to participate more in the nurturing of the child and do more of the housework. Women are saying to the men that they should seek more of their ego rewards in the home as a father and husband. But this is unrealistic. Oh yes, men can do more housework, and they can feed a bottle to a baby. They can also cook, but for pure ego enhancement, they need the larger societal stage. This is not to ignore the fact that if men became more involved in family life, it would be a definite benefit to their children. They are the second most important significant other in the life of any young child. But the Libbers are kidding themselves if they think that the family will ever have the same focus for men that it has for them. You can put an apron on a man, but you cannot turn him into a Hausfrau.

Unlike men, women are more likely to do things for their intrinsic rewards. They like a clean house, flowers, polished nails, and clothing. For its own sake, women adore shopping. They tend to be in love with love, beauty, and all manner of aesthetic pleasures. This suggests that women are probably more intuitive and naturally more introspective than men. These are all qualities that make the character of women more compatible for home life, and it is particularly important to mothers when they per-form as their child's "I." With his natural predilection for the larger societal stage, there would be little ego enhancement for the father performing in this capacity, even if he enjoyed his role as a significant other.

Women must understand that if they are to reorganize the family, as we have known it for hundreds of years, then they must take into consideration factors that go beyond learned behavior. There are psychic and ego functions of men and women that cannot be ignored. For this reason, I emphasize the fact that the overall treatise in this book is not about keeping women barefoot, pregnant, and homebound. Although I am certain I will be accused of that, but what I am trying to do is make a case for social realism accord-ing to our innate selves and not our socialization.

There is yet another point to be made about the psychic and ego basis for the family relationships of men and women. Marx, who is best remem-bered for his analysis of the capitalist economic system, was much more of a social philosopher than a political economist. In this context, he had this to say: A man has a spiritual need to work on his external environment, to put his mark on the corporeal world as it were. Indeed, Marx's entire theory of social change is posited on this idea. We can wonder if he also believed that women had the same need as a man in this regard? Perhaps not, because this spiritual need of a man is innate, and it speaks to the male's more aggressive tendencies. Marx even saw this aggressiveness as helping to bring about the class struggle.[9] And most importantly, man's need to shape his environment has also given rise to modern society, as we know it.

Actually, women have helped men shape the external environment, but it has been in an indirect way. Much of what men do in the external world is to please them. They have always competed for the female's favor, and women have always been able to manipulate men into doing things they want done. These things include building them a home to nest in, getting them food, and giving them protection when they are pregnant and nurturing young babies. When men use their aggression as a provider, it does give them the great sense of ego enhancement.

Being a family provider has always been an impetus for men to engage themselves in outside activities, but now women are putting pressure on them to turn away from the outside world. This is causing many men to feel frustrated, and it is creating a lot of bad blood between husbands and wives. As a consequence, fuel is being added to the fires of the male's natural aggressiveness, and we are seeing men using that aggression more and more against women. When there was a wilderness to conquer and wild animals threatened him, a man could take out his aggressions in that natural setting. But in modern America, there are very few such opportunities, except maybe for the occasional hunting and fishing. Unfortunately, because of these circumstances, too many men today feel justified when they take their aggression out on their families.

I have been talking about the problematical nature of the modern family as it relates to our innate, human character, and I have been contrasting the needs and instincts of women with that of the needs and instincts of men. The purpose was not to pit one against the other, but rather to draw attention to the fundamental natures of both. Of course, I am talking in broad generalities, and consideration must be given to innate individuality. That means the X-factor is always in play. With the family being co-opted and used as a service institution for society, only lip-service is offered for the development and nurturing of the child's individuality. The innate self of a newborn is compromised from the very first moment a parent begins to socialize him.

The family has always been a cultural institution of teaching and learning, and that is the way most social scientist talk about it. But to better understand how the family has deteriorated as a private institution that once served its members in the first instance, we have to look at the family in a different social context. The family is used by society as an organizing principle, and this principle is used to take control of our social consciousness. Since society is constituted by a series of interlocking institutions, the organizing principle helps to give us the emotional frame of reference that will allow us to develop institutional behavior. If I have not made the point clear, an institution is a repetitive, formal way by which important societal functions are carried out.

We have noted that the family is given the responsibility for the primary socialization of the child. Through his significant others, the child is introduced to the larger social world he will someday have to participate in. Unfortunately for him, the socialization process is conducted on the basis of reward and punishment. The child must learn that if he does the right thing, he will be rewarded, and if he does it wrong thing, he will be punished. He also learns that the determination of what is right and wrong is not his to make. It is something that is imposed upon him. The determination is made by his significant others, but as he grows older, and enters the larger social world, that determination is made by society. The child is learning to respect authority and the right of others to have power over him, power that is represented by, parents, teachers, police officers, government, the church, revered, historical documents like the United States Constitution, and institutions generally. Without this respect for authority, society could not exist, as we know it.

As a child, we submitted to parental authority because they took care of us and provided us with food, clothing, and shelter. This is the basis for our belief that if we submit to societal authority then society will also take care of us, too. However, the larger society is much different than the family unit. There are many different classes and ethnic groups vying for social success. Our society is hierarchical and stratified. In such a social structure, inequality is built into the system. This means that inevitably, some groups will be taken care of better than others. In this sense, the family is being used, as an organizing principle, to train individuals to accept bias and inequality in society. Allport acknowledge just this very thing.

Learning to respect authority in the family forms the basis for the belief in a supreme being. Belief in God is a matter of faith and not reason. People say that there is a God because they feel it to be true. From where does the feeling come? Very likely, it was initiated in the unconsciousness of the child during the critical 0-3 year period. This is when the organizing principle takes hold of us emotionally when we have no way to fend off the influence, and especially because it is taught to us by our significant others. We want to please them because we must get the love, affection, and nurturing they can give us. If we are socialized to believe in a Supreme Being at this time, the majority of us will be unable to deny it later in our lives.

Society has used this belief in a Supreme Being to develop religious institutions, and these institutions have always been important to human social systems. Next to the family, religion may be the second most important institution. However, most Americans would tell you today that they do not have much religious faith. Their sense of an Almighty Being is much more secular. In our new action-oriented consciousness, the old God in heaven is just a shadow of His former Self. In fact, there is a new Supreme Being that has arisen in the form of science, technology, and specifically television. For the younger generation, the new God is likely to be an electronic mechanism.

According to Durkheim, people in general have always had a misconception about the deity, no matter whomever or whatever it was. The Frenchman said that He was never the savior of souls. He was established to help keep order in society. Durkheim said that societies must have social solidarity among its people.[10] Therefore the system requires that its members function in an orderly, predictable manner. This means that everyone is expected to conform to the rules, norms, and values of society. Thus, all newborns must be socialized to the satisfaction of their significant others, and the child is made to feel that he must bend his will to suit societal needs. With their own behavior as examples, it is family members who teach the child that conformity is good. The organizing principle involved tells him that being different is bad, and you will get punished if you do not conform. As a result, the child can grow up feeling that conformity and survival is the same thing.

This message is carried over into the larger society. The individual should strive to belong, to be accepted, to be like everyone else. Starting with our elementary school days, and now it may be beginning in preschool day care, we learn early on that we are expected to fit in and cooperate with the group. A child is stigmatized early in life if he is different or he tries to be different. If he is raised to feel that he must fit in, to be disgraced this way can be very traumatic. It can be taken as a form of rejection, and in mature individuals, it can develop into a fear of ostracism. So, most individuals will try to talk alike, dress alike, look alike, and even think like everyone else. And the capitalist economy plays on this fear to sell products, set trends, fads, and styles.

Using the family as an organizing principle of conformity helps to maintain the political balance in society between the haves and the have-nots. When the child leaves home and enters the larger world, he is told that conformity is necessary so that there might be harmony between him and his fellow citizens. But this is predicated upon the notion that society will treat all citizens the same, equal justice and so on. However, we know this is not possible in a capitalistic, hierarchically, stratified society. But what conformity does do is help to maintain the status quo and keep things as they are. As such, it helps to keep the powerful people powerful and the powerless people powerless.

America is also a multiracial, multiethnic, and multi-religious society. There are people here from every corner of the world, and these differing groups of people ban together in many subcultures. They develop their own family neighborhood enclaves and lifestyles. Conformity begins first with ones own social, reference group, and this is the first level of identity for most people. The individuals in all these groups may identify themselves as Americans, but they put their ethnicity first. Specifically, conformity works against the harmony and cooperation it is suppose to stand for. How fascinating. The family, as a community institution, was supposed to bring members of society together, but it is not happening in our modern world.

Today, the family is seen more as an economic unit, and it is the materialistic side of the family that is stressed above all else. It concerns itself with cost of living, standard of living, and lifestyle. Family and religion used to go together and share in the early training and socialization of the child. The child's moral health was seen as being just as important as his physical health. In this context, the spiritual needs of the child was being recognized. He needed inner spiritual guidance to realize that human beings were much more than just their physical body. Jesus talked about our immortal souls, and it needed nurturing along with the rest of us. But this part of the human character is no longer regarded as important in modern society. Under the aegis of the new God of technology and electronics, it is only the corporeal reality that concerns us. For we are riding the wave of materialistic hedonism, and we must keep finding ways to give our bodies pleasure, pleasure for pleasure's sake.

We have an economy that is dedicated to meeting our materialistic wants far beyond our needs, and if we conform and fit in, we are told that we will be provided with a gluttony of pleasures. We have been led to believe that life is just a bowl of cherries, and that we have a right to keep eating them without end. We have cultivated this insatiable, hedonistic appetite that drives us like a whirlwind. Where did this compulsion come from? Well, let it be said that it is a function of emotional deprivation. Having been denied the unconditional nurturing of affection and love that we needed as a child, we have grown up feeling unfulfilled as a person. To relieve ourselves of our deprivation, we are led to believe that all we need to do is become a materialistic hedonist. But to do this, we must inevitably give up our belief in the reality and importance of the human spirit.

An emotionally deprived person will grow up feeling inadequate, unfulfilled and spiritually empty. The organizing principle here is the process of emotional deprivation itself, which undercuts the child's sense of I and inhibits the development of emotional independence. Indeed, the reward and punishment way of socializing the child is sure to prepare him for emotional dependency. Even as an adult, he will find something outside of himself to become dependent on. If it isn't materialistic hedonism, then it is sure to be something else: drugs, alcohol, sex, smoking, and even criminal behavior. While the overall influence of society will tend to push most people into the circles of materialistic gluttony, there is always the individual's X-factor, which will have its say in the choice of dependency. It can be almost anything, from the good, to the bad, to the ugly. It can even be, murder, my sweet?

Allport said because the family exercises absolute dominance over the child, he would grow up respecting authority and power. This can be stated in another way. He will grow up believing that there must be Chiefs and Indians in society. Because the young child must be taken care of completely by someone else, there is this natural dependency between the small child and his significant others. If two adults were involved in a dependency relationship, this would not be normal. However, emotional deprivation makes a person dependency prone. He is therefore open to such relationships, and society prays upon it. For example, American society is hierarchical in nature, and it is bureaucratically organized. Both these systems are authoritative, leadership and command structures. For them to work, there must be obedient enlistees, the supervisors and the workers, the boss and the minions, the Chiefs and the Indians. The early family background of the child prepares him for playing either role as the Chief or the Indian. But since the number of Indians far out way the number of Chiefs, it is much more likely that the average child will eventually find himself performing as an Indian.

With the Chiefs and the Indians, the organizing principle is the belittlement of the self. The dependent person in a relationship is always the lesser person. For instance, take our relationship to God. If we say He is omnipotent and Almighty, we can only be something less by comparison. We acknowledge that there is a force that is much greater than us out there in the universe. In the face of that force, we are made smaller. In the same fashion, if God is the Holy Father, then we all must be His children. We are in that context His dependents. It was Max Weber who said belief in God prepares our consciousness for the acceptance of other types of authority. God is the ultimate big Chief, and we are His Indians.

The structure of the American family is nuclear, and Parsons said that it was an isolated nuclear family. He meant it was cut off from what used to be an extended family unit. Industrialization, urban living, and a high level of social mobility were specifically the cause of the change. Does the nuclear family create isolation for its members today? There is some question about that, but there is no doubt that the nuclear family has it own kind of organizing principal. It has been noted that since there are only a few members in the smaller nuclear family, relationships tend to be more intense. There is more pressure on everyone to cooperate and live together in harmony. But with mother and father out of the home working, with television performing in the role as the chief significant other, and with electronics and action motion pictures constantly massaging the emotions of young people, the chances for cooperation and harmony in the family is not close to what it used to be. And, since parents spend so much time away from home in their job lives, and children spend so much time at school, malls, movie houses, concerts, and so on, the family has a different meaning for its different members.

When the family was organized around agrarian pursuits. All its members had the same common purpose. They worked together, shared together, protected one another, and loved one another for the purpose of survival. From the children to the adults, everyone had duties to perform that kept the family unit going. It was through the group effort that food, clothing, and shelter were provided for all. In the nuclear family, there are clearly productive and nonproductive members, and this has come to be a source of conflict and dissension in the home today. This is particularly true in middle class suburban homes. These homes stand as the epitome of the family as an economic unit. In such families, income is praised above all else because middle class suburbanites strive to live a bourgeois, materialistic lifestyle, and in America, you have to make a good salary to afford it.

Furthermore, because the relationships in the nuclear family are more intense, and there is a greater need for cooperation and harmony, additional pressure is brought on the significant others, the mother most certainly, to see that the standards of conformity are met, particularly as it relates to house rules in suburban middle class families. These standards are endemic to the lifestyle, and at an early age the child is coerced into adopting them. There are scheduled times, on a daily and/or weekly basis, for work, play, school, bedtime, dinnertime, and the family hour. Very often, this timetable is dictated by the parents' commuting schedule, to and from work. In the order of priorities, the needs of the nonproductive family members must take a backseat.

As the young child grows up, he must conform to the household schedule, to the times for the different types of social interaction. This need for conformity will also bring about a greater amount of pressure on the mother to succeed with primary socialization of the child as quickly as possible. Seeking to get fast results, training the child on the basis of reward and punishment can seem to be her first best option. It may seem more viable because the household schedule may not actually give her much "quality time" with her child.

All factors would indicate that emotional deprivation is sure to be heightened in the nuclear family. The intensity of relationships and the isolation of its members guarantee it. The nuclear family is specifically a product of our time. It exists because our society has need for it. To be sure, fundamentally it is the capitalist economy that gives a great deal of support to the nuclear family, and conversely the nuclear family gives much support to the capitalist economy. This occurs, in part, because the nuclear family helps to energize the engine of emotional deprivation, and in this we can see a direct connection between society and the problem we have been exploring. It may well be that there is a pure, exacting functional relationship between our society and the process of emotional deprivation. Indeed, this would seem to be consistent with Freud's pronouncement that society, by its very nature, generates frustration in people by suppressing basic impulses and restricting individual freedoms. Since the family is the basic institution of society, it should come as no surprise that it would be used to further the ends of this functional relationship.

The family is a very powerful institution that has a tremendous influence on the development of the child's psyche and psychology, particularly in respect to social relating. During primary socialization, the child is taught in very repetitive fashion about the values and norms of acceptable behavior. In his non-consciousness days, this repetition creates an emotional context for the child that causes him to believe that the social edicts he is being taught are true, proper, and correct. When he matures and develops consciousness, he already has the psychological and emotional frame of reference that allows him to have a taken-for-granted attitude about the values and norms he has come to believe in. This sense of "knowing" that one's beliefs are correct deepens as the person grows older, and he comes to accept that his way of thinking about matters is the only right way to do it. At this juncture of his life, the person has entirely internalized the beliefs that he has been taught. They have become a part of him for all practically purposes.

However, these beliefs have come down to him from society. They are not his alone, but they are of the generalize other. For most people, socialization has caused them to have the beliefs of the social majority. It is believed that this will make it easier for cooperation and harmony to take place among the social members. But implicit in the taken-for-granted attitude is a very serious psychic problem that can take control of the person's social consciousness. The taken-for-granted attitude is more than a compilation of beliefs. They are convictions that are thought to be demonstrably true, and as a consequence they become a controlling, devastating organizing principle.

Robert K. Merton has observed that in social situations, all too frequently, we are motivated by a self-fulfilling prophecy.[11] He posited the notion that any belief about a social situation maybe true or false. However, if one acts upon a false belief as though it is true, then the belief becomes true to the person who believes it. A taken-for-granted attitude has this element of a self-fulfilling prophecy in it. Take this example: A student is going to have a mathematics examination in the near future. He does not like math, and he believes that no matter how hard he studies he will not pass the exam. So, he does not study much, guaranteeing the fact that he will not do well on the examination. There is no way that the student could have known that he would do badly on the exam if he had studied properly, but having not done so, he was unprepared to succeed on the test. Therefore, his belief became reality. This is the devastating nature of the taken-for-granted attitude. With the self-fulfilling prophecy, it establishes its own truth, a surrealistic phenomenon.

A taken-for-granted attitude locks the person into the truths mandated by his social reality. For instance, in America there is racial prejudice, and Merton pointed out that it is difficult to solve this problem because of the self-fulfilling prophecy that influences white attitudes towards Afro-American citizens. The majority of whites take for granted that blacks are inherently inferior to them. Even with a mountain of scientific evidence to the contrary, they will still believe it because they are locked into this social truth. An errant belief has taken control of their social consciousness.

Allports says that the structure of the American family, and the relationships within it, help to produce a personality that will exhibit racial prejudice. A taken-for-granted attitude would support such a personality, and such a personality will support this attitude. This is an organizing principle with such power it distorts true reality and creates its own. This is monstrous in its effect, and as surrealism, it comes straight from the id. Therefore, the American social reality may be based on truths, half-truths, false-truths, or no truth at all. Most people are so locked into their taken-for-granted attitudes they do not have the mental or emotional capacity to evaluate the so-called truths they live by.

Beginning with socialization in the family and its organizing principles, we come to accept what society tells us about life, living, the world, the cosmos, the Almighty God, and ourselves. Explicitly, we are taught to take society's edicts for granted, but in doing so, we give up a critical human function. We relinquish the right to evaluate our social reality on the basis of our innate needs. And failing to do so, we end up acting like herd animals; or at worse, no better than the artic lemmings. Like the lemmings, we are rushing to commit mass suicide. Another way to think of it is like this. By denying our own individuality, we are dehumanizing ourselves. What can be more violent and self-destructive than that?

And that is the bottom line. We live in a society that has turned us into our own worse enemy. It starts in the family, and progressively we are taught behaviors that cause us to prey on ourselves. For example, in the name of hedonistic pleasures, we learn to eat too much, smoke, drink, use habit forming, addictive drugs, and be sexually promiscuous. All these negatives behaviors are driven by emotional deprivation, and the need of capitalists to make a profit off our dead minds and dying bodies. Oh yes, we know these behaviors are a threat to our natural lives, but we cannot stop ourselves. Our society has created a feel-good, surreal world that has us locked into a social consciousness of self-debasement and self-defeatism, and no matter how badly it debilitates us individually and collectively, we will not give it up. The truth of the matter is, we can't give it up without destroying the only selves we have ever known.

Compulsive Masculinity

So then, at the close of the twentieth century, we Americans find ourselves engaged in self-defeating, self-destructive behavior that is controlling us more than we control it? Moreover, this behavior has turned us into our own worse enemy, and we don't seem to have to the power to stop it. What a predicament to find ourselves in. Of course, to ease our conscience, we would like to believe that some mysterious force has somehow surprised us in causing this situation, but there is no truth to that notion. We have been living with the cause of our predicament since the first moment our mothers started babbling baby talk with us, and now it is time to pin the tail on the donkey. Unfortunately, the donkey happens to be us.

Emotional deprivation is the force behind our predicament, and we need to take a closer look at how it affects our ongoing social behavior. But first, it must be noted that emotional deprivation impacts in different ways upon the behavior of males and females. Let us look at the males first. An emotionally deprived male grows up being ambivalent about who he is. He feels he is not the man he supposed to be. Therefore, because of his libido and ego, he must prove his manhood to himself and others. However, males will find themselves inhibited by their family background and upbringing. Their initial relationship with their mothers can get in the way. We can learn about this from the work of Talcott Parsons.

Parsons pointed out that in a nuclear family, boys are vulnerable to the formation of a feminine identification. He makes this statement because in the traditional nuclear family, the father was away from the home at work most of the time, and the mother would largely raise a boy child. As his chief significant other, she would also become his chief role model.

49

Being dependent upon his mother for love and affection, the boy child would likely adopt her behavioral patterns in order to please and win her favor. Add to this the fact that emotional deprivation will cause a child to grow up with a weak sense of I this makes the boy even more prone to copy his mother's behavior. In effect, he would be acting like a female, but he is not a girl and he will not grow up to be a woman. Therefore, he is developing a pattern of behavior that can lead to an identity crisis.

Having been raised by his significant others on conditional love, to the denial of his innate self, a boy child is likely to be uncertain about himself as a boy in any case. This feeling can be carried over from boyhood to manhood. It is a feeling of male emptiness, and it cries out for prove of self. And growing up without the love and overall nurturing needed amounts to a prescription for emotional debilitation; and this, too, can lead to an identity conflict for a boy child.

This identity conflict becomes apparent to the boy once he begins playing and associating with peers, particularly in school. He is likely to be shamed and rejected if he acts like a girl. He learns very quickly that a sissy boy is to be scorned, and he also learns that society looks down on females as compared to males. Women are thought to be inferior to men. A sissy boy then is no better than an inferior girl, and among other boys, such an individual is to be ostracized from his male peer group. To try to break out of this negative identity pattern, Parsons says that boys will feel this need to demonstrate their masculinity. They will adopt and assimilate behavior that exemplifies society's image of the male character, such behavior as the love of sports, being aggressive, acting tough, withholding emotions, expressing bravado, taking chances, and seducing girls.

Much of these demonstrated patterns of male masculinity are nothing more than acts of role-playing in the very real sense of the term. Many males, because they initially behave like their mothers, may suffer deep-seated anxieties and ambivalence about their sexual identity. They can feel confused about it. There are common instances of mother fixations, and it can be the basis for a series of neurotic, and even, psychotic problems. As a consequence, Parsons says, they can develop aggressive behavior towards females who they unconsciously blame for their identity conflict. Males then find themselves with repressed hostility towards their mothers, and they can develop guilt feelings about it.

Once they are interacting with their peer group outside the home, boys begin to feel pressure to prove their manliness. This comes directly from other boys and from various institutions of society. Since males are thought to be superior, boys can feel compelled to demonstrate this character out of fear of being belittled, or worse, ignored. By almost any account, subtly and otherwise, they can feel driven to prove themselves, and this can become a neurotic compulsion. The effort of males, young and old, to uphold the ideals of societal manhood, causes them to suffer from the distress of compulsive masculinity.

Compulsive masculinity should be thought of as psychological and emotional pressure that is being bought to bear upon males to prove themselves worthy of their manhood. The difficulty here is in the obvious fact that there can never be an absolute standard of manhood for all male personalities. There can only be broad categories that reflect a certain cultural bias, social coloring, and characterization of a collective persona. Due to the X-factor, there will always be differences in expressions of masculinity. In this context, prove of ones manliness will be to the self in respect to others. Consequently, compulsive masculinity transpires in the person's mind as he thinks of himself being viewed by others. He wants others to see him in the best light, which is perhaps how he does not see himself. Therefore, he is inclined to exaggerate, boast, and even lie about himself. This kind of posturing can become a part of his male persona, and fantasy can easily become accepted as reality.

Bowing to various kinds of vicarious expressions, males living through their fantasies have become a major problem in America today. The media is constantly talking about charismatic personalities from Presidents of the United States and movie stars, to TV personalities and sports figures. The fads and fashions of "role models," in behaviors and dress, are copied, duplicated, and mimicked. Through images projected by the media, males are pressured to submerge their sense of innate self in the plasticity of the mass-produced personality. That means the role models of today are media products, manufactured for public consumption. They have little, if anything, to do with life in the real world, and this is precisely the point. A vicarious style of self-expression does not want the person to live in the real world. It calls upon him to live in a fantasy world, a world that keeps him out of touch with his innate self. But by the same token, it keeps a channel open, so to speak, directly to the individual's id. It is from the id that the psychic energy comes that supports living in a fantasy world.

Because males feel pressure to prove their masculinity to themselves in the first instance, they therefore live with a sense of being constantly on trial and in the spotlight. There is the feeling of being watched all the time, and indeed this is true. Each individual male is always acutely aware of his own behavior. It is a manifestation of his ego, and he is always trying to put his best foot forward, particularly in the face of females. It is only the female who can give him that absolute recognition of being a man. This comes about when she invites him to share her bed. This is the primal recognition that all straight males desire in the end. Therefore, the proof of masculinity is never in the male's control. It comes from without, and the acknowledgement can be given arbitrarily and capriciously. In any case, prove of masculinity is something that has to be continuously reaffirmed.

Because of his ego, the male will feel very competitive about proving his masculinity. Whereas, it is the female who can really authenticate his manliness, the individual will think of his prove as coming from competition with other males. He thinks he must prove that he is better than the other guys while at the same time he must feel that he is one of the boys. There is always this ambivalent quality in his relationship with other males. He wants to be accepted as a legitimate member among his peers, but he also wants them to recognize that he is the better man. Now here is the rub. In a group of males, everyone can have this same agenda, and it can be source of subtle unrelenting competition and conflict between them.

Of course, the members of any group of males will have varying degrees of strengths and weaknesses. One person will be better at one thing and weak at another, and in friendships among males, you will often find buddies giving into each others strengths while playing up individual weaknesses. It is an odd form of ego enhancement that demonstrates deference to the other guys, but at the same time their weaknesses are used against them. Male friendships are invariably of a complementary nature. The drive to prove ones masculinity is so strong among them; it is truly difficult for them to be in relationships where all members are of equal status. True buddies have interlocking friendships where their weaknesses and strengths fit together to form a bond. This has come to be recognized today as male bonding.

Women do not have the ego of men, and they do not have the need to prove to themselves they are women, except in the biological sense as a progenitor. For this reason, they find it difficult to understand what male bonding is all about. The modern feminists have tried to duplicate this among women, but their efforts have not been very successful because the basic human ingredients for it are not present in the female character. Women are more apt to reject female bonding because it interferes with the natural state of competition between females to get the best man to father their offspring. Women are more about procreation than girl relations.

In the same fashion, the best relationships between a male and a female will have the same elements of complementary nature that occur in male bonding. That is to say, in such a relationship the female will behave in a manner that enhances the male's sense of ego, and she will give him ample opportunity to demonstrate his manliness to her. Because of their compulsive masculinity, men will be drawn to women who favor them in this way. But, under the aegis of the new feminism, it has become harder and harder for the males to find such women. This is due to the fact that the feminists say that there should be equal partners in a relationship. However, from the point of view of the males and females, that could only be possible if the social, emotional, and biological needs of the two are the same. That has never been the case with men and women. Nature made the two different for a reason. Opposites attract naturally. Forced homogeneity forms a blend that looses its potency.

To put it simply, the male ego is not going to change, and no amount of feminist demands or philosophizing will make a difference. The male ego is based on biology and not society. Compulsive masculinity verifies this fact. But this has not stopped women from bringing their own form of pressure on males, and they are causing men to further repress some of their innate male feelings. This can cause some males to be uneasy around females, and they can feel that they must prove their masculinity by punishing women. The punishment usually takes the form of some kind of abuse, psychological, emotional, or physical. And the males will get all the energy they need to do bad things from their ids. Because of their repressed feelings, there are always monsters within them ready to come forth to do their bidding.

The importance of sports to compulsive masculinity is obvious and unmistakable. Professional sports in particular are based upon a high level of competition, extraordinary expressions of the collective ego, a great deal of male bonding, and an adversarial need of individuals to prove themselves among the boys. Plus, for the professional sportsman there is always the opportunity to be an exhibitionist, and indeed to get recognition and financial reward for it. Professional sports are compulsive masculinity personified.

At the nonprofessional level, sports are used to bring the young boy into the world of competition. When a male child first leaves home, he comes from a relationship where his mother is the model for his behavior. If it is a good relationship, with the child suffering only minimal emotional deprivation, and he has not been badly affected by sibling rivalry, then he will have had little or no experience with social, egoistic competition. But once he gets among his peers and goes to school, he will begin to know the pressure to prove he is one of the boys. In this context, it is absolutely necessary the boy become adversarial minded. He must learn how to compete, how to stand up to others and defend himself. He must learn the importance of being a winner. And further on down the line, he will learn that the girls go for the winners, and they don't care much for losers. In short, sports will give him a vehicle to express his compulsive masculinity.

The sports industry has become a dominant, massive feature of our twentieth century cultural life, and it comes as no surprise that one of the reasons for it is that professional sports have hooked up with television. The world of sports is brought into our home everyday with the news and other programming. The result is that many sports personalities have become almost like members of the family. Between a movie star and a sport's star, the latter is thought to be much more of a role model because he or she does their communicating in the real world, out front where we can see, and sometimes even touch, them. They are absolutely real people like us and, they are not celluloid figures. For this reason, it is much more likely that vicarious bonding will occur with sports persons more readily than it would with movie actors. Also, with the sale of team hats, shirts, jackets, sneakers, and entire uniforms, to the sports fan, young people can seemingly transform themselves into the image of their baseball, football, basketball, or hockey stars.

What is the message these sports figures are sending to the young people of America? They seem to be saying that life is nothing but a game, and we are all players in it. However, only the strongest, the fittest, the meanest, and the most aggressive can become winners in the game of life. Everyone else must be a spectator on the sidelines. And in the public's eye, winners become larger than life characters, and we view them as heroes. As such, they take on a godlike stature among common, ordinary people. Their skills, their physical abilities are hyped and extolled as virtues by the mass media, and we are naturally belittled by the propaganda. Oh, if we could just touch the hem of their garments, how happy we would be.

The mass media gives a tremendous amount of publicity to our sports heroes, and television is constantly flashing their image in our face. They have been turned into national celebrities, and they are paid as such. In comparison to the income of the spectators, they are paid an obscene amount of money that goes far beyond any sense of economic proportion-ality. This is an expression of the capitalist notion that money is the end all and be all, and it confirms the fact that the golden rule is even more golden for athletes (whoever has the gold rules). These sums of money, in the millions, encourages the professional athletes to assume a marketing attitude about their work, and they can come to see themselves as a fran-chise, selling their skills and talents to make a profit.

Fifty years ago, most professional sports had more of a working class economic base for the players. The owners were not making barrels of money either, even though they were doing better than the players. Then along came TV with its package of guaranteed money, in the hundreds of millions of dollars that owners and players now use to bankroll themselves. When salaries were low, professional athletes played their games more for the fun of it, but now they play their games for the money. While players say that the money they make is of secondary interest, the salaries of pro-fessional athletes continue to rise.

Professional athletes used to play for the pennant, the Stanley Cup, the right to go to the World Series or the Super Bowl, and hopefully get a championship ring. They were more interested in individualistic, aesthetic rewards. But now they play for the money in new contracts and commercial endorsements. These players are more capitalist than sportspersons. Michael Jordan of the National Basketball Association fame is the perfect example of this present day phenomenon. These professional athletes have sold their skills and talent for a pocket full of gold, and to that degree they are no longer in control of their own destinies. They have now become a commodity like any item that is sold on the commercial market, and mar-ket forces will largely determine their careers. And, in functioning like a commodity, they have alienated and dehumanized themselves.

Professional athletes know that the teams they play for must win if they want to get the big bucks, and market forces are relentless in creating pres-sure for success. As a consequence, the Vince Lombardi decree has taken over the sports culture: in professional sports, winning is not the most important thing. It is the only thing that matters. Nobody really respects the person who is second best. To count for something, you have to be number one, and players feel compelled to keep trying to climb to the top of Championship Mountain, even though they are fearful of the fall if they make it to the top. Somehow they know that there is no aesthetic reward up there, but the ghost of Vince Lombardi keeps driving them on.

For too many professional athletes, the Lombardi decree has captured their souls and they have become manic-depressive about their desires to become a winner. A manic-depressive is an individual who is severely emotionally deprived. Indeed, it is a person who is unable to control the swing of his or her emotions. Think of all those athletes playing scores and scores of games and experiencing exaggerated feelings of pleasure or pain, acceptance or rejection by the fans, because a game is won or lost. Think of the heights of ecstasy they can go to when they make a strong come back and win a game they thought they were going to lose; or the deep sense of frustration and depression that can befall them when they lose a close game that they should have won. Think of the mind games they must play with themselves when they are in a slump.

The Lombardi decree, in itself, is enough to cause manic-depressive problems for pro athletes, but being driven by market forces also exacerbates the situation. They are after the championship because they are competing for the almighty dollar as a franchise. If the player's team does not succeed as a winner, there will be no reward in profits; and when teams fail to make the playoffs, players get shipped out and traded. Except for an unusual few, there is little financial reward for players when they are moved off the roster. Add to this the fact that the careers of most professional athletes are very short. Therefore, they have personal pressures on them to go after the big money contracts and commercial endorsements.

The professional athlete knows that he must be competitive among his peers if he is going to play on a regular basis. That means being one of the fittest, meanest, and most aggressive guys available. A manic nature will give a guy all the emotional push he needs to assume this type of character, and these manic displays are sold as virtues to the fans by the media. There is much shouting, gesturing, and braggadocio, and the public has come to think that such behavior is quite suitable for our heroes on the ball fields and in the arenas. We want them to be strong, tough, and manic when they are performing for us. When players are aggressive, that is how teams win championships. Also, this is the action mode that we can relate to best, and it allows vicarious bonding to occur more easily.

The character of professional sports has definitely changed in recent years. Participants come to play ready to do battle with an enemy, and each team prepares for a game as though it is a military campaign. The coaches, managers, and team owners pressure their players to perform like they are on a battlefield. Skill, and the ability to use it, once was the most sought after qualities in a player, but now management looks for aggressiveness in players and their willingness to commit brute force. This has had a severe impact on the personalities of the athletes. They come to the game with a killer mentality. It is not enough to win in the competition; your opponent has to be beaten in physical, emotional, and psychological terms. And if players need to act like thugs to do it, that's okay, too. Taunting and intimidating talk, abusive language, obscene gestures, threats, and assault and battery are all regularly a part of the games. All major sports venues have now become a more subtle form of the Roman amphitheaters. Fans go to the arenas expecting a fight, and maybe a game will breakout.

Fighting has become institutionalized in all the major sports, and what is most interesting about this is that the games have changed in such a way that they lend themselves to provoking violence. It is said that baseball is America's national pastime, which is to say that baseball is America's most popular sport. And as our most popular sport, it too has become more violent. Every baseball fan knows that the most dangerous and violent thing that can occur in a baseball game is the bean ball; when a pitcher throws a ball at a batter's head. Brushing batters back from the plate has always been part of the game. When it happens, it might very well produce a fight between the players on opposing benches. These incidents were usually quite rare overall. But in recent years, the game has changed and become dependent on specialists like the closer pitcher. The sole purpose of the closer is to come into the game and shut down the opposition in the last inning or two of a ball game that his team is winning.

A good closer is an intimidator. He comes into the game with an attitude that the opposition cannot hit his best pitch, a fastball, a slider, a sinking curve, or whatever. And more often than not the pitcher is right because he knows where he is going to throw the ball. The batter can only guess. The closer can be arrogance personified, and that does not sit well with opposing players. He can have a trick pitch that he uses to embarrass them. Pitchers who show up batters are not to be liked. As one major league player was quoted as saying, "Pitchers, why they aren't even human."

A manic-depressive personality does not take well to stress and ego-deflating pressure. But the confrontation with the closer, as an individual batter, or the team in opposition, has become a daily occurrence. This has brought a level of anxiety to players in the late innings that was not experienced prior to the era of the closer, and the level of overall violence, hit batsmen, bench clearing brawls and angry confrontations between players and umpires has certainly increased. There is much less sportsmanship between the players, and the game is perceptibly different than when I first became interested in it fifty years ago. I am not sure just what all the reasons are for this, but the players are angrier than they used to be.

In pro basketball, the players have sprouted up like Redwood trees. Seven foot plus players are more plentiful now than ever, and overall basketball players are bigger, stronger, and more athletic. Even the smallest players can jump above the basket rim and dunk the ball. The basket on a basketball court is ten feet above the floor. A seven-foot player, standing below the basket, can practically put the ball in the hoop without leaving his feet. Much of the strategy of a pro basketball in recent years was planned to keep the big men as far away from the basket as possible. "Putting a body on the big man in the middle" was the way this was done.

That is, the opposing team members would lean on him, and push him, to keep him away from the basket. But according to the basketball rulebook, if you push on a player, lean on him, or otherwise impede his movements, that is a foul. However, the players were allowed to get away with this all the time because a big man, down close to the basket, would be able to score very easily, and that would make opposing players look like chumps.

Fouling is permitted wholesale in professional basketball, and these are big powerful men, weighing upwards from two hundred to two hundred and fifty pounds. And no one likes to be pushed and shoved around, especially when it is in a basketball game. It is even more upsetting when you are being watched by thousands of people in the arena and on TV. And just as the fans need their sports heroes to vicariously bond with, so it is that the players use the fans to energize them. For the home team in basketball, the fans are the sixth man on the court.

Not only is fouling permitted in keeping the big men away from the basket, but also the guards and forwards are allowed a much larger variety of fouls. Defending players are always hand checking their opponents, setting picks, and pushing off. Not a play goes by without multiple fouls occurring. Obviously, the referees cannot call all these fouls because players would be constantly at the foul line taking free throws. Therefore, the referees decide which fouls they want to call, and their decisions are very personal, arbitrary, and capricious. Any given push, shove, or hand check maybe called a foul or it may not be. It is entirely up to the referees. For this reason, frequently the players do not know the reason for any given foul call, at any given point in the game. Because of their foul-calling authority, it is the referees who can, and do, decide perhaps most of the games that are played in professional basketball. To this degree, the game we see in the National Basketball Association is not basketball the way it was originally supposed to be played. In fact, it is a hybrid that should be more accurately called "Refball."

Basketball was designed to be a game of skill where players would be nimbly moving about the floor, dancing and dribbling around each other in an effort to get a good shot at the basket. Originally, the most important shot was the two-handed set attempt, and lay ups were incidental. Then came the big men, and the small players developed the jump shot to get up and over them. But, in the professional basketball, big men became even more important to the game because of the twenty-four second clock. The team that has the ball must take a shoot in that length of time. Big men were needed to get rebounds. The more you have the ball, the more shots your team can take, and the better chance you have to win.

Therefore, with the need to keep the big men way from the basket, with the further need to crash the boards for rebounds, and because of the twenty-four second clock, there is tremendous pressure on the pro basketball player to be aggressive. And given all the other factors, being champion, financial rewards, and their likely manic-depressive game behavior, is there any wonder that professional basketball has become so mean-spirited and ugly to watch? The in your face, hard-fouls, punish-your-opponent basketball is exhibited for public consumption, and the media announcers keep talking down these activities. They say the players are just playing hard, good, tough basketball.

But, this is not true. Pro basketball players in their new action mode are not just playing hard. They are playing violently, and they are sending a message to the impressionable young people that to play in the game of life, not only do you have to be aggressive and win, but you must also humiliate and punish your opponent. The game of life is really not a game at all. It is a war, and all real players are warriors. Mistakenly, or otherwise, some pro basketball players have come to look like the soldiers of the Mongol Genghis Khan. They have shaved, cue ball heads and tattooed configurations all over their arms. These tattoos can be signs that imply strength and power to the opposition, the enemy players. It is an attempt to subtly intimidate them. The ball head makes the player stand out more. The tattoos make him seem more mysterious and threatening.

Now, if there is any doubt that professional basketball has evolved into an aggressive, violent game, it all comes to fruition with the dunk shot.

These big, strong, athletic players have made dunking the basketball their consummate statement about their attitude towards the game, the opposing players, and to some degree the fans. It is the singularly, most important purpose of the game to put the ball through the hoop. It takes a great deal of skill to do it on a consistent basis by shooting at the basket from fifteen to thirty feet away. Dunking the ball does not require much skill at all. With these big, tall players, they just jump above the rim and jam the ball down through the hoop. And to be sure, they do this angrily and with power, and the harder they slam the ball in the hole, the more the fans seem to like it. To score this way does not give the player any more points nor does it do anything worthwhile for the game. What it does do is make a statement. I am an aggressive, angry young man out to do whatever it takes to win. Don't get in my way or else I'll run over you. Dunking has come to epitomize the violent tendencies in professional basketball, and the fans have shown that they like it. TV pipes this violent action right into our homes, and we say it is great entertainment.

At the start of the 1999 NBA seasons, players were told that they could no longer push and shove the big men down under the basket, and excessive hand-checking would also not be allowed. It was an attempt to cut back on the violence, but these rule changes did not alter the power of the referees to arbitrarily call fouls. "Refball" still lives.

We do not need any in depth analysis of football to say that the game is a violent sport. Indeed, professional football is just another name for organized violence, and college football is not far behind. A pro football player is rated by his fortitude and meanness. There is a parallel axis to his performance: his ability to take pain and his ability to deliver it. He has to be able to take a strong, even vicious hit, and he has to be able to give one back when necessary. With all the talk of strategies, running games, passing games, defensive and offensive maneuvers, the essence of the game comes down to this: the toughest team will usually win most of the time. The reason is because the game is all about brute force. Football seems to tap into our primal nature, and the process may be stimulated by emotional deprivation.

In pro football, players of both teams are supposed to beat up each other. A football game is very much like a street fight, just as explosive and just as dirty. The fans do not see most of the sneaky, underhanded stuff. They are too far away from the action to notice it. Coaches teach their players that the only proper way to play football is to be aggressive and very physical. You cannot be timid and be a good football player. On every play, players are matched up one on one, and a person on the other team has to be blocked, knocked down, or run over. It is get him before he gets you. Football calls upon the participants to be guided by their most basic instincts, the will to survive. This is what the learning in the non-consciousness stage is all about, survival. It is tremendously dangerous on a football field, and any player is always just one hit away from a life-threatening injury. Understand that players are out there on the gridiron to do bodily harm to one another. It is truly the mentality of the caveman, the survival of fittest.

Football is a game that is played for territory. This is very indicative of our primal nature, and consistent with McLuhan's idea that modern man would return to a tribal society. In the game, each side must defend its goal line, its end zone, from infiltration and occupation by the opposing team. Defending territory takes the players emotionally back to the days when humans were forest creatures. It was a time in our past when we had to stake out territory to use for hunting, foraging, and living purposes. It was no game to defend ones territory against other animals in the wilderness. It was a struggle for survival, and often-mortal combat ensued. Every encounter was a desperate one. It truly was kill or be killed. To the victor goes the spoils, and the prize was life itself. Can there be unconscious feelings such as this that help to motivate the football player? It may seem strange to suggest it, but consider this. What does it take for the average person to want to harm someone even when the individual has not offended him in anyway? What has turned him into an enemy is simply because he declared himself your opponent in an insignificant youth game of territorial invasion?

Is there a primordial mentality to the football player? To be sure, like the caveman he must enjoy physical contact, the smashing, crashing, and crunching of human bodies. He must enjoy the fighting and organized mayhem. He must like to taunt and tease adversaries, and he must get pleasure from being sneaky, sly, devious, and a thief. He also must like to hurt other people in order to make himself feel taller and better than they. The point is that all these attitudes and behaviors express basic human emotions, emotions that flow to us from the primordial past when we were governed by raw, unconscious, survival instincts, and these are the feelings that can bring out the kind of nasty, mindless aggression it takes to be a good football player.

And we cannot ignore the dramatic similarities of the modern football stadium to the Roman amphitheater either. Our modern gladiators are on the field fighting for the right to go to the Super Bowl and compete for a championship. They are being urged on by the fans in the stands, who tend to be in varying degrees of drunkenness because of all the beer they have been drinking and the mob mentality that controls them. To be sure, they are all revved up in a vicarious action mode, and they are shouting and exhorting the home team to destroy the visitors. Show them no mercy. The fans want to see violence on the field to compliment the violence they are committing on themselves in the stand.

Our modern day gladiators do not use spears and swords to fight with, but they are just as dangerous as their former counterparts. As physical specimens, they are muscle bound Adonis', but don't let that be misleading. There is an image problem here. Through special training programs, weight lifting exercises, special diets, and the use of various kinds of steroidal compounds, football players have turn themselves into deadly, human weapons. For instance, there are three hundred pound men racing around out there on the gridiron, and when they throw themselves through the air at an opponent, they become flying missiles. And make no mistake about it, professional football players want their opponents to see them as lethal weapons, ready, willing, and able to punish the opposition in defense of their territory.

Baseball maybe the great American pastime, but football is this nation's most popular sport. More people attend football games and watch it on the TV tube than any other sport. As the lifestyles of our culture have taken on a more action mode, games that are in that same mold have become more popular. Football, basketball, hockey, and soccer have increasingly put baseball on notice that they, too, have fan appeal. Specifically, football has overtaken baseball because its violence communicates more directly to its fans. By contrast, it is commonly said today that baseball is too slow and boring. Fans today want to see action and not a lot of guys standing around waiting for a ball to be hit to them.

However, there is one aspect to baseball today that does get much fan attention, and that is the home run. In 1998, Mark McGuire and Sammy Sosa had a home run duel to see which one would break Roger Maris' single season, home run record of sixty-one four-baggers. The entire sports world focused on the competition, and baseball took its place at the top of the sports hierarchy once again. This occurrence in no way changed the fact that football is more compatible to our present day societal action mode. In fact, the home run race between McGuire and Sosa would seem to confirm the analysis.

Sports fans around the nation became caught up in the home run race because in baseball the ultimate expression of power is the long ball. Within the game itself, the most energetic, aggressive, and yes violent thing that a player can legitimately do is that of hitting a home run. It was probably this expression of power and aggression that caught the attention of the sports world. For the action-oriented fans, the home run in baseball is comparable to the dunk in basketball. The television camera can even let the fans fly with the flight of the ball. Is this not the magnificence of electronic communications, and is there any wondering that young people can feel like they are psychologically wired to their electronic machines?

Professional hockey and wrestling have also become very popular today, not to mention boxing. All three sports are purposefully violent, and they are all prominent on home TV. Hockey is probably the most demandingly aggressive, professional team sport in America. Since the athletes are on skates, there is constant action. It is a swiftly paced game, and very much like the computer games that the young people like to play. The players and the puck go flying up and down the ice at a very rapid speed. The fans have to keep their eyes glued to the panorama of action if they want to keep up with what is going on.

Included in the game of hockey is checking. Players are allowed to smash into each other in an effort to control the puck. This angers players and causes fights. But what is even more incredible, hockey teams have players who are designated as the enforcers. It is the purpose of these fellows to go into a game to hurt, and I do mean hurt, a specific opponent on the other team. Is this not the height of purposeful aggression? And it is what the fans go to hockey games to see because the players and the fans have tapped into the reservoir of free-floating aggression. Not only could an enforcer ruin a man's career, but he could also cause a player to sustain a life threatening injury. Intentional violence of this sort is psychopathic.

Wrestling and boxing personifies violence. It is combatants going at each other one on one. In professional wrestling, the violence is choreographed and symbolic like the action in a motion picture, but the message is not lost on the fans. For almost all the major sports, fans are given a false message that violence is unintentional and incidental to the game. But, in boxing, violence is up front, totally exposed and personal. The object of a prizefight is not just to win the bout, but it is really to knock your opponent unconscious. It goes without saying that fighters have been killed in the ring. And now that championship boxing is broadcasted over cable TV, pay per view, no sport's figure is rewarded more richly for committing the worse kind of violence on his fellowman than the prizefighter. What kind of human priorities are we teaching our young people with this kind of message?

Hockey, wrestling, and boxing also emphasizes, in the extreme, the message that you have to be mean, tough, and aggressive if you want to be a winner in the game of life. Is this the type of message our so-called entertainment industries should be sending to members of our society? Of course not, because it is a prescription for violence, and by treating violence as a spectacle that we should enjoy rather than abhor, we are desensitizing and dumbing down our emotions. But we need to ask, where do suppressed emotions go? Nowhere, except deeper into our unconscious mind. Then they may erupt as monsters from the id.

All this sports violence rolls into our homes day after day, night after night, week after week, and all year long. The TV has become our main form of communications and entertainment, and it has become our new chief significant other. Therefore, it is absolutely ridiculous and silly to think that young people, and all of us, are not affected by it. The violence in sports is a reflection of the pervasiveness of the violence that is exhibited throughout our society, and we have already mentioned it in terms of war, racism, sexism, capitalism, crime, and the gun culture. I could also talk about the violence of child abuse, road rage, school shootings, and poverty among many other expressions of it, but the purpose of this study is not to give a list of all the violent acts in our society. The purpose here is to talk about the common root to all the violence, emotional deprivation.

Perhaps the chief role models for young boys today are sports figures. TV is also trying to move young girls in the same direction. It is a merchandising ploy, but it could have a tremendous negative impact on girls. Generally speaking, girls do not have the need for ego enhancement from sports like boys. To say it again, they do not have to prove their femininity like boys feel compelled to prove their masculinity. Nevertheless, the feminist and the TV marketers are trying to create a manufactured form of compulsive femininity based on the hero-worshiping of female athletes. Actually, little girls maybe even more susceptible to vicarious expression of themselves because they find it easy to identify with another woman. They had their mothers as role models. Nevertheless, I hope that most little girls refuse to get sucked into the deadly sports culture of America with its violence and rampaging monsters from the id, and I think they will avoid it. Most girls do not have that strong competitive urge to do well in such a culture, and they will, as females, be better off without it.

To take note of the extent that American males live a fantasy and a vicarious lifestyle, one only has to look at all the clothing items and paraphernalia of sports, movie and TV figures that they wear and use. Compulsive masculinity makes them want to puff up into the image of their heroes. They get a feeling of being their heroes from the clothing being worn with the team logos, the names and numbers of outstanding players. There are advertisements and commercials telling the individuals what kind of food, drink, soap, and deodorant their role models are using. So, not only can the individual dress like his hero, but he can eat and smell like him, too.

The very fact that professional sports have become so important as a form of entertainment also speaks to the presences of compulsive masculinity. The need for males to live vicariously has created a welcomed audience for sports activities. TV feeds this need. Television focuses on young males, especially when it comes to sports programming. This speaks to the fact that the three major sports, baseball, football, and basketball, are fundamentally youth games. They were invented primarily to be a form of exercise and fun for kids. The sports were not meant to have any more meaning than that. But the professionalization of these sports have turned them into something surreal and larger than life, along with the players being elevated to the status of heroic icons. To their detriment, all too many of the players have the emotional makeup of kids, but that is the only way they can take their job performance seriously. They are, by all accounts, compulsively driven personalities, and they put a great deal of pressure on themselves to prove that they are the best among their peers.

As I pointed out, all professional sports are essentially children's games. The games are set up as good guys and bad guys in adversarial situations. In professional form, they have developed into vocations of skilled competition that seem to turn mortal persons into petty gods. So it is that the professional games have come to allocate a certain status of superiority to winners and inferiority to losers. This mantle also falls to the fans that follow the teams. The male ego calls upon the players to be the best. Therefore, the compulsively driven personality will wrap himself up in the image of a winner, as a player, or a fan. There can be a form of bonding between players and fans, and a male's sense of manhood can be strengthened by such relationships.

Compulsion, by its very nature, produces aggression. To be a good ball player, the person has to be aggressive. Aggressive behavior is taught and legitimized for young males through sports participation and fan activity. The aggressive behavior in sports also matches with a need to express it because of the frustration that immature males have to endure through socialization. It is also part and parcel of the general free-floating aggression in society. Players can be aggressive, and they can be rewarded for it, too. Now fans are becoming aggressive like the players they mimic.

The fact that beer is sold at all professional sports events increases the likelihood of aggressive behavior on the part of the fans. Males go to the games because it gives them the opportunity to express their masculine admiration for the sports, and they can be compulsive about it. They can get drunk, paint the team colors on their faces, heckle the players on the opposing team, and boo the referees and officials of the games. And in doing this, they will be applauded for showing strong fan support for their team.

Sports teach males that the aggressive, masculine personality is a winning personality. Compulsive behavior can be seen as being necessary to be a winner, and by implication gaining almost any kind of success in the game of life. So, to be a man is to be a winner throughout, at home, on the job, among other males, and especially in respect to women. To be "a loser" is a crushing blow to any male's ego. Individuals will put enormous pressure on themselves to be winners and to get recognition of that fact. What really is the point about all the awards and championship that are given out in sports to players? They have little to do with the lives of the 99.9 percent of the human population on this planet. These awards feed individual players' egos and vicariously their fans. It is, therefore, a means of reward-ing compulsive, masculine behavior.

Because of television sports, compulsive masculinity is placing even greater emotional demands upon American males to demonstrate their manly character. TV is constantly presenting the best players as role models and specifically encouraging young males to emulate these star professionals. But the truth is that these stars are even unusual among their professional peers. Most sports figures are not of the same level of talent as stars like Michael Jordan, Mark McGuire, or Dan Marino. How can an average group of fans expect to measure up? They can't, but that will not stop them from trying. And, for many, it will engender more frustration in them and raise more questions about their male character in comparison to the sports icons they are trying to emulate.

To emulate professional sports figures in seeking to prove ones sense of masculinity is to judge oneself by standards of a child's game. That is to say, to use sports in this fashion is to restrain ones own emotional devel-opment and maturity. By the same token, to see sports as only a game with no value in it, other than the enjoyment a person gets from playing it or the fan by watching it, would be to take away its importance as a means for individuals to demonstrate their masculinity. But this is the proper way to look at sports. It should not be seen as a means of defining the male character because sports games are, by their nature, capricious and filled with surprises. No two games are ever alike, and consequently there can never be any true, set of standards to judge the male character by.

The only way one can take a child's game seriously, as the professionals and the sycophantic fans, television and news media do, is to act like a child towards the game. This means giving a surreal, larger than life importance to it. Grown men will break down and cry if they lose an important game. Such a lost can make them angry and mad at the world. Professional players are known to throw tantrums, throw items around the clubhouse, and break chairs, mirrors, windows, and their own hands. Such actions are indicative of manic-depressive behavior. The players take losing and winning so personally, one might think that their lives depend on the outcome of the game. I can assure you that this is never the case. All this is to say, professional sports helps the individual maintain an immature outlook on his life, and this makes the personality more suitable for expressing compulsive masculinity.

Sports and television have inadvertently brought to the social surface an old problem for the compulsively driven male personality. Bonding with sports figures has males feeling that they, too, are in the spotlight generally. But national television has also been pushing female sports, professional basketball, soccer, tennis, and boxing. Women are taking away some of the spotlight from the men. There is no doubt that the networks, and especially the cable television sports channels, are trying to create competition between the men and women in professional sports. Unfortunately, the male athletes may be bothered by the old nemesis of an identity crisis now that women are taking some of the television spotlight away from them. If nothing else, the male athletes are likely to behave more compulsively than ever in order to keep them from being eclipsed from the TV spotlight. Their egos will demand it.

It is rather odd that the producers and managers of television sports are pushing so hard to have female professional games compete with the males. Television sports are very important in our culture because they service the male ego, but the fostering of female professional games will undercut this purpose. One reason is the fact that males are not able to identify with female athletes as role models, even though professional female athletes are beginning to act as aggressive and violent as the males. Indeed, such identity would seem to go against the male's social nature. And to be sure, females do not have a need for sports bonding, as do males. Where are the producers and managers of TV going with this?

There is a hierarchy among the sports as to which are most favored by men. Even with all the women who are now engaging in one form of professional sports or another, the cultural value of the sport is still measured by male standards. The more the sport exemplifies masculinity, the more men will relate to it. In this context, the most masculine of sports is prize-fighting, professional boxing. The heavyweight champion of the world is always held in the highest of masculine esteem. When Muhamid Ali was the champion, the mass media declared that he was the most recognized athlete in the entire world. The reason that boxing is so admired it allows an individual man to go against another man, one on one. It puts the character of a real man on display, where he can express his fortitude, his physical power, his prowess, and his ability to confront and defeat an adversary. But most importantly, the professional boxer is allowed to turn himself into a monster from his id, and it can be the ultimate display of compulsive masculinity.

Sports games were originally intended to engage participants. The real fun is in playing, not watching. But, with the professionalization of sports, the purpose of it has been turned around. The public has come to believe that it is better to watch highly skilled players rather than engaging in a clumsy game themselves. And to be sure, professional sports have been with us for more than a hundred years, which suggest that the causes of emotional deprivation, as Freud noted, and its offspring compulsive masculinity, are not something new to the history of our society. But since the coming of TV, sports have grown in cultural magnitude, and it now seems to have become indispensable to the survival of our way of life. There has been an evolution of the relationship of males to professional sports, and it may be due to a greater severity of emotional deprivation among baby boomers and the succeeding generations that have grown up with television. Because of their dependency on electronics generally, they have a consciousness that is very different then the population of sixty years ago at the start of the Second World War.

The Second World War, with its atomic bomb, took away the personal, masculine meaning and purpose of war forever. Like the prizefighter, the soldier was the very symbol of male aggressiveness, bravery, and heroism. The fighting man was no doubt a real man in full character. But with the atomic bomb, war from the American point of view became a battle between eastern and western technologies. Yes, there was the Korean War and the Vietnam War with thousands of American ground troops involved. But in both cases, they were just the end game to the start of a new military era. And as the real testing fields of battle decreased, the void was filled by more and more of a vicarious lifestyle for males. TV suddenly appeared to push the process along, and motion pictures and professional sports quickly fell in line. Decade by decade, electronics invaded our lives with toys, games, computers, and so on, until our children had become human electric cords in constant need of a charge of energy to function in a hyper active world of action.

The energy of the ego is the chief stimulant for compulsive masculinity, and the ego likes to have the individual exhibit his body in energetic, forceful ways. This makes sports perfect for compulsively masculine, exercises. But since the ego is involved, we are talking about the raw energies that come directly from the id, the place of the monsters. This speaks to the fact that sports have become so violent today partly because of an ego-id connection. At the same time, this connection can lead to even more deviant, criminal expressions of ego energy from the id. There are all kinds of monsters tramping through our society, rapist, murders, serial killers, and child molesters. It is then quite obvious to say that some criminal behavior maybe distinct expressions of compulsive masculinity.

As well, it is interesting to point out that ballplayers and criminals have similar modes of behavior. For instance, some of the most aggressive people in our society are professional sports figures and criminals. This is not to say that ballplayers and criminals have similar motives or similar personalities beyond this trait, and I am not trying to stain the character of professional players. But these two groups do example daring, aggressive behavior, and they wear the male persona like a suit of armor. The most interesting thing is that they both exhibit compulsive behavior, and they both are driven to prove that they are better than their adversaries, members of the opposing team and officers of the law.

Both professional ball players and criminals help to tune in youngsters to the prevalence of aggressive behavior in our society. Once young males begin to participate in the outside world beyond the home, they learn early on from peers, magazines, movies, sports, and etcetera, that males are thought to be naturally aggressive, just as women are thought to be generally more passive. In the present time, aggression matches up very well with the action focus of the American lifestyle. Males are made to feel that they must be on the go and be a take-charge-guy. Just as one has to be aggressive when playing sports, the person must be aggressive in the game of life. Males are thought to be leaders. They want to be out front. The world is a stage, and all of us are actors on it. The aggressive person, the successful person, is always center stage. He wants to be the center of attraction wherever he goes. It is an ego thing, and compulsive masculinity demands that he make the effort.

Being aggressive also means making one stand out in a crowd. Ego and the X-factor can cause males to do odd and even bizarre things to accomplish this. They can become devils or saints, bullies, racists, sexists, and even clowns. The purpose is to get that attention and command center stage. In school, young males learn that it is important to be at the head of the class. If they are going to get the most out of life, then they must try and become the best at something. Trying to be the best can become a compulsion in itself, and it pits males of the same peer group against one another. School boards, with their grades and promotion systems, inadvertently encourage this kind of competition, and it exacerbates the feelings young males can have with their compulsive masculinity.

The fact that young boys are made to feel that they must become the best at something, even if it is lying, cheating, or harassing the girls, causes them to become dreamers at a very young age. They can have dreams of rising to the top of some social or vocational ladder. But, for the overwhelming majority of the young males, they will never get to the top of anything. There are too many aspirants for the very small number of places at the top of the social hierarchy. The majority will strive, but only a few will succeed. This has always been the case in societies that are stratified and hierarchical. Therefore, compulsively masculine behavior will lead to only frustration for most of the male population in America. No matter how hard they try, most of them will not be allowed to succeed. But they will mimic the media blessed role models and acquiesce to vicarious forms of living instead.

The aggression that comes from compulsive masculinity results from the frustration induced by society. Therefore, males can harbor an instinctive dislike of society, and they will try to find ways to overcome the power they think society has over them. Their drive for success is a desire to best the system. Men are often driven to gain power, wealth, status, and authority to put them above the control of society. To be sure, this is the ultimate meaning of success for the capitalist. This is why we always find the businessman and the politician in bed together. In America, there is a symbiotic relationship between them. Indeed, American society is crowded with rich, power-drunk, power-crazed men. Think of it: why is the goal of a rentier capitalist constantly about making more and more money when he does not need it? At some point, the money becomes not a means to an end, but the end in itself.

Deviant and criminal behavior are even clearer examples of how some individuals will try to put themselves above or outside of the control of society. For these groups, their social paths can be seen as a form of self-ostracism. They take these paths not as a matter of choice, but rather because they cannot help themselves. They are emotionally compelled to do what it is that ostracizes them. Like the smoker, the alcoholic, the gambler, and the junkie, the compulsive personality suffers from an emotional addiction. In this case, the compulsive personality is unable to control his deviant and criminal behavior. In fact, his errant behavior is controlling him.

Aggressive behavior and the action mode of our society do go hand in hand. Everyone is caught up in this mode in one way or another. Therefore, aggressive behavior has become a norm, and we have spoken of this in the form of films, sports, and so on. But because it is a norm, we have come to dumb down our emotions, and we have become less sensitive to the real negative nature of aggressive behavior. We may talk about the good qualities of an individual who takes charge, and is bold and energetic, but that is just the other side of the coin from being aggressive, pushy, and militant. We reward this kind of behavior in a man's world. Jesus' pronouncement that the meek shall inherit the earth does not apply here. If you turn the other cheek, you are likely to get your butt kicked.

Because of ego and the X-factor, all males will not, and cannot, react the same to aggression as a norm. Indeed some will resist complying with the norm because they fear the power that society may have over them. Others may feel that society is, like their mothers, demanding their obedience as she did during socialization. They might then rebel against the demands of society. Rebellion is very much within the character of the male persona in this culture. It is the idea of taking a stand, challenging the odds, and standing up as the underdog. It means being stubborn and doing things on your own when matters call for it. All of these character elements are richly sought after by the compulsive male personality. These virtues are extolled in the behavior of the rugged individualist. Just think of the movie persona of John Wayne.

Rebellion is thought to be a natural reaction to the status quo and the older generation by young people. Which is to say, social rebellion is very much a youthful exercise. As this speaks to the phenomenon of compulsive masculinity, it reaffirms the idea that all the fuss about proving ones manhood is an attitude of an immature person. No surprises here. The reliance on sports and hero worship confirms this. And youthful rebellion is often a reaction to pressure from the older generation to conform. It is usually one's mother who symbolizes that older generation. Fathers tend to be more tolerant of their sons. But, since mothers are likely to want their male offspring to comply with the norms of society, some males will turn their aggression specifically on their mothers. They may hold them responsible for the pressure they feel to conform to the norms. Thus, mothers are getting what they justly deserve, or so the young person might believe.

Males may also turn their aggression against their mothers because of the identity conflict they may be experiencing and because of the misguided belief that their mothers are responsible for trying to sissify them. They are likely to feel guilty about exhibiting such behavior, but their compulsion will drive them to do it anyway. This same sense of guilt may actually cause some males to acquiesce to the belief that they have been sissified, and they may further believe that that is the behavior their mothers want from them. The identity conflict is then resolved in favor of effeminacy. As a consequence, a reverse course of compulsive masculinity can occur, but the male homosexual is likely to be just as rabid about his masculinity as the so-called macho man.

Young males are very sensitive to any hint of sissification, and they will use aggressive behavior to show their toughness. Indeed, young males learn quickly that boys are supposed to be tough, meaning hard nosed. This attitude is contrasted with girls who are supposed to be sugar, spice, and everything nice. Little boys learn that they are expected to be like vinegar, ice, and nothing nice. Nice guys finish last, and they usually are sissies. Acting tough is always expressed in comparison to girls. And being tough means not giving into pain, not showing emotions, and absolutely no crying. Nothing denies manhood more than crying. It is girlish, and demonstrates a specific lacking in the male character, or so the belief in the male persona goes.

Males are compulsive about being tough because they have an inner dread appearing weak. Weakness is thought to be a female trait, and every fiber in their being tells them that women do not like weak men. For procreative purposes, women have always been drawn to strong, tough males. The most desirable men in our society are the successful men who tend to be compulsive and aggressive. Acting tough lets women know this. The tough guy is very attractive to females. They have a raw aurora of masculinity that is appealing.

In civil society today, the tough guy image is played down by females, in particular the new feminists. But at the same time, under the guise of women liberation, those same feminists are calling for women to be treated equally in the military, in sports, and generally across the social board. Given the way the major institutions in society function, women have found themselves adopting the role-playing of males, and they are competing with men. They try to be tough like men, but it is difficult for them. They do not have the ego or the compulsive drive that keeps pushing men along. Without that sense of compulsive masculinity, many women find it all but impossible to keep up with the men on a one to one basis.

As every male knows at a very young age, acting tough means putting on a performance. Acting tough is never a spontaneous act. It is always a plan in the person's mind, and the performance completes the plan. It is another obvious reason for the role-playing that males engage in. Indeed, acting tough is, in Erving Goffman's phrase, "a presentation of self."[12] Or, at least that is what the person thinks he is doing. But all too frequently, it is not the innate self of the person that is being presented in the performance, but it is a role that has been designated by society. We may pooh-pooh the tough guy imagine, but we certainly have not given up on it. If nothing else, the males think they need it as a function of their masculine persona.

Compulsively, the tough guy image is kept alive in the news media, in motion pictures and on TV. There is the dedicated cop, the hardboiled private eye, and the gangster, which are all characters in movies and teleplays. We can recall the performances of Frank Sinatra, Humprey Bogart, and Edward G. Robinson in these kinds of parts, and there is always another crop of these tough guys playing on the big and little screens. There is Clint Eastwood, Arnold Schwarzenegger, and Steven Seagal. These film characters are not real, but they keep alive the image of the tough guy so that young males know what to strive for. They are important to the compulsive personality because it tells the person how to act tough in language, facial expressions, and demeanor.

The fact that toughness is a performance tells us that it is an image thing and very much a direct expression of the ego. Whenever the ego is involved, so is the id. And, when the male acts tough, he uses it to put someone off and even frighten him. Success depends on how good is the performance. People who act tough usually do it in loud, obvious, and conspicuous ways. They are attempting to manipulate someone's emotions. To do this, they have to make a strong impression on the individual, and scaring the person can often accomplish this. The manipulator may then draw upon a monster from his id to demonstrate his toughness. This may require him to be verbally abusive and vicious, or it may cause him to commit violent acts towards that other person. The motivation and energy for the monster will come from the unconscious mind, and the individual may have little conscious control over his actions. Indeed, this is how compulsion works.

When a person acts tough, like being loud and boisterous to intimidate someone, it suggest that he is putting on a front to hide his true feelings. Maybe the person does not feel tough and strong, but rather he feels weak and frightened. He may then have fears that someone will question his posture and suspect that he is a phony. This can cause him to exaggerate his toughness to an unrealistic degree. Young people in rebellion are examples of this kind of phenomenon. They feel they must put up an irredeemable front because they suspect that adults will not take them seriously. This is why young people are constantly pushing the social envelope and climbing out on tenuous emotional tree limbs. Compulsive masculinity goes well with this kind of youthful attitude. It supports that natural, breakaway, rebellious mentality.

Youthful rebellion invariably begins in the home, and as such a boy will frequently exhibit toughness towards his mother. He may be unconsciously stimulated to try to breakaway from the sissified influence that he feels he has learned from her. Because he has been emotionally deprived, a boy can feel that his masculine self is repressed and smothered when he is at home with his mother, and that is why he feels he must rebel against her. But later that same need to express toughness can be transferred to other women who can come to represent the mother as a stand-in. As a cultural persona, in their romantic relationships, men often find themselves wrestling with the ghosts of their mothers.

Acting tough is role-playing and a function of compulsive masculinity. Therefore, the person can feel ambivalent about it. Role-playing is a reminder of mother as a role model. This can heighten a male's identity conflict, and make him feel more like his mother than he consciously wants to admit. Consequently, it can cause him to double his efforts at being tough, even if it puts him on the outs with society. Indeed, being on the outs with society is a confirmation of toughness. This is clearly the case with hoodlums and gangsters. They are in a battle with society that started with socialization back in the home. These individuals may be the extreme examples of toughness derived from compulsive masculinity.

Hoodlums and gangsters contest the authority of society by breaking and flaunting the law. They know they will be incarcerated if they are caught. Therefore, they are mindful of the fact that their activities put them in jeopardy. Nevertheless, their compulsion to be tough can be so keen; these individuals will even put their lives on the line to prove it to themselves and society. After all, in our culture, a defiant death is the ultimate expression of toughness. It shows that a person is willing to give up everything to prove just how strong he really is. In motion pictures, TV programs, legend, and song, a defiant death is extolled as a virtue and a true statement of masculine pride and fortitude.

In the motion picture *White Heat*, James Cagney, the consummate movie gangster and tough guy, made this most telling statement on the present subject. The tough guy can think of himself as fighting against his mother, society, and the world. Playing a gangster in the motion picture, Cagney finds himself trapped by the police on top of a huge oil tank. The police are closing in. If he surrenders, he would be admitting defeat, society will have subdued him, and his veneer of toughness would be shattered. But the character has no intention of giving himself up. He has a gun in his hand, and he waves it in the air as he screams, "Look Momma, I'm on top of the world." He then fires his gun into the oil tank and blows himself up.

In the motion pictures, tough guys, be they bad like the James Cagney character or good ones in the John Wayne mode, they are all presented as folk heroes and romantic icons. This makes them very appealing to the eyes of young people, and of course the movie industry plays to this. The producers of motion pictures make a concentrated effort to seduce the kids into a following for tough guy characters. Toughness, as motion pictures portray it, is a metaphor for power, strength, and bravery, and these attributes are all thought to be masculine ideals.

It is most interesting to point out that a tough guy is thought to be someone who is persistent, a person who does not give up easily. Richard Nixon used to say, "When the going gets tough, the tough get going." For him, toughness was a call to action. This attitude fits securely with the action mode of today's culture. In this same sense, being tough is enhanced by the compulsion the person is feeling when he is acting tough. It is the feeling of action within action. Mr. Nixon thought he was tough because he could act tough, but when his feet were finally put to the fire because of the debacle of Watergate, his real frightened self came out in the open. It was then that he retired from public office. He could not face the humiliation of impeachment. If he had been convicted, he would have been confronted by his own demons in the form of monsters from his id, and he would see himself as having lost the battle to show the world that he was a real man.

Traditionally in our culture, toughness was thought to be almost entirely a male trait. But the new feminists are furthering the notion that females can be, and perhaps should be, just as tough as males. The motion picture industry and TV programs are presenting images of tough women in sports, the military, the police force, in business, and as politicians. Much of it is pure hype and characterization, but the feminists are pushing the images hard on the young girls who have yet to reach maturity. I am not sure where this is going, but I can say with a definite certainty that it will not eliminate emotional deprivation in females or compulsive masculinity in males. It is inconsistent with a woman's nature to try and act like a man. In fact, it is likely to deepen her sense of alienation.

Contrary to men acting tough, today's feminists have attacked males for being unable to express their feelings. Women say that men withhold their emotions, and it is unhealthy. In keeping their feelings inside, this can cause them to explode angrily from the built up emotional pressure. But what disturbs women even more is the fact that men do not openly express their feelings for them. Men have difficulty saying they care for, and love, a woman. One of the goals of Women's Liberation was to get men to open up more, and be more emotionally expressive like them. But whether women like it or not, the male nature is one that is less expressive of his inner feelings than a woman. Essentially, no amount of feminists browbeating is going to change that.

Yes, with pushing and urging from a new feminist credo, some men have tried, and I guess to some degree succeeded, in acquiescing to the wishes of women. They have become more expressive with their feelings. But in truth, most men are not comfortable with this new mode of behavior. The reason is quite obvious. It is not natural for men to overtly show their emotions. They can make it a part of their act, make it a new bit of role-playing, but they generally do not take such behavior seriously. They may do it because their female friend or spouse wants it, but given their druthers, they would do otherwise. Just as women should not try to be men, they should also stop trying to get men to be women. Being unemotional was thought to be a part of the armor of the chauvinist pig that the modern feminists were against. For that very reason alone, men should not try to alter themselves because women want them to do so.

There is another way of understanding the ambiguity of this situation. In being non-emotional, males have come to think of it as expressing strength. This attribute is firmly part of the male persona. It is consistent with the idea that big boys and men don't cry. They are expected to control their feelings. We can see how this is in contrast with women who have the tendency to cry at the drop of a hat, when they are happy or sad. This is a clear emotional distinction between men and women, and I would suggest that it is innate. The feminists would have us believe otherwise. They say that men withhold their emotions because society has taught them to do so, but then I would ask the feminist, why do women cry much more readily than men? Did society teach them to do that also? If the feminists were honest with themselves, they would have to answer no.

I don't mean to say that society has not exploited this natural difference between men and women. For instance, there is this cultural belief that a man is being strong when he withholds his emotions, and a woman is showing weakness when she cries easily. But neither one of these descriptions are appropriate for the two behaviors. The difference is there, but it does not mean a good characteristic for one, and a bad characteristic for the other. Men are innately what they are, and the same applies to women. There is no way to truly or reasonably compare innate qualities of the sexes. We are what we are, and there is no legitimate way to qualify a better or worse situation for either.

Because there is this false notion that women are inferior to men, showing emotions is thought to be a non-masculine thing. To this degree then, males learn at a very early age not to show their emotions to girls. Boys think that the females will not respect them as a real male if they do. In the past, when human beings had to do battle with the elements and the beast of the forests, women were naturally drawn to the strong male individuals who could protect and provide them with food, clothing and shelter. They did not want weak, crybaby men who acted like women. This is still true today, but then it begs the question. Why are the feminists "pussifying" the men, turning them into wimps that go against their natural grain? The feminists are surely confused in what they are doing.

Males express compulsive masculinity because they are trying to break out of the pattern of behavior they learned from their mothers. That pattern evolves from the natural relationship between mothers and their children. It develops because children want to please their mothers. It is the same as pleasing themselves when they are in that period 0-3 years old, but a boy child will find himself in conflict with his innate sense to be reserved when he displays his emotions. For this reason, there is always a repressed component to males expressing their emotions. There is a part of the person that wants to do it, and another part of him that does not want to do it.

If a person is withholding his feelings, hiding his emotions, he is perpetrating a lie. He is lying to himself and to others. And if he is presenting himself falsely, then he is living a lie. It is an act of suppression and repression against oneself. This can trigger reactions from monsters of the id. When monsters start trampling, all kinds of bizarre things can occur. The person may try to hide from himself, but this will be difficult because his innate self will not be denied. It will find ways to express itself. Therefore, the person may very well seek out other means to help him hide. He may become a substance abuser, with alcohol, amphetamines, Prozac, heroin, or crack. The individual may go after whatever he thinks will help him control his feelings. It might even be a lifestyle of wild promiscuity.

One of the chief disorders of a person who holds back his emotions is the disease of manic-depressiveness. It is an old illness, but it is quite prevalent in our society today, particularly in respect to sports and the rabid fans that follow them. This disease is very interesting because the two extreme supports each other. A person is manic to force himself from being depressive, and he is depressive to avoid expressing his manic behavior. The problem is obvious. To suppress one is to call up the other in a never- ending cycle. This is truly a self-perpetuating monster from the id.

Males have an aggressive persona. Females have a more passive image. However, it is the males who withhold their emotions in a passive fashion, and the females who express their emotions more openly and readily. This is another reason why there is emotional conflict in both males and females when it comes to expressing their feelings. For each one to live up to their social expectations, they have to suppress their innate feelings to do the opposite of what their socialization has told them to do. This twist of behavior flows directly from the problem of emotional deprivation.

With men having a natural tendency to withhold their emotions and women having the tendency to openly express their emotions, there is a certain emotional compatibility between them. One acts to form a balance with the other. But things are changing. Due to the attitude of feminists, women are calling upon men to show their emotions and be more like them. However, the feminists do not seem to realize that they are asking men to go through another form of socialization. And this can trigger in men the memory of their mothers who caused them to experience an identity crisis. As women ask men to be like them, their request may be taken as an attempt to wipe out their male identity completely. Men may think that women are trying to steal, or prevent them, from expressing their manhood. In the gangster phrase, the guys may feel that the women are trying to rub them out.

Women pride themselves on their sensitivity and intuitiveness. Yet, they seem to be unaware of the undue pressure they are putting on men in trying to get them to be more expressive of their feelings. Forgetting socialization for the moment, the bottom line is this: if men wanted to express their inner feelings more, they would do it, and they would not need women pushing and pressuring them to do so. All too frequently women want to mother their men, and they persist with the idea that all men are nothing but little boys on the inside. Women should realize that this is an attitude that exacerbates compulsive masculinity.

When young males are growing up, they learn soon enough that image is more important than substance. They learn that pretending is basic to the male character and persona. In trying to live up to the cultural image of a man, the male will be effectively a role-player, and role-playing is basically an act of pretending. Again, this attitude of being a pretender gives legitimacy to a vicarious lifestyle. It makes for easy bonding between the public and their motion picture, TV, sports heroes, and it gives verification to the idea that whole world is a stage and we are all actors on it.

Consider what these heroes represent. They symbolize rugged individual-ism, the John Wayne kind. He stood for law and order, morality, bravery, nobility, and protection of the little guy. Young males will model their behav-ior after these heroic icons, in particular the motion picture personalities. It is easy to do it because their exploits are presented in dramatized stories, with music to match that tingles the spirit and helps to bring the actors alive and closer to the viewer. These characters are seen as being larger than life, and making the impossible seems ordinary. But it sends the wrong message to young males that they must perform like their role model heroes if they want to succeed in life and reach the top of the heap in America.

But in truth, real people cannot match up to the behavior of the motion picture and TV heroes. Their actions are unreal and choreo-graphed. They are following a script, and they are always winners if the story calls for it. Because of their action orientation, and their electronic connections, young males will feel that they must be like their celluloid role model heroes. Though they cannot be as a brave and successful as those icons, they will still put on a front and pretend that they can be all the same. The fact is they will be displaying bravado, and bravado, in and of itself, is a form of vicarious behavior.

From motion pictures and TV stories, young males get the message that they live in a culture that is dominated by the values of social Darwinism. Society functions on the basis of the struggle between the classes, the races, ethnic groups, the rich and poor, women and men. The capitalistic economic system, the political institutions, and the adversarial nature of the criminal justice system inspire it all. To survive in this system, you have to be brave and aggressive; or at least project this image for others to see. Social Darwinism confirms the idea that the strong win in the game of life; and once again, it speaks to the importance of sports.

Sports allow males to be aggressive and violent, but it is also used to bind males together in behaviors that in the overall constitute the male persona. The individual ego pits one male against another, but in sports, team sports that is; it allows males to combine egos for a common purpose.

With all the compulsive masculinity going on, if there were not some apparatus or institution like sports, men would take more of their aggressions out on each other and women, too. John Dollard said that because society has a reservoir of free-floating aggression, there must be outlets devised by society for its use. The perennial racial, religious, and ethnic scapegoats are always available, but because of the new electronic culture, games and sports have become more useful as a way of letting out aggression.

This new form of releasing aggression is more surreal than real. It is a pretender's way of presenting an image for public consumption, which is precisely what motion pictures and TV are all about. At the same time, when a person is pretending, putting on a false face, then he is hiding himself, or he thinks he is. When one is being aggressive vicariously, it is not the same as being truly aggressive towards the real world. Instead, it is another form of suppression, and such action forces itself down into the unconscious mind and brings into play the power of the id. This is likely to generate, in bravado terms, walking, talking monsters.

A person will present the face of bravado to give others a false impression of him, and to try to convince them of his sincerity. He may not feel very comfortable about doing this, but he is more afraid of being exposed as a phony. Bravado is a defense mechanism, and it is used, in part, because so much of the male persona is just pure role-playing. Since role by definition is false, the male knows that his grand masculine behavior is bogus, but he goes on acting out the phony business because it is something all the males are doing. Even if he were not inclined to engage in bravado, his ego would still call upon him to participate in the exercise like other males. Because of a need to bond, many males have a tremendous fear of being ostracized from the group of their peers. This will keep them acting out their role-playing because it allows them to fit in.

Compulsive masculinity brings pressure to bear on males to act tough and brave for the sake of their persona, and it points to the ambiguous nature of the male cultural character. It even suggests that there are many different reasons that cause males to behave in a rational or irrational manner. How do you define a calculate risk? Because we live in a bureau-cratic society, we have tried to make our system function rationally, but it is not going to happen. For instance, males in our society are being driven by compulsive masculinity and that is not rational. Indeed, in many ways it is down right neurotic, if not worse. Ambiguity reigns supreme, and no amount of rules, regulations, laws, role model heroes, or anything else is going to change that. The male has an ego, and it has more influence over his innate behavior than anything the culture has yet to come up with. I don't see that changing in the future. One of the best statements that I have ever heard about the ambiguity of the male character was made by Gregory, "Papy," Boyington. Boyington was a flying tiger and a Marine Corps pilot who won the Congressional Medal of Honor during the Second World War. He was a first class hero, a role model of sorts for young people, but this is what he said about the hero. "Just name a hero and I'll prove he's a bum."[13]

Compulsive masculinity, masked as heroism, can cause men to pay the ultimateprice, death. It occurs often in combat situations during wars. Soldiers and other military personnel will seemingly give up their lives for the cause, their buddies, or for a military objective. Individuals may know ahead of time that they are going into a no win, no return situation, and that death is a foregone conclusion. Yet, they carry on and do their duty, with the knowledge that they will get no reward for their sacrifice. Such individuals maybe motivated by heroism, but Emile Durkheim had another name for it. He called it altruistic suicide.[14]

Men are thought to be braver than women. This is supposedly due to their egos and natural aggressiveness. But once again the feminist are try-ing to change this male-female dynamic. They are pushing the idea that women are just as brave as men. The fact that women want to be warriors in the military, cops, firemen, and astronauts indicates this. And women think they should not be excluded from any job just because it poses a threat to human life. But whether women can do the same job as men is really not the issue. With men and women in the same workplace, many men are finding it more than a little uncomfortable competing with females. In this context, for a man, having a job has lost some of its meaning, and many a guy is bedeviled by a nagging thought: if women can do the same job as men, then maybe men are not so damn superior after all?

In fact, there is one way that men are definitely inferior to women. As we have been talking about it here, compulsive behavior is caused by emotional deprivation, and men are more susceptible to it than women. As a consequence, when under pressure, real or imagined, severely emotionally deprived men often find themselves functioning out of control. And when a person is out of control, he may not be cautions and careful. Indeed, such individuals like to take chances. Taking chances, pushing the emotional envelope, putting oneself in harm's way, these are attributes that are very much a part of the male persona today. From this, a young male comes to realize that life is a high stakes game, and sometimes you have to gamble based on assumption or gut feeling. Indeed, he learns that to be a big winner, you may have to be foxy and slick. Therefore, men are expected to be daring and willing to throw caution to the winds when the need arises, and whenever there is the opportunity to grab the brass ring.

Taking chances means relying on ones inner feelings and intuition. Intuition is a function of the unconsciousness and the psyche, and this puts the action at the level of the id where monsters may be stimulated. Similarly, taking chances means challenging the unknown. In the *Star Trek* sense, it means going where no man has gone before. It means having an interest in adventure, the bizarre, and mysterious things. It means experimenting. Which leads me to ask, why do so many young people get involved in alcoholic drinking, smoking, and drug taking, especially when there is so much evidence to tell them that it is bad for their health? And why do so many young people get caught up in cults of one sort or another, religious, political, cultural, or artistic? Maybe it is the emotional need to take a chance, to experiment.

Of course, living a vicarious lifestyle is also a way of taking a chance, and it cannot be exaggerated how various forms of this have taken over the behavior and personalities of Americans today. This is extraordinarily true for young males from fifteen to thirty-five, and this is no accident. Young males are the prime targets for motion pictures and TV audiences. It is they who respond most readily to the present day action mode of society. As such, males are very willing to take chances because they feel they are mimicking their fictional heroes. Because of the movie going and the TV watching, the avid fans feel embolden by the chances they take. They see themselves as the heroes they imitate, and it makes them feel larger than life. But, unfortunately for them, they will have to learn that they are but human, and they cannot accomplish what scripted heroes can. But, they can still be fearless because they are living through some hero's make believe experience.

Motion pictures and TV programs have come to be guides as to how males can, and should, take chances. The characters on the big and little screens do a lot of drinking, smoking, and drug taking. All this hedonism is presented as a means of having great fun and gaining meaningful pleasure. But we all know these activities are bad for our health. They are killers. However, they may offer something that cannot be gotten any other way. The smoking, drinking, and drug taking can bring euphoria and ecstasy of a magnitude that makes taking the chance worth it. Our celluloid heroes are telling us, this is what real men are into these days. They are taking these stimulants to fortify themselves in the difficult game of life. It is rough out there, and a little help from these stimulants make things go better.

We are taking chances when we use drug stimulants, but taking chances has other rewards. A person is putting himself in jeopardy, psychologically, emotionally, or physically, and this sense of being in jeopardy can make the adrenalin pump faster inside the individual. This rush can give him a charge like a feeling of compulsion. Men will do all sorts of things to get an adrenalin rush. They will even do foolish and dangerous things, like engaging in criminal behavior, being a racing car driver, test pilot, tightrope walker, wrestle alligators, and put their heads in the mouths of lions. Young people are very much into risk taking, but it tends to be of the rebellious kind. For young males, it can be just another expression of their efforts at compulsive masculinity. In any case, for them, their cause is always genuine and unique.

When one gets an adrenalin rush from doing something dangerous, it is a kind of high, and such euphoria can have a strange effect upon individuals. One particular effect is autoerotism, and for this reason, some men will seek out an adrenalin rush for that added pleasure it brings. It makes acting out the male persona just that more worthwhile and enjoyable, and it gives a hedonistic dimension to compulsive masculinity that encourages males to behave in their role-playing fashion. Men have been known to go beyond an erection in these circumstances. Indeed, some men have reached climax and ejaculated in the face of danger. If there were any one thing that might help women understands that men are basically different constitutionally than they, perhaps knowing this occurrence would help. I cannot image women being afraid, and then they have an orgasm as a consequence of it. They are more likely to pee in their pants and let it go at that.

Males are more daring than females because of their ego, and if they were not driven by compulsive masculinity to prove their manhood, they would still be risk takers. There is also a stimulus that comes from the natural competition between males for the favor of females. By the same token, women have always tried to prevent their men from taking too many chances because they need them to protect hearth and home, especially when children are very young. When women address men in this manner, the men may see them as acting like their mothers, and then out of defiance they may conduct themselves precisely in the way they were asked not to do.

In effect then, when women try to hold men back, men may perceive this as an attack on the male ego. The males will likely act very strongly against women, in these instances, because they will feel the need to defend themselves. The tendency to be a man will be backed by compulsive masculine behavior. Undoubtedly, in American society, this is one of the chief reasons why there is so much strife in relationships between men and women. After thousands and thousands of years living with men, women are still doing battle with the male ego. It would be better if they acknowledged it and came to terms with it. Women can never understand what ego really means to a man; just as men will never understand what love really means to a woman.

Once males reach puberty, the emphasis of their compulsive behavior is to impress, and eventually to seduce, females. Making out and sleeping with girls becomes the most important focus in a young man's life. This continues into his adult years. For many, males, from the ages 15-45, sex becomes the strongest motivating force in their lives. If a male is having an identity crisis with his mother, what better way to put it to rest than by seducing females? Getting over with the girls should help to establish a guy's sense of sexual identity, and it should give him prove positive that he is a man. If there is one requirement nature puts upon the male and his manliness, it is his participation in the function of procreation. Only a male can impregnate the female: ergo, masculinity is established.

But, compulsive masculinity pushes men to seek out sexual relationships for the pure enjoyment of it. A sexual orgasm reaffirms the innate self. Consequently, men are largely motivated by lust and a desire to have unrestrained, erotic pleasure with a woman. Planting their seed is of secondary importance. That men can satisfy their lust and impregnate women at the same time, it is nature's way of ensuring procreation. Also, seducing and seeking sexual gratification from a woman is a way a compulsively driven male can feel he is being aggressive, and for some men this can be a sublime expression of their manhood. Of course, it is mostly imaginary, but then that is much of the force behind compulsive masculinity.

Therefore, it goes without saying that there is an instinctive drive in men to seduce women, and women also have a tremendous need to give themselves to men. They are motivated by one of the strongest forces in nature, the desire to reproduce and continue the specie. When women are prime for impregnation physically and emotionally, it does not take a Don Juan or a Casanova to seduce them. This is to say that because of their biology, women will be responsive to compulsive masculine behavior. When seduction is the game, the biology of a woman takes over, and she is no more in control of her sexual self than is a man with his ego.

Now let me be clear. I am not saying that when a woman is in heat she will have sex with just any man. However, there is the likelihood that any man would have sex with any woman under such circumstances, if for no other reason than the fact that he is being driven by his compulsive masculinity. But there is always the X-factor to be considered on the part of the male and female. And women still have a natural urge to mate with the best, biggest, strongest males who they feel will give them healthy, vigorous offspring. The stronger the offspring, the better the chance of survival for the child and the specie. In this sense, procreation is the male's prerogative.

How very interesting. The feminists have been styling the debate about women's liberation around the notion that it is men who have screwed up their lives with a chauvinist pig attitude of keeping them home, barefoot and pregnant. But if women have an innate, biological need to be procreative, then home is where they ought to be, and men cannot be blamed for it. But more importantly, if procreation is a male's prerogative, then women have taken the wrong stand on their right to an abortion. The decision to have a baby was never their privilege alone. Therefore, they should not have the sole right to decide to terminate the pregnancy. In any case, a compulsively masculine driven male would find it shocking that a woman would want to terminate his baby. He would perceive it as an attack on his ego.

As its been said, women have always chosen the biggest, healthiest, strongest men to mate with. They were usually the rugged individualist type. But could you imagine John Wayne consenting to his wife having an abortion? He would not likely do so. However, the days of the rugged individualist are gone. There are still the celluloid images, but in the real world there are only semblances of the Tarzan Man and the Frontiersman. Physical strength and prowess has been replaced by wealth and social status, but these characteristics are poor substitutes for raw masculinity. As well, wealth and status is by its nature circumscribed. Only a few people can have it, while the majority cannot. This situation has caused non-elite males to be very hyper in acting out their compulsive, role-playing, male personas.

So, we come right back to where we started. Males are driven to prove their manhood by seducing females, and this compulsive behavior can parallel the sexual drive because they are both energized from the id. However, this can be a dangerous combination that makes men go sexually wild. When sex and monsters from the id get together, this is sure to lead to violence. Isn't this what we see in motion pictures and on television all the time. The combination appeals to something inside of us, and it also raises a question. Can compulsive personalities get meaningful gratification from their sexual engagements? Because, as some honest men would willingly tell women in a candid moment, few sexual encounters with females actually live up to their billing. There is too much dishonesty and illusion involved.

The modern feminists are bucking the tide. They want to copy this male, compulsive sexual behavior. They have ordained that the passive, Victorian woman is dead, and she must never rise again. For centuries in the western world, men had sexual freedom that was out of reach of women. Men could have wives, paramours; visit prostitutes, and involved themselves in all kinds of sexual shenanigans. They could seduce many females and sport their success like a badge of honor. But if women did the same thing, they would likely be branded a whore and a slut. However, now there has been the sexual revolution, and women see themselves as being free to engage in premarital sex to the same degree as men. And they are asking the question, "What's love got to do with it?" But the better question is, "What has compulsive masculinity to do with it?"

THE BIOLOGICAL IMPERATIVE

If men are being driven by ego and compulsive masculinity to seduce women, why do women so willingly give in to them? Indeed, the question may well be, "What's love got to do with it?" And the answer is, in the romantic, poetic sense, probably nothing. Sure, women like to hear men say, "I love you," but when women submit to men, they are responding to something that is much more primal. Compulsive masculinity may have been an inducement for women to change their sexual behavior, but it has not caused them to change their biology. And it is biology that matters more than their sociology. When are we all going to get that through our heads? There would not be the problem of emotional deprivation if we would accept this basic fact. But of course, that is more easily said than done. Therefore, let us take a look at the impact of this problem from the point of view of the girl child.

To begin with, it comes as no surprise to say that a girl child will associate herself very strongly with her mother, but unlike a boy, the girl will not suffer an identity crisis about it. However, she will still have emotional problems because of the deprivation she experiences during the first years of her life. Talcott Parsons says that a girl's mother is a personal role model for goodness, wifehood, motherhood, and homemaking. The girl is made to feel this should be the direction of her life, and doing these things will give her emotional fulfillment. And, as a consequence, she will be relieved of her deprivation. But, when the girl becomes a woman, to accomplish these things, she must "catch a man," and this activity is very anxiety provoking for a female.

The feminists today have decried this notion of a girl's life being directed to homemaking. In a male dominated society, women have been pressured to see themselves as family providers first and little else second. They have been socialized, so the feminists say, to think that the best thing they can do with their lives is to be wives and mothers. Indeed, if one accepts the Adam and Eve theory, then God wants women to do these things, too. That makes the case for Holy Destiny. The feminists say that this is the worst kind of chauvinistic fatalism.

However, in making these statements, the feminists are being naive and more than a little disingenuous. What essentially motivates women towards marriage and motherhood is the inherent need within humanity to perpetuate itself. Women must bear offspring if humankind is to continue to make history. We can talk about the power of social institutions, male domination in society, and the obnoxious, sexist, chauvinistic pig, but in the end it is none of these things that force women to get married and become mothers. In the same way that men can be emotionally driven by compulsive masculinity, so it is that women are driven by a biological imperative, the drive to perpetuate the species.

This does not mean that every single woman in the world, health permitting, will become a mother. There are always social differences, cultural pressures for and against motherhood, and the X-factor, to be considered. But, by far, the overwhelming majority of women everywhere want to become mothers. In fact, most women will feel that their lives are incomplete if they do not have a child. Indeed, in societies outside of the Western world, procreation is thought to be more of a consecrated function. It is a duty performed in the name of the Holy Spirit. In American society, child bearing is thought to be an individual, personal choice. Therefore, the notion of a biological imperative is dismissed or played down. But still, we know that Western women hear their biological clocks ticking when they start approaching the time of menopause. Women do not have babies because society wants them to, but rather they have babies because their bodies demand it. Biology will overcome social philosophy every time.

Why is trying to "catch a man" so anxiety provoking for the female. Parsons says that a woman discovers that there is a lot of competition out there in the world, and all the young men seem more interested in seducing rather than marrying her. Of course, the males are being motivated by compulsive masculinity. In any case, the female is ambivalent about this because she is likely to be aware that a guy tends to have a Madonna complex about his woman, but at the same time he hopes she will be a sleazy slut because he wants to sleep with her. The female deals with her ambivalence by falling in love. Love constrains guilt and gives the woman license. She can now engage in fornication, with the hope that premarital sex will lead to marriage.

The feminists take issue with this description of a woman's sexual ambivalence and the anxiety provoking nature of it. They say that women have just as much right to be sexually free as men, and they should not be considered sluts for it. This is not the Victorian Era, and women today should not be bound by that old moral code. It was unhealthy then, and it is just as unhealthy now. The Madonna complex is, and has always been, a figment of the male imagination, something they wanted to believe in for their own sense of sexual lust and turn on. And women do not need to be in love to have sex. They can get just as excited for a one-night stand as any man.

In any event, Parsons states there is something else that is even more disturbing to the female. She is expected to become hedonistic about sex because that is what the male wants. He wants a wild woman to satisfy his lust. However, girls grow up believing that sex is a family function, and it is not to be done just for the pleasure of it. This will cause women to restrain themselves, and their lovers are likely to be less than satisfied with their performance. Under these circumstances, women will become anxious about having sex, and their relationships will suffer. But, they will still be motivated to sleep with guys anyway because of their biological imperative.

And the situation gets even more complicated. Emotionally deprived women are also emotionally immature, and when they are fulfilling their biological imperative by becoming mothers, they can be setting themselves up for unanticipated psychic problems. In seeking emotional fulfillment, they must play the role of the chief significant other for their children. To do it properly, they must give unconditional love and affection to their offspring. Consequentially, a situation can develop in the family where the mother is competing with her own child for emotional support from the father, other significant others, and herself. This can make childrearing for the mother an experience of emotional winners and losers, and the child is definitely going to be the loser. To be sure, growing up under these circumstances, a child is sure to be severely, emotionally deprived.

Moreover, after having great expectations, Parsons says that eventually women come to the conclusion that marriage and family does not automatically remove their feelings of emotional deprivation, and because the society puts so much stock in it, they tend to look to material rewards as an alternative means for relief, in clothes (furs), diamonds, gold, houses, cars, or whatever. The majority of the women will depend upon their husbands for these things, and they will have sex with them in return for such favors. In effect, they find themselves involved in marital prostitution. I would suggest to you, this is quite common in America, and it is somewhat a function of a materialistic society. At the same time, the feminists are calling for women to be more economically independent of men so they can avoid being a party to household harlotry. But this is looking at the situation from the end perspective and not the beginning. To stem the tide of emotional deprivation, the problem must be nipped at the start, in the bud.

Most married women find out soon enough that the promise of emotional fulfillment in motherhood and family bliss is not easily obtainable, and they reluctantly fall into a status of martyrdom and frustration, playing emotional games with their husbands to see who will control the temperature of the bedroom. However, men will resist women's attempt to control their sex life. In the past, men were inhibited from taking any direct action against their wives by custom, norms, mother-fixations, the law, feelings of right and wrong, and the tradition of marriage. But as the feminists have called for women to be given no special treatment from men, husbands are turning on their wives with vengeance. Men have come to be extraordinarily freewheeling and violent towards their female sex partners.

Women's Liberation arrived some three decades ago with the ideas of the feminine mystique, and the movement engaged in a power struggle with men. The chauvinist pig had to be defeated, and the way to defeat men was to make them more like women. Men should be pussified. Down with machismo. There should be no bravado and no male bonding for the boys. It was time for men to show their feelings, to play more of a role in the care and nurturing of the children. Men had to stop grading them-selves by the size of their penises. "My joint is bigger than your joint." Since Women's Liberation began, women have assaulted the male's per-ception of his manhood, and the males have given into a lot of the females' demands because of their orgasmic imperative.

The Women's Liberation movement has brought the battle of the sexes out into the open, and there is a bare-knuckle cultural and political battle going on. The fighting has become vicious and nasty because both parties are being motivated by their biology. Emotional deprivation has created an impossible situation for them. Sociologically they are at odds, but at the same time, biologically they know they need each other. They have their differences, but by natural selection, they are drawn to each other. Biology will overcome the demands of society every time. Learned norms and values can influence behavior, but ultimately, biology cannot be rationalized.

On the other hand males, in their compulsive masculine roles, are driven to be the person society says they should be. Their ego demands that they put themselves on display and compete with other males for the favor of females. The image of what they want to be, their sense of manhood, comes from outside of themselves, and that image is more a function of the *Me* than the *I*. It is a collective sense of self. On the other side of the social equation, females are driven to be the person they were born to be, and it is the universal call for all women, motherhood. Therefore, the biological imperative drives women towards men even when emotional deprivation will make a relationship with them problematical and quite difficult.

Because women naturally grow up with a biological need to be mothers, emotional deprivation causes them to seek out sex more readily. They can imagine that sex will bring them the love and affection they want, and it can lead to the motherhood they desire. This suggests that the greater the emotional deprivation, the greater the female urge to be sexually active. Moreover, this activity is likely to begin at an early pubescent age.

The relationship of emotional deprivation to sexual activity has much larger implications for our society. Our social structure is a stratified, hierarchical system. The system is designed and maintained so that the few can dominate the many. Wealth and power is in the hands of a small elite. There are the haves and the have-nots, and inequality is built into the system. It is the multitudes that suffer most from this disequilibria among the populace. If we go down the social hierarchy, from the few elites at the top to the masses at the bottom, material deprivation increases progressively. And even if we did not have socialization, there would still be emotional deprivation associated with this, and it seems to influence the biological imperative. Ergo, girls from lower socio-economic backgrounds will be sexually more active, and this activity will began at an earlier age. As a consequence, many of these young girls do become pregnant. In an historical context, the social circumstances of this event are not so unusual, but in our society, out of wedlock children have become a burden for the poor and minority communities.

American lifestyles today are measured by jobs and incomes. Poor and minority communities tend to be economically depressed areas. As well, their educational systems and their infrastructures are sure to be outdated, outmoded, and even dysfunctional. High school dropout rates are very high. There are few job opportunities, and unemployment is five to seven times more than the national average. The majority of young girls who have babies under these conditions are not emotionally and financially suited to be mothers, and their children tend to grow up in poverty. The cycle of emotional deprivation keeps spinning and stimulating the biological imperative of the girls in these communities, and it gives birth to a culture of poverty. This is perpetuated by our stratified, hierarchical social structure. Clearly, this is not an accident, and it means that the biological imperative is being used in a political way against these communities. The elites have a vested interest in keeping the poor, poor.

It is quite true that males dominate our stratified, hierarchical social structure, and therefore the system does serve men first and women second. Our social philosophy is, by and large, a function of the male consciousness. In the dating and courting rituals, men can, and do, make chauvinistic demands upon women, and the women feel they must comply if they are to be a chosen one in the competition for "catching a man." Driven by their biological imperative, females will try to present themselves in the way they think men want to see them, and in many cases, they may go to absurd lengths to do so. For instance, they have gotten it into their heads that blond-headed, large-breasted, big butt, small waist women have more fun and more often get the man. So, millions of women are regularly dying their hair, slimming down and puffing themselves up to meet these specifications, and now this type of fake, blond-headed woman is proliferating throughout society like milkweed in a grassy meadow. And it is no coincidence that a large number of female actors and TV talking heads have that phony blond look.

Changing the color of one's hair is only the tip of the iceberg for women in their attempt to present an image that they think men want to see. They are doing aerobic exercises, running, gym calisthenics, and they are into bodybuilding. Moreover, cosmetic surgery is booming, and women have taken to silicon breast implants. This latter occurrence is utterly dangerous and perverse. Women get implants to make their breasts bigger, and it points out just how far they will go to get the male's attention. Imagine putting a dangerous, alien substance into your body for appearances sake. Of course, it is the biological imperative that is making them do it, and this underscores once again that it is not the chauvinist, male society that is forcing women to become wives and mothers. It is something that is inside of the women themselves.

Since they were small children, girls have been told they must keep their bodies clean, be neat with their clothes, and just generally keep themselves looking attractive. How they appear to others, specifically members of the opposite sex, is very important, indeed crucial, if they are going to "catch a man" someday. Girls grow up with a love for nice clothes, cosmetic makeup, and hairstyles, and they will be constantly making themselves over to suit fad and fashion. Whatever look is in at the moment women feel they have to be a part of it. They cannot take the chance of being excluded and ignored. They tend to have a feeling inside of them that says, "I must be liked, and I must belong." And there is enormous pressure from family, peers, and society for girls to conform to the social norms. Their situation is quite different than their male counterparts. Boys must struggle with the masculine behavioral image, while girls must struggle to perfect a pictured, ideal image of the body beautiful. They feel compelled to do it because that biological force inside of them demands it. And superficially, the image is constantly changing from era to era. Is there any wonder that trying to "catch a man" is so anxiety provoking?

In all the attempts by girls and women to remake and remodel themselves to fit the prevailing female social image, they have forgotten a fundamental fact. They must first lose self-confidence in, if not come to dislike, the innate person they were born to be. With propaganda, scare tactics, fashion models, role model starlets, subliminal advertisements, and crass appeals to their vanity, women are made to feel insecure about their God given looks. They are ridiculed, chastised, and made fun of if they do not look like the Barbie Doll of the day. They are made to feel that in a world of perfect, beautiful women, the women of motion pictures, TV and the slick magazines, they are rejects. A result of this is that many women develop a form of self-hate.

Self-hate is a kind of violence because it is an expression of the denial of one's innate self, one's individual human nature. Certain types of violence in the movies tend to underscore the self-hate that women exhibit towards themselves. This is within the overall character of the world that is communicated to us by motion pictures, which is a violent one. Motion pictures and TV dramas reek of violence in blatant and subtle forms, and the level of it has increased precipitously in the last forty years. One of the reasons for this has to be our increasing dependency on the picture media as the primary means of communicating information. Emotionally, the present generation of electronic nurtured kids is in action mode just about all the time, and they want their information to be delivered to them in the same way. Motion pictures and TV dramas follow this prescription.

There is no better example of a violent personality than a killer, and over and over again, we see motion pictures and TV dramas giving us portraits of killers. We are treated to gangsters, outlaw cowboys, serial and monsters killers. We are shown people being sliced, diced, bashed, smashed, shot, and blown to bits. And with computer graphics, there is no limit to the gory details that can be displayed. The moviemakers know that their audience has the taste for blood, and they make every attempt to deliver.

In Hollywood motion pictures, violence is used as a form of entertainment and perhaps other things as well. Think of the enormous number of movies about women being threatened with violence, being physically, verbally, and psychologically abused and assaulted. Think of the genre of serial murderers. Invariably the serial murderer is a male who kills women. Given the indigenous sexism in our society, what kind of message does all this mayhem against females suggest? It tells us that men have some very deep seated, unresolved emotional problems with women. I suspect the problem goes back to their childhood, and the ugly hand of emotional deprivation is probably involved in it. Yes, there are laws to protect women from harassment, abuse, rape, etc., but the truth is that if a man wants to hurt a woman, there is little to stop him. One of the most dangerous things any woman can do today is get married.

In recent years, Hollywood has cashed in on a certain genre of movies like Halloween, Friday the 13th, A Nightmare on Elm Street and Scream. All these movies have one basic theme, kill young people, primarily young women. If there was any doubt that Hollywood moviemakers have some terrible ill feelings towards women, watching any of these types of motion pictures will take away your doubts. If you take these films literally, it appears as though the male incarnate feels threatened by the female, and the only way he seems to be able to defend himself is by going ballistic and chopping her into a lot of little pieces. The level of violence in these films can be so flagrant, it would suggest that the producers and directors of such movies are closeted, repressed sociopaths.

And who are the individuals who go to see movies like Halloween? They are young people, and in particular girls. In their action mode, they are getting an electronic fix, and the young people are being told how they should behave toward one another. It is the values of brute force and fear of the male as an instrument of power, the arbiter of life and death. And isn't it very interesting that this group of motion pictures have come about in the wake of twentieth century feminism and Women's Liberation. It is as though the male psyche feels under attack, and it is striking back in symbolic terms against the female's wish to knock the male off of his high horse.

Horror films as a genre have been around since Hollywood first started making silent one-reel motion pictures, and monsters like Frankenstein, the Wolfman, and Dracula have always terrorized women. But these creatures were monsters in the otherworldly sense. Not so with the Halloween genre. The monsters in these movies are psychotic males who have been driven mad by females, and now they are seeking revenge. A prime motive in all these movies is vengeance, and when you go after a person in this way, you want to really hurt him or her. This is another behavior that the movies are teaching our young people. Never take your lumps lying down, and always payback double in spades.

There is a startling fact about these hate-kill movies. Women go to see them and find them entertaining. This is very strange. These hate-kill movies acknowledge the authority of men to overpower and kill women, even if only symbolically. For women, who find these films entertaining, it would seem to be a form of self-flagellation, if not self-negation. There maybe an element of a self-fulfilling prophecy indicated here, and women should ask themselves a serious question. What is it about these movies that they find entertaining?

The same violence in Hollywood motion pictures is to be found on the family TV. Television has become just another outlet for the movie industry. But the Hollywood movie takes on another dimension when it becomes a part of the home. Now the communications is up front and personal. As Marshall McLuhan pointed out, we have a different relationship with the TV than with a theater motion picture screen. The television is like another significant other in the home, of the magnitude of ones mother or father. Once upon a time, youngsters initially learned their values and role-playing from their parents, but now television is responsible for much of it.

There is no mistaking the physical violence, and some of the psychological and emotional violence, that are seen in movies. But there are more subtle forms of violence in films that perhaps go largely unnoticed because they masquerade behind seemingly other purposes, like the shrill expressions of enjoyment and playfulness. And it is all presented to the moviegoer as the good life, the lifestyle of the beautiful people. For instance, with all of the medical evidence about the dangers of smoking, the drinking of alcoholic beverages, and drug abuse, why do the people in the motion picture industry continue to show actors and actresses engaging in these dangerous, addicting, life-threatening behaviors?

There is no good reason for it, and there is no excuse for it. I know the argument is made that the movies are just depicting what goes on in real life. But that is a stupid argument because what is presented in the movies can never be like real life. Movies present us with manufactured drama that is scripted and played out by actors in a role. And we need to recall that role by definition is false. Moreover, we should keep in mind that these addicting, life-threatening behaviors are presented as the essence of the good life, and in some cases the ultimate of hedonistic pleasures. However, living the good life in real life has nothing to do with smoking, drinking, and taking drugs. These are all negative, debilitating behaviors, and people should not be encouraged to engage in them. But that is exactly what motion pictures, and their subsidiary, television, are doing. They make these deadly, habit forming, drugs appealing. This tells us that the moviemakers of today are Judas goats, leading their flocks of viewers to slaughter.

From religion, we learn that the body is a temple of God. To defile it is to violate a holy covenant. To pollute our bodies with smoking, alcohol, and drugs is not only sinful, but it is also a form of violence. Without a doubt, such behavior is certainly self-defeating and self-destructive, which makes it violence of the worse sort because it can be correctly classified as a form of suicide. From Emile Durkheim's analysis, we can describe it as egoistic suicide,[15] and it is time for the American public to get smart. We should stop patronizing motion pictures that are encouraging us to commit ourselves to a slow and agonizing program of death. And understand, we are being programmed, and this is a calculated effort by the motion picture industry based on a simple axiom. "Give the people what they think they want, even if it kills them."

At this stage in our social evolution, we have indeed forsaken the written word, but in a strange turn of events, we have become more dependent upon the spoken word; that is a certain type of spoken word. Nowhere is this truer then in the present crop of motion pictures. The dialogue of these films has fallen on extremely hard times. In their attempt to give the moviegoers what they think they want, the Hollywood writers have been doing what Senator Daniel Patrick Moynihan has termed "Defining Deviancy Down."

Language has always been available as a weapon for those who wanted, and had the ability, to use it that way. For that reason, our society, and I would say all societies, classified certain words in their vocabularies as proper and improper, profane and sacred, sophisticated and vulgar. Then there are the words that are totally beyond the pail in polite society, words that define the user as a deviant. These are obscene words like shit, fuck, asshole, motherfucker, and cocksucker just to mention a few. These words were not acceptable in decent conversation, not long ago. There was a time when they were rarely even seen in books, and they were never spoken in motion pictures. To be sure, they certainly were not said on television.

Today, thanks very much to the motion picture industry; former deviant words have become part of everyday speech. It is hip and in to use these words, and an entire generation has now grown up using them as common vehicles of communications. Let us be clear about something. These are brutal words that tend to ride on waves of anger and aggressiveness. In many respects, they are mindless words that are used to excite, denigrate, and emotionally beat down another person. They do not appeal to cool heads, soft talking, and reason. They are, more often than not, a call to action. They are used to heat up discourse and not calm it down. They are spiteful words, and even when they are spoken softly, they still carry the power to disturb and provoke. The public has become comfortable with these words because emotionally they suit our action mode. These words deliver a punch whenever and wherever they are used.

Scatological words are blasphemous and dehumanizing, and they must surely attack the sensibilities of others. When so directed, by their usage, they constitute an act of violence towards another. This is precisely how these words are being used in motion pictures today, but it was not always that way. During the early days of Hollywood, the moguls, who were practically all immigrant Jews, ran a tight studio system of writers, actors, and directors. These men had come to America to escape the persecution and insecurities of the anti-Semitism they suffered in Europe. They came here looking for comradeship and community with the American people, and they put their dreams on film in the myth of the ideal family-oriented small town. They sought communal love and tranquility that had been denied them in European society. At the same time, they did not come to America to upset the social applecart by drawing attention to themselves.

Their output tended to be films of inclusion rather than exclusion. Their motion pictures tended to understate their desires to assimilate. Their dreams were presented to us in satire, comedies, musicals, and fantasies. Reality played backseat to the message. The scriptwriters of the day had to be adept at saying metaphorically, in fact covertly, what was not to be professed openly. Everything had to be done with subtlety, with genteelness and often with suave affair. The writers did not always accomplish their task well, but the effort was there. And there were some very good scriptwriting done in those days. But the studio system is gone now, and independent filmmakers are competing like racehorses for production dollars. The only message they are paying any attention to is their profit margins. Market studies show that more can be accomplish with less when you give the audience what they think they want. And the consciousness of the movie audience is more fickle today. It is largely the mind of young people who don't care for subtlety. They want action, and in words that means engaging in scatological language.

The motion picture industry is giving us wholesale violence and calling it entertainment. Why do we accept and feel comfortable with this ruse? Where is our common sense? Is it that our emotional motors are stuck in action drive? Or, to paraphrase Timothy Leary, perhaps we are too turned on, and too tuned in, and we are unable to drop out. But in the final analysis, we really don't need elaborate explanations of the message that Hollywood is sending us. The bible tells us that violence begets violence, and in the end, if Hollywood is trying to give us what it thinks we want, the solution to the problem lies not with the moviemakers per se, but it rests with us, the viewing audience.

Women are loath to admit that there is any self-hate involved in their desire to make themselves look better. They will even say that making themselves look nice and attractive has nothing to do with the opposite sex. With women striving to fulfill their biological imperative, I find that hard to believe. The feminists also say that what may seem like self-hate is nothing more than women attempting to wrest the control of their bodies away from men. This is quite an ambiguous notion. Of course, I cannot get inside the heads of women, but there is some subtle, if anecdotal evidence to indicate that women do have more than a modicum of ill feelings about themselves.

To begin with, if women really thought well of themselves, they would not be so easily influenced and intimidated by false images of perfection and beauty they are constantly being exposed to, and they would not allow themselves to be exploited and manipulated by fad and fashions so readily. And why are so many women addicted to dieting? Is it because they like their overall appearance? I don't think so. And how often have we heard women say, as a Freudian slip, "I hate the way I look." But then, we should not take that comment seriously because it is only a flippant remark. Right!

However, the best clue on this subject is to be found in motion pictures. Movies about serial killers are very popular today. Women flock to these shows in droves, and they get some kind of perverse pleasure out of watching screen action where a series of women are murdered in very graphic detail. The setting, plot line, and details of such motion pictures are pretty much the same. An evil man murders a beautiful woman, and very often, by explanation or implication, a message is delivered to the audience that the woman is killed because she is beautiful. Since viewers today tend to strongly identify with motion picture characters, why would women want to be beautiful like the person in the movies if it might invite their own murder?

But the women are only looking at a movie, you might say, and a motion pictures are fantasy. They can't hurt anyone, and the viewer knows that. But one has to think about the symbolism of it all. Fantasy is a highway to and from the id. We are talking about an unconscious mechanism that we do not control. For instance, why do we get frightened in the motion picture theater? We all know that what we see on the big screen is not in fact real, or is it? Think of it as being surreal, and the experience is like each person being in his own dream.

To try to seek perfection of any kind is nothing but fantasy. It is no wonder then that in the face of the perfect female body type, women have come to reject themselves and suppress their innate beings. This means they are in denial of the biological imperative. Their sense of self then retreats into the unconscious, and this brings reactions from the id. Chasing a surreal, beautiful, ideal image, women have created their own kind of monsters to bedevil themselves with, the monsters of self-doubt, low self-esteem and self-worth, anorexia, bulimia, and the mirror-mirror, ugly duckling syndrome. But the most monstrous thing of all is the stuffing and slicing of their bodies in the pursuit of good looks. They can get surgery to "correct" almost any physical deficiency they may think they have, from a nose job to reconstruction of the labia of the vagina. They may call this cosmetic surgery, but in fact this is psychic, intrusive, mutilation. Surely, the impact of breast implants is a good example. To understand this, just consider the opposite: breast removal. It alters the entire psychological and emotional perception that the woman has of her self. It is also as though some ruthless monster has torn her body apart and violated her.

This is not a whimsical comment either. Children are brought up in our society to believe in monsters, the dragons, goblins, ogres, and sea serpents, just to mention a few. And invariably, these monsters chase after beautiful girls. Women have been brought up to believe in these fantasies. It begins with fairy tales and the Prince on the white horse who saves the girl from the monsters. He does so because he loves the girl, and girls learn early in life to believe in, and to strive for, love. Because of the female's natural sensitivity and intuition, she is more susceptible to believing in fairy tales. As a result, she tends to have a more active pathway between her consciousness and unconsciousness. She is then more open to her demons from the id. They are more actual and real to her, and she is comfortable functioning on an imaginary plain where the impossible is possible. Consider this: why is it that women cannot see the folly of chasing modeled images of perfection? Why do they get hung up on the treadmill of dieting? Why do they believe that love will conqueror all? They believe these things because these matters are not logical or rational. They are fanciful. But then, why do women have such an attitude? It is an investment in the mind and spirit of a progenitor. To fulfill this purpose, women should feel that they are special, but emotional deprivation causes them to suppress this feeling. In an attempt to reclaim it, women seem to have declared war on their own bodies.

During the various stages of socialization, girls are not treated the same as boys. There is always deference shown to them. They are treated more tenderly and perhaps with greater affection than boys. They are thought to be "sugar, spice, and everything nice." And all significant others know that girls are special because they may be mothers some day. It is not spoken of that way, but the implication is always there. When little girls are restrained from playing roughhouse games like cowboys and Indians, it is not just an act of male chauvinism. It is a way of protecting them for their important, future responsibility. The feminists say this is poppycock. Girls should be allowed to engage in whatever activity they want if it pleases them. To this extent, I agree. But the truth remains that most girls are not interested in the traditional activities that have engaged boys, and no amount of feminist urging is likely to change that. More often than not, biology will dictate.

Some people will say that I am preaching biological determinism, and that women are more than the sum of their body parts. They say it is not biology that dictates, but it is socialization that has put women at odds with their own bodies. But this is certainly putting the cart before the horse. Society does not give rise to biology. It is the other way around, but emotional deprivation has caused women to be confused about whom they are and their purpose in life. Women feel a double barrel of pressure on them to "catch a man." They are pushed by their biological need to be a mother and their sense of being unfulfilled that comes from emotional deprivation. As a result, their social and biological desires are all scrambled together.

The baby boomers have produced a generation of young women who see themselves in very different terms than their mothers. They speak of themselves as being liberated women who have careers outside of the home. The feminists have convinced most of them that marriage, mother-hood, and homemaking does not have to be a woman's destiny, that catch-ing a man should not be their first priority. Women are being encouraged to become doctors, lawyers, warriors, and Indian Chiefs. They have been told, and many have accepted the notion, that being like their mothers will not be emotionally fulfilling for them. They need a vocation where they can express their minds and use their intellect. So, over the last three decades, more and more women have taken their place in the work world along side of men.

The occupational world outside the home has been, for centuries, the province of the males, and the nature of these jobs, along with the charac-ter of the institutions that ran them, were all a function of the male con-sciousness. All the bravado, posturing, and aggression of men were built into that system. When women became involved, they discovered that in order to fit in, they would have to behave more like men because that is how the system worked. Women had to assume a masculine mask over their femininity.

However, being a workingwoman has not greatly diminished the desire of most women to get married and be a mother. Women have achieved substantial job status in all of the major professions, but they still have that natural urge to cohabit with males. No matter what vocational success the average woman may achieve, she is likely to feel incomplete and unfulfilled if she does not have a baby. Indeed, there is pressure to be successful in a career and as a mother, and in the present situation; to meet the need of one is to highlight the absence of the other. So, many women are having their troubles fitting into the mold of the new woman. The demands of being a wife, mother, and having a vocational career are putting a tremendous strain upon them physically, psychologically, and emotionally. To be home or not to be home, that is the question? And many women are finding themselves on the horns of a dilemma.

It has been difficult for working mothers to balance their time between home and job. Time for childcare has suffered. The need for day care centers and surrogate parents has ballooned. I have already stressed the fact that putting a child in a day care center when he is under three years old is inviting definite emotional deprivation to be visited upon him. In trying to comply with the aegis of the new, modern woman, women are been encouraged to turn their backs on their children at a time when they need their significant others the most. Young women have generally accepted the idea that their careers come first, and being mothers and family comes second. However, for many career minded women, this is but a rationalization they cannot sustain emotionally. They find themselves in conflict over commitment to job and home.

This has produced a strange kind of problem for women. Like men, seeking material rewards, they are driven to succeed in the work world because of emotional deprivation, but they can feel a nagging discomfort about being away from their children. Not only does the child need his mother's, individual, personal care, but also the mother has a biological, emotional and psychic need to give the nurturing. This process begins in the womb, and the mother's body, mind, and spirit, throughout the gestation period, prepares for it. When women abandon their children before their children reach three years old, they not only doing emotional damage to the child, but they are also doing damage to themselves.

To say that a woman is strongly motivated by a biological imperative, is to point out that procreation not only defines her as a woman, but it helps her function in the capacity she was born to fulfill. There are no alternative experiences that can be substituted for this. The feminists have sold young women a phony bill of goods. They have tried to make the case that a woman can become a careerist in some vocational activity, and it can be just as rewarding and fulfilling as motherhood. This is, of course, a lot of nonsense. The most aesthetically rewarding thing that any human being can do is something that is creative, something that bespeaks of the individuality of the person doing it, and something that no other person in the entire world could have done. Women have the unique ability to do this naturally.

If we praise the creative artist for writing books and poetry, composing music, and being painters, how can we not recognize that a woman is being creative when she carries a child in her womb for nine months and gives birth. Indeed, no other human act of creation can equal it by comparison. It is the creation of new life that is infused with the Holy Spirit, and it is this creation that gives rise to all other forms of human creation. Without the child, there is nothing, no society, no culture, no Mozart, Beethoven, Shakespeare, or Picasso. How can any other job, responsibility, and any other human effort be more important? Why do we keep trying to put society before biology?

There is at all times a powerful voice within women that speaks to them about their maternal creativity. It demands that they heed the call for the sake of species survival. But, at the same time, because of the feminist call, younger women have tried to turn a deaf ear to their maternal instinct. This is an act of suppression, a suppression of their innate selves. Because their biology is making the demands, women may then turn on themselves. Their bodies can be seen as the enemy that is trying to keep them from participating fully in outside world with men, and from the id the monsters of anorexia, bulimia, and the dieting treadmill may emerge. And once these monsters are unleashed against their bodies, the absurd can set in. Why are women having cosmetic surgery on the labia of their vaginas? This goes to the heart of a woman's sense of discomfort with her body. It is the pressing demand of the maternal instinct, which is a function of the vagina. If it represents the enemy, then why not attack it?

Emotional deprivation has caused ruptures in the way women think and feel, and in doing battle with the first enemy, themselves; they have developed a need to have an adversary, the chauvinist pig. But the contest was always between their *I* and their "Me." Now that they are in the work world, it has allowed them to externalize their problems more, and they have become more openly aggressive and more susceptible to committing violence. It has been a natural path of development. When women entered the outside world in the occupational sphere, and when they began competing with men in the same job classifications, it was inevitable that they would become more aggressive. And as women became world-lier, they have picked up the worldly habits of men: the excessive smoking, drinking, drug taking, and promiscuity. Like the men, TV and motion pictures have given them role models to copy and imitate, and the fictional women characters are becoming more and more hardnosed.

Women are also learning Karate and various forms of defensive maneuvers, and they are buying and learning how to use guns. It is a dangerous world outside the home, and these are survival tools and techniques. On its face, these activities may seem to be good for a woman's protection, but all this aggressive posturing is contrary to a maternal instinct. Mothers should focus on nurturing and not hurting people. Aggressive behavior does not help women fulfill the promise of womanhood. Being an absentee mother and developing aggressive habits is helping to turn women away from their innate selves. But it is impossible for anyone to really run away from himself. So, women are constantly into disguises, in changing fashions (clothes), hairdos, wigs, makeup, and the ultimate attempt at transformation: reconstructive surgery. If they can't get away from their inner selves, then they will hide it.

In the action mode of our society today, many women are trying to be super moms. They want to manage a career outside the home, but they want the fulfillment of children and family also. They juggle their time and commitment in trying to accomplish this, but unfortunately they maybe asking too much of themselves. There are only so many hours in the day, and a person has only so much energy to expend in a span of hours. But the feminists have put women between a rock and a hard place. They have been politicized to believe that they must do more than just be a homemaker if their lives are to be meaningful, but their biological imperative tells them that if they do not become a mother than they have not fully developed as a woman. These are competing urges in conflict. Super mom may not be able to do justice to both of them, but the new woman is determined to try to make a go of it. Unfortunately, the two can not be reconciled and women need to recognize this for what it is worth.

If a mother is not with her child during that first, critical period of his life, emotional deprivation will be. And remember, there is no second chance in this regard. If women put their careers before their children, emotional damage will be done, and they should not buy into the idea of "quality time." The years 0-3 are finite. The chief significant other must be there at that time in an ongoing capacity. If she is not, then the opportunity to help her child develop a strong sense of "I" is lost forever. Can any job or profession be worth that? I honestly believe that the majority of women who have babies do love them, and want to do the best for them. But emotional deprivation has caused them to accept a feminist philosophy that is misguided.

It is rather sad that many women have really taken to heart the feminine mystique notion that the family, children, husband, and homemaking were used to deny them the opportunity to have fulfilling and meaningful lives. This attitude has turned many women against the family and against children. They rationalize that children will keep them from having a full and productive life, whatever that means, professional careers, big paychecks, more clothes, and vacations, etc. The feminist philosophy has always been about "me," about women supposedly beginning to think about themselves first instead of their children and their husbands. Basically, I have no qualms with this.

Women, or anyone else, have the right to live their lives in a manner of their own choosing, as long as they do not purposively hurt others in doing so. Yes, women have a maternal instinct, but they essentially do not have to become mothers if they do not want to. But women have been trying now, for thirty years, to have their cake and eat it, too. A result is that their relationships with their children have suffered tremendously. With so many women being working, absentee mothers, a cadre of children have become emotionally deprived by default. It is a guarantee that the effects of the present day emotional deprivation will be with us well into the new millennium. The super mom must face the fact, that the best mother is not a part time participant in her child's life. If a woman is not prepared to give her child the full attention he needs in the first three years of life, then perhaps she should reconsider having a baby. In our society, it is perfectly acceptable if a woman does not want to have a baby.

It is extremely important to note the impact of emotional deprivation on women because they are the bedrock of society. It is because of them that the family came into being, and from family we get community and society. When women begin to change their traditional patterns of behavior, then change is inevitable throughout the society as a whole. So, the structure of the American family has been changing because it has become common for women of all classes to be working outside the home on a regular basis. Along with the change in family has come a different sense of community. The idea of community used to mean a residential area where a person lived. It was a place where friends and neighbors coexisted, raise their children, went to church and lived their lives away from their professions and their jobs. This old picture of community is quickly going by the boards, and the notion of a "bedroom community" is now taking on a whole new meaning.

The family home used to be the glue that held the community together, and central to the home was the mother, the lady of the house. She was there as a wife and a nurturer for her children. She was also there to make the home a physical and emotional refuge for family members, and to connect with other neighborly homemakers. This made for a rather stable residential area, but with so many mothers now at work, the family and the community have become less stable. Mothers are not available as before to give emotional support and guidance to their children. Working parents must rely upon surrogates. Very young children are detached from their parents, and older children have become wandering, latchkey kids who create peer group families to replace the ones they have lost at home.

The traditional family and community is going through many changes due very much to a new role that women are playing in both of them, but the innate need of women to be mothers and nurturers has not changed. However, under the pressure of emotional deprivation, women are playing down these qualities in favor of opportunities and success in the occupational system. They are denying their desire to fulfill their maternal instinct. Once again, this is suppression, and it constitutes a form of self-alienation. Judging from the stress that working, super moms confess to feeling today, this seems to be a significant emotional problem for them.

Self-alienation is a unique kind of emotional problem. It is an indicator that a person feels that she does not know herself. She can feel like she is harboring an alien inside of her. When looking into the mirror, there are times when the person does not recognize herself or she is displeased with what she sees. This is that mirror-mirror, ugly-duckling effect. It is an irrational feeling that makes women want to change themselves, their appearance, their bodies, their essence. The body is demanding maternal fulfillment, but a woman can refuse to recognize it. Psychic barriers are erected to deny the truth, and the self-alienation deepens. Emotional deprivation itself may become a refuge as a woman may seek to live in her past, retreat to the fantasies of her childhood memories when the body was not her enemy and did not make demands on her.

In thinking that there is an alien inside of her, a woman can conjure up strange thoughts about who or what that alien might be. From her id can come images of all kinds of monsters and demons, incarnations from her childhood fantasies and fairy tales? Even images from motion pictures, TV, and books can become real in her imagination. The thought of a baby in her womb can be seen as an alien that may try to possess her. This idea was fictionalized in the motion picture *Rosemary's Baby*, a 1968 classic horror film, and all of this is essentially concerned with the fear women have generated about motherhood. Having a baby is not thought of as "a blessed event" like in the past. For the new, liberated woman, it can be seen as a debilitating impediment to a fulfilling, productive life.

Of course, there is a social and emotional dichotomy here. The woman's biology is demanding one thing, and the philosophy of the new woman is calling for something else. A woman can feel trapped in her psyche between two competing forces, and it can be quite frightening to her. She can try to relieve herself of this pressure by supplementation, rationalization, and transference. Humans do not like to accept responsibility for their own individual shortcomings. Invariably they will try to shift the blame to something or someone else. Struggling with their trapped feelings, which they cannot control, women often over-compensate for it by behaving in a hyper-emotional state. They hide behind their emotions because they feel they are not capable of controlling them. Or, they develop exaggerated notions, and the self-fulfilling behavior to go along with it, about how wonderful, beautiful, and extraordinary they are because they are frightened that others will discover they truly feel otherwise. The idle rich often suffer from these kinds of neuroses. However, most women will try to deal with this problem by involving themselves in some form of transference.

Trying to catch a man is anxiety provoking because of the competition. And men are constantly after a woman's body, and they try to turn women into sleazy sluts for their own carnal pleasure. It is the men who impregnate women. Therefore, men may think of women as being nothing more than a hole they can use to plunge their egos into. In this regard, women believe that men see them only as sex objects. With these kinds of attitudes about men, it is quite easy for women to blame them for feeling trapped by their competing emotions. But the essential culprit is thought to be sex. A woman's body can yearn for it because that is the focus of the biological imperative, but giving into sex for many women opens up a Pandora's box of conflicting emotions. Enjoying it can make them feel sleazy. On the other hand, if they restrain themselves, they might not reach an orgasm.

This leaves them frustrated. So, they are damned if they do, and damned if the don't.

To complicate matters further, American sexual mores are still weighted down with many values from the Victorian Era, and they constituted a fall back position for many women who can use them to justify their problems with sex and an inability to achieve orgasm. When women were primarily homemakers, they accepted their martyrdom and sexual frustration as a trade off for family life and the security of a home for themselves and their children. The situation may not have been ideal, but women could still feel a certain satisfaction with themselves in that they were fulfilling their maternal instinct. Indeed, this may have produced undo pressure on women to be the perfect Mom and wife, and inadvertently there was more than a little of self-exploitation. But when women began to rebel against their role in the family, it was the husband who was blamed for their discontent and lack of happiness.

But the discontent was a function of self-alienation, and that is an individual problem. It is in the mind, and of the spirit, of the person experiencing it, and generically, alienation has a larger meaning. One can be alienated from others and from their sense of community. Thus women find themselves beset with creeping alienation that can make them feel isolated from family members and people of their traditional, residential community. This alienation is now a natural development because many women are giving greater time and commitment to their jobs and other outside interests. And younger women are making a concentrated effort to find rewarding, fulfilling personal experiences away from family and the home. With both parents working, there is much less time for them to spend with the children, or with themselves, and children are often being raised and supervised by surrogates.

Workingwomen have less time for neighborly get-togethers like afternoon tea parties, bridge games, PTA meetings, and friendly gossiping. Cultivating friendships and being neighborly used to be very important in the community because it helped to support a network of adults that watched out for the children and property. As a result, residents felt as though they had a personal investment in the community and the people in it. But with the breakdown of the traditional family structure and women becoming outside wage earners, the present day communities, particularly suburban communities, have become more like way stations for transients. People are constantly popping in and out of their homes, commuting to work, going shopping in the mall, or visiting the movies or a restaurant. All of these can make workingwomen feel estranged from their homes and communities.

Alienation has also bought another problem to the surface for women. It is a problem of disconnect. Innately, and for the sake of specie survival, women were born with a purpose. They were born with the ability to be progenitors. They do not have to honor this purpose, but as an instinct and/or imperative, it was there to be considered and respected. The liberated woman has abandoned this purpose as the means for validating her life, but she has not been able to come up with a comparable alternative. Positions in the occupational system do not give women that same sense of a comfortable, natural purpose for themselves in life, and as they become more involved in the work world, they are finding it less rewarding. Many women may want to revert back to a more homemaking style of life. We can see this in the way they are trying to bring job and home together, but they can feel trapped by their circumstances. They have accepted the feminist negation of family in favor of an out-of-home career, and now they don't know how to face up to the possibility that perhaps the feminists had exaggerated their case.

As it has been said, the occupational system has been traditionally a man's world. But in the last three decades, women have increased their numbers in the system enormously. Because of their egos, men feel threatened when they have to compete with women. So, the occupational system has been unyielding to the full participation of women in many respects. To combat this, women have been trying to feminize the system. They want to make it over to serve them. Surely women have every right to receive the same pay as men when doing the same work, and they should be given the same opportunities for promotion, but must the workplace, among other things, become a reflection of the female's battle with her body? Recently, women have been using the law to beat up on men in order to force them to feminize the occupational system. Since Supreme Court Justice Clarence Thomas was accused of sexually harassing Anita Hill, sexual harassment court cases have run wild across the land. Sexual harassment law has become a political club that many less than honest women are using against men. President Bill Clinton certainly knew about all this.

I'm not trying to make excuses for the immoral, illegal, shabby behavior of many men. There is no doubt that for many long years, men who were bosses and employers used their positions to take sexual advantage of women. This was dead wrong, but how many women have used their bodies to gain favor and promotion from their bosses? We will never know? Keep the harassment laws on the books, but men should not be prosecuted for telling an off-color, sexual joke among themselves that was overheard by a woman, or because they have a risqué calendar of a female in their offices. Women go to the movies to see females exposing themselves totally nude, and they never complain. There are "women's programs" on cable television that are as pornographically frank and sexually bawdy as you could ever want to see and hear. "Sex and The City " on HBO cable television is one such program. Women adore these shows and praise them for their outspoken frankness. Now isn't there some great inconsistency here that I am not getting? This leads me to believe that all this fuss about sexual harassment is not really about how men treat women, but it is really about how women treat themselves.

In Emile Durkheim's term, the modern, liberated, workingwoman is suffering from anomie.[16] She has all the classic symptoms. She lacks a genuine, fundamental purpose for her life. She is without a sense of identity, and she is bereft of social mooring. She is uncertain about where she belongs, at home or in the work world? Women, because of their innate character, their role as mothers, have a special need to feel wanted and to know that they belong to somebody. This is what love is all about for them. They go through their lives seeking it. They can be like the perpetual Princess looking for her Prince. And to be sure love is just a poetic metaphor for initiating the procreative process. To do this, a woman must catch and belong to a man, but the workingwoman plays down this need to belong to a man. How liberated could she be if she thought that?

Durkheim concluded that anomie could produce dire consequences for individuals who might be caught in its grip. The need, he said, for human beings to belong to the group, to someone, is so strong that without it, a person might even commit suicide. This is the ultimate act of human violence, self-murder. To make the point even stronger, Durkheim discovered that unmarried, lonely women are more likely to commit suicide than those who are married or in a relationship. Of course, lonely old men also have a high rate of suicide, but this seems a function of individuals being tired of living and who are ready to bring their long lives to a close. Women tend to kill themselves for romantic reasons whether they are young or old.

Durkheim also made another interesting observation. He said anomie and deviant behavior tend to increase in society during times of rapid social transformation. Examples of this can be seen when social values are changing, when there is increased technology, and when elements of the social structure are changing at different rates. Indeed, that is a perfect description of our society at the turn of the new millennium. Durkheim was right on both counts. Anomie is widespread and deviant behavior is rampant, and women have been caught up in this wave. They are becoming standouts. By increasing numbers, they are turning to lives of crime, and the female prison population is growing rapidly.

However, we should not blame the Women's Liberation movement, the sexual revolution, or our increasing dependency upon technology for the personal dilemma women find themselves in. It is socialization and its outcome, emotional deprivation that is at the heart of the problem. We can speak of alienation and anomie, but in our unconscious mind we know what is really bothering us. I don't mean to be simplistic, but the solution is simple. Women, and all of us, can be emotionally better off if we show more respect for our innate selves that socialization has caused us to suppress. Women should acknowledge their biological imperative, but this does not mean that every woman who is capable of having a baby will have one. It just means that women have to be respectful of who they are and not live in denial. Let the X-factor be considered for each individual and nature's course will follow. Their inner spirit and their heart, and not social philosophy or a political agenda, would then guide them.

In the final analysis, the biological imperative is not about women per se. It is really about babies and the perpetuation of the human species. Women's Liberation and women's family frustrations should always be framed with this in mind. However, the feminists have tried to make this a non-issue. Women need not think of themselves as progenitors in the first instance. In the credo of the "me generation" of the 1970s, women have been told to put themselves first, ahead of children, husbands, and family. But, for the good and bad of it, these are the things that have traditionally given meaning to a woman's life. Was that all a mistake? Every fiber in a woman's body says no, even when her liberated mind says yes.

Let us be clear about this. Women will continue to have babies because the biological imperative is orgasmic relatable. Nature was not going to leave the perpetuation of the specie up to the whim and fancy of the human mind. Men and women will seek out sexual relations for the pleasure in it, and for most women, eventually pregnancy will occur. So then, babies will continue to be born. The question is how will they be nurtured and raised? If women approach motherhood with the notion of me first, then the future of this society is in trouble. The young child needs his mother to be fully engaged in the nurturing if he is to develop a strong sense of I and avoid the pains of emotional deprivation. He needs love and attention, and he should not have to compete with his mother to get it. John Bowlby did a study of infant children, and he discovered that if they were deprived of loving care, they would be unable to give love to others when they mature. They will also have problems coping with love when it is given to them, and they are likely to have other kinds of severe emotional problems.[17]

We see the elements of a loveless society all about us: there is crime, killings, the high divorce rate, break down of the family, racism, bigotry, and ethnocentrism. Without the emotional capacity to love, people will, in the same community, even across the whole society; devise other means by which to relate to one another. Hate can be viable when used in this capacity. Like love, it is a strong force that can unite people. Other options are hero worship and vicarious living, but one of the most active social elements, in this regard today, is the stereotype. It is more suited to the pictorial mode of our society, and it gives us the quick reference we want in an action-oriented world. When you get right down to it, hero-worshipping and a vicarious lifestyle is also based on a certain kind of stereotyping; the John Wayne type of rugged individualist, for instance. And the muscle bound athlete who is not too bright intellectually, but has tremendous instincts and physical abilities. There is also the blond-headed, blue eyed Caucasian, sexy bombshell, i.e., Marilyn Monroe, who always has more fun.

There is another good reason why stereotypes prevail in our society. Our society is an adversarial world. We live amidst good guys and bad guys. We live with rights and wrongs. A hierarchical, stratified society is by its nature an environment filled with tension and hostility. As well, because our society has a capitalist economy, there is the constant competition and struggle between entrepreneurs to make a profit. Within this arena, it is useful to be able to easily define your opponent because your actions can then become a matter of a self-fulfilling prophecy. When women were more at home, they were not so deeply involved in this environment, but that has changed. They, too, are assuming more of an adversarial attitude in their social behavior. As women once saw themselves being stereotyped as barefoot and pregnant homemakers without individuality, now they are applying this same stereotype prospective to men: they are all chauvinistic pigs.

In their struggle to free themselves from the shackles of old, the modern woman has turned men and children into adversaries, and many women have declared war on their enemies. Men are chauvinist pigs, and their children have come to be their little piglets. Now, there is truly the battle of the sexes that is going on, and each side has sent forth their monsters from the id to fight for them. Presently, it is common for a relationship between a man and a woman to be fraught with psychological, emotional, and physical abuse. Indeed, some form of abuse, and even violence, has become a normal means of communicating and relating between couples. A man may be abusing a woman every 12 seconds of the day, but women are beginning to fight back in that thirteenth second.

It is tragic that men and women have to engage in physical and emotional battles because in the overall there is no way that they can disengage themselves. They need each other. Neither can reach their full potential as a human organism without the other, and this is in the context of procreation. The biological and orgasmic imperatives will force them to come together, but seeing each other as adversaries ends up driving them apart. This contest between men and women, while lamentable, is at least understandable within the historical context from which it has risen. But how do we explain the dismissive, abusive, and even violent attitude some women are having towards their own children today? If men exploit women in the home, are children to blame also? Some feminists would seem to say yes. As piglets, children make demands upon mothers that limit their mobility and outside activities. This is not conducive to the lifestyle of the liberated, working woman.

I repeat: a woman does not have to become a mother if she does not want to, but if she does she has the ultimate responsibility to fulfill the task. No one else in the world, in the entire universe, is capable of optimally taking care of her child as she can, and for the best welfare of the child, and ultimately the species, it is something that cannot be relinquished by the mother. The gravity of this should weigh upon every woman who thinks of having a baby. A woman can have no greater responsibility than looking after her child. But social philosophy has come between a woman and that reality. She has been told that she is a thinking being, and no biological imperative can tell her how to use her body. Women are telling themselves that having a child is an option and not a human requirement.

In this same fashion, women have opted to back away from their status as the chief significant other in their child's life. They have convinced themselves that a young child wants love and affection from an adult. But it does not have to be the birth mother, and it can be any surrogate. This kind of thinking is so Victorian and pre-Freud. With women seemingly so enlightened about sex and their bodies, it is difficult to understand how they can be so regressive about their relationship to their offspring? If there is such a thing as the biological imperative as I have been speaking of it, then it points up how deeply women have been affected by emotional deprivation. Even the simple female animals of the forest, fields, and jungles know they have the ultimate responsibility to see that their young, and their species survive. Psychologically and emotionally, today's American woman is trying to dissociate herself from that responsibility. The struggles women are having with themselves, as to whether they will be mothers or moochers, is at present unresolved.

The ultimate question of this chapter comes down to this: Is there really such a force as the biological imperative for women? The feminists will tell you absolutely not. Women, they say, have sought validation for themselves as wives and mothers because they were socialized to see their worth that way, and because for many years they were not allowed to participate fully in occupational world of men. But this is only half true. Women have suffered because of bias and sexism, and it is also true that men have used women for their own social and sexual advantage. This situation developed at time when women were very dependent upon the men to take care of them and their children. They admired, and still do, the strongest, bravest, and most virile men. They respected the rugged individualist, and they willingly gave themselves to these men because it ensures them and their children of the best chance for survival.

When the environment humans lived in was thoroughly wild, filled with vicious, threatening animals and uncontrollable climatic conditions, women were quite content to stay at home and let the men do battle for them in that hostile world. They were using men to serve their procreative interest. But once nature had been tamed, men became less important to women as guardians and food gathers per se. Women then developed other expectations from men. They wanted to be emotionally cared for and loved. For this to happen, the male had to change his behavior and become more "civilized." And the way women got men to do it was by the giving or withholding of sexual favors.

Over a long historical period, men bent, bowed, and genuflected to the wishes of women who, initially, were seen as made in the image of goddesses; and in the process, an elaborate social system of etiquette, decorum, mores, and courting rituals developed. As groups of people settled into permanent residential areas, progeny became very important. Thereafter, marriage became institutionalized and culturally regulated. No doubt, women gained a measure of security from this, and yes men did exploit them. However, women were more willing participants than the feminists would have us believe today. What has always been present in the relationships between men and women is the trade off. Each has something the other wants, and they are constantly maneuvering to put themselves in the best position to get it.

If there is a biological imperative, then women need men to fulfill it. Men certainly have an orgasmic imperative, and they can only consummate it fully with women. Even in this period of the Women's Liberation movement, if you ask a woman what she wants most out of life, she is likely to say, in one fashion or another, a good relationship. Is this socialization talking? I don't think so, and any woman who is willing to be honest about her feelings would agree with me. Women want to be wanted, and they have a need to be needed. Women like to be cuddled and held, and they have a proclivity for nesting. This is consistent with the way women get joy from their bodies, by being touched and caressed. Is this because of social-ization or biology? You really don't have to be a mental giant to distinguish the difference. And who can fulfill all these needs for a woman? It normally means a man.

You put a man and woman together, and let them hug and caress, this will surely lead to sexual relations. There is no doubt that this is a biologi-cal experience no matter how much society has influenced the behavior of the participants involved. And when members of the opposites sex start having sexual relations, pregnancy and babies are sure to follow. This human process is constantly occurring around the globe in millions of communities. The social reality of the many groups may be quite differ-ent, but the biology of the experience is always the same. That is the uni-versal connection here, and society may influence it, but it does not give rise to it.

In America, we have the cult of the individual, and it is a belief that the individual is more important than the group. This is a social philosophy that is an ideal, but it is not carried out in practice. Nevertheless, the belief strongly influences our political and criminal justice systems. The individual is thought to have certain inalienable rights that cannot be abridged by mor-tal men or governments. Individuals are expected to have control over their own lives, and for long weary centuries, because in status they were subordi-nate to men, women felt that the control of their lives had been denied to them. With the Women's Liberation movement, the sexual revolution, and the civil rights movement of the 1960s, women felt politically motivated to gain control of their lives. Changing their social status had become a new means of validation. Issues that had evolved from the problem of emotional deprivation became confronted by feminism, but because individualism implies free will, any idea or theory that had a biological connection, was rejected as deterministic.

For over thirty years, women have been riding on a wave of the new feminism, and they have had a number of successes with their liberation movement. The housewife of the 1950s is gone forever, and women have increased opportunities for higher education and positions in the occupational system. They are more economically independent and politically motivated, and they are now more active in every sphere of our social life. However, women do not seem to be any happier today than they were before the coming of the liberation movement. According to the feminine mystique, back then women felt alienated and estranged from their families as they do today. They found themselves in an identity crisis then, and they are in one now. In commenting on the present state of womanhood, Gloria Steinem said that women are particularly susceptible to feelings of self-doubt, self-hatred, and the sense of incompleteness. Why?

Like men, socialization has caused women to suppress their innate selves. This would certainly give rise to self-doubt, self-hatred, and feelings of incompleteness. These are some of the classic symptoms of emotional deprivation. In this, women should understand the roots of their emotional problems do not essentially have to do with men. It is with themselves. Emotional deprivation is a problem of the self. That is why alienation always plays a role in it, and the woman can feel that there is a stranger inside of her. It makes it easier to cultivate self-hatred because the hate can seem to be directed at the stranger within. But when a woman turns on herself this way, she becomes an incarnate of a monster from her id. It is the self, fighting with the self, and even the *Me* maybe left out of it. This is a prescription for catatonia, and it is a mental disorder that specifically works against the physical behavior of the body. The disease maybe the extreme end of the scale of the problems caused by emotional deprivation.

The fact that women focus so much of their attention, in the positive and negative sense, on their bodies, tells us that their biology is indeed unique to the validation of themselves as women. The biological imperative is just a term used to express this. Besides, no rational, intellectual argument can ever make the case for the importance of a woman's body in the human scheme of things. The awareness of it must come from within women themselves because the answer to their confusion and alienation is inside of them, as it is inside all of us. And to be sure, because women are so necessary to the maintenance of species survival, nature gave them the means to overcome the problems of self-doubt, self-hatred, and feelings of incompleteness. It is called motherhood.

When a woman is nurturing her child during the days of his non-consciousness, she is performing as his I, but for the mother to act as the child's I, and help him develop a strong sense of self, the woman needs to function as the innate person she was born to be. The child made his special connection with that element of her being when he was in the womb. In functioning as her innate self when nurturing her child, a mother is enhancing her own sense of I and purpose in life, and she is doing it on the physical, emotional, conscious, and unconscious levels. Motherhood validates womanhood.

In impoverished nations around the world, millions of women are faced with enormous obstacles that prevent them and their children from having even a marginal standard of living. Starvation, drought, and disease keep daily company with them. Survival is a day-by-day proposition, with no guarantees of what the morrow will bring. But, by and large, these women are not confused about their purpose in life. They want to have babies and be mothers. Even in their abject poverty and social misery, they seem to know that having children is a blessing, and they understand that it is children who make their lives worthwhile. With our standard of living, how wonderful it would be if American women felt that way?

However, in our society women believe that having a baby is just another one of their options as individual, liberated persons. They don't feel any sense of responsibility to do it, and they certainly are not going to be dictated to by some biological imperative. These ladies have an attitude. "We've come a long way, baby, and we are not about to turn around now." As social commentary, this is one of the saddest jingles ever conjured up by the ad-boys on Madison Avenue, and interestingly enough, it sounds very much like famous last words.

WOMEN'S LIBERATION

Oh yes, women have come a long way, baby, but the question needs to be asked, "Do they know where they are going?" Better yet, can it be said that they are progressing or regressing? The majority of the feminists would have us believe that it is certainly the former and not the latter. But in fact, the jury is still out, way out. Some of the old guard feminists, like Gloria Steinem, Gloria Allred, Camille Paglia and Christina Sommers, are now wondering if feminism has gone too far? Paglia and Sommers, in particular, criticize the radical feminists for promoting male-bashing, female chauvinism, and "totalitarian feminism."[18] All of this makes one wonder: are pork chops from the chauvinist pig still a priority on the feminists' political menu? This development needs to be explored.

To begin with, let me point out this basic fact. American society today has fallen under the spell of a cultural conundrum. Both men and women are quite confused about their social identity and purpose. On the surface, this situation seems puzzling, but in fact there is no great mystery about it. The conundrum exists because emotional deprivation has stolen their sense of individuality. While everyone has been deeply affected by the problem, men seem to worry less about it than women. They have the dominant roles in almost all of the major institutions in society, and they can easily rationalize that what they do outside the home is meaningful and important. For centuries, women did not have that privilege. Women felt alienated and isolated from the outside world, and the confusion they came to feel had to be dealt with up close and personal. Their bewilderment concerned itself with what it meant to be a woman in the role of wife and mother.

Traditionally, women had to depend upon their family role to satisfy all their basic needs and aspirations. This was due to the fact that their major responsibility in society has always been the nurturing, rearing and social-ization of the children. To be sure, the social contract says that youngsters have to be taught the norms and values of the society. If the children learn these matters properly, they become social conformists, and other social members would respect them for it. This would reflect well upon the morals, etiquette, and social standing of the family, and it was thought that only a good mother could produce these results in her children. In this way, a mother could feel a sense of meaning and importance in her life. And since mothers were concerned with their children's long-term survival, to raise them to be good members of society meant they would have the best chance to accomplish this within the system. This is what the society wanted, and psychically the mothers would know that they were fulfilling their natural responsibility as progenitors. This was a mother's reward, and because of it, for a long time, women could accept their role in the home as being important and worthwhile.

But, their role was based upon a delicate balance. As long as the majority of the children of society, especially the bellwether middle class kids, accepted conformity and sought a place in the establishment, mothers could feel right about what they were doing at home, but two overlapping, socially shattering events occurred that would begin to change young people's attitudes, the Great Depression and the Second World War. The former caused people, young and old, to lose faith and confidence in the social system. As a conse-quence, by the late 1940s, the beatniks had arrived. They were middle class kids who turned their backs on the establishment, and they took enormous delight in castigating bourgeois family values. They sought a new socially creative purpose for their lives.

When the men returned from the war, they came home looking to rekindle their family life anew. It was the time of the baby boom, and wives were under heavy pressure to be perfect homemakers to smooth their transition back into civilian life. The middle class was growing, and many urban women suddenly found themselves living a new lifestyle in suburbia. They became dependent upon cars, and they had to change their shopping and recreation habits. There were no neighborhoods in the suburbs like there had been in the city, and therefore no neighborhood schools. The children had to be bused to and from their educational centers. The man of the house became a weekend husband and father because of the daily commute to his job in the city. A whole new way of life was evolving for women who had been raised as urban dwellers. By and large, the new middle class and suburbanite women were not prepared for all these changes. Initially, they had trouble coping with them. Then, to top it all off, through the 1950s an increasing number of middle class young people were beginning to reject their middle class values.

Under these circumstances, the old rationalizations women used, about their self-worth and importance in the home, no longer sufficed. And interestingly enough, discontent was brewing in the middle class family just as discontent was breaking out in society at large. In 1954, the Supreme Court rendered the Brown Decision that outlawed segregation in public schools. In 1955, Rosa Parks sparked the Montgomery, Alabama bus boycott, a protest against segregation in public transportation. And, students from North Carolina A&M College sat in at a Woolworth lunch counter in 1959 and the civil rights movement was underway.

As the battle against segregation was beginning to grip the nation, a new group of disaffected middle class youths appeared in the 1960s. They were the hippies. They took a stand against the government, the Vietnam War, and they joined forces with the civil rights movement. Collectively, young people were rising up against the establishment. They were challenging traditions, and they called for substantial political change, equality and justice for all. Social change was pulsating throughout society, and it was infectious. Group after group was stepping forward to redress their grievances: African-Americans, Native Americans, Chicanos, gay men and lesbians, farm workers, and college students. From every quarter, the establishment was being assaulted, and it seemed that everyone was getting into the act. Women felt inspired. They took a look at their situation and concluded that they had grievances, too.

For three decades, beginning with the Depression, American women had been feeling less and less secure about their role in the family. With the increasing suburbanization of their lifestyle, they were no longer the center of the family unit. In the newer middle class communities, the home was just a way station where members came to eat, freshen up, and sleep. The role of women in these families was as a cook, a maid, a chauffeur, and occasional lover. By the time of the civil rights movement, many middle class women came to realize that their lives were as unrewarding and sterile as their beatnik and hippie children said it was.

In 1963, Betty Friedan published *The Feminine Mystique.* In her book she explored the causes for the frustrations of modern women in their traditional roles in American society. Her book became a rallying call for women, and just like that the Women's Liberation movement was underway and a whole new generation of feminists burst upon the social scene. Friedan seems to have articulated the unhappiness many women were feeling about their dissatisfaction with being a housewife and mother. The problem was recognized, but what was to be done about it? Discussions, conferences, and debates were held. Women intellectuals wrote news articles and academic papers, and gradually they came to the conclusion that they needed an organization.

As a result, the National Organization For Women (NOW) was eventually born. NOW was to become a political action organization, with the specific mandate to change the legal status of women, but the Women's Liberation movement was more about women changing their traditional roles and image in society. From the discussions and debates, with individuals like Betty Friedan, Kate Millet, Gloria Steinem, Wilma Scott Heide. Alieen Hernandez, and Dr. Ann L. Scott, a philosophy developed that was to guide the movement. It was very much an expression of the political atmosphere of the 1960s, a call for women to be treated equal to men in all matters legal and social. The philosophy was a reaction to the belief that American society was a male-dominated system, and the roles of women were greatly determined by the superior position of men. To understand the Women's Liberation movement, one needs to know how women saw themselves in their traditional role as housewife and mother.

Simply stated, the traditional image of a woman in America was that of a *Hausfrau*. It had its beginning at a very early age, when a young girl was made aware that her social destiny lay in the fulfillment of this image. The feminists noted that through socialization, the internalization of cultural ideology, family pressure, peer pressure, and the limiting of social options in education, jobs, and generally in public life, the developing young woman was made to feel guilty if she did not yearn to fulfill this home-maker image. In terms of social esteem, community recognition and acceptance of being a mature person of good moral character and of sound mind, this was practically the only area of society that was truly opened to the vast majority of women.[19]

Of course, the feminists played down the fact that there were some sound reasons for society wanting women to become mothers and home-makers. Biologically, only women could bear children, and as a consequence they are suited to nurture the offspring. Moreover, all societies have an interest in perpetuating themselves. Children are needed towards that end. But, there was a contradiction here. Apart from the biological realism of wanting women to become homemakers, the social roles involved called upon them to develop distinct types of attitudes about themselves as members of society. These attitudes were like self-fulfilling prophecies; or at least until recent years, they seem to have such power. That is to say, once women accepted these attitudes about themselves, even with reservations, a certain road through their social life became a fait accompli.

As well, it was very anxiety provoking for women to try to fulfill the social obligations being called for by these attitudes because they first had to "catch a man" or allow themselves to be "caught by a man." This was in recognition of the fact that women saw their social functions as growing out of a man's social roles; which meant that women were dependent upon men for their social recognition. Now this point was more than a bit of a stretch for the feminists. Biologically speaking, women have always been independent of men, except in the procreative sense, and their roles have always been based more on biology than their social status. If women accepted the notion that male roles are more important than those of females that does not make it so in fact. It is just a judgment call by the women.

In any case, women were saying that they were not free social agents, but rather they had been socialized to believe that they belong to men; fathers before marriage and husbands afterwards. It was pointed out that Freud, in his psychological theories, gave support to the notion that socially women were to belong to men. Theoretically, Freud developed the ideas of the Oedipus complex and Penis Envy. In the Oedipal situation, a young female child competes with her mother for her father's affection; or she competes with her mother, it could be said, for the right to belong to her father. Freud, of course, saw the young male child competing with his father for his mother's affection. But in the case of the female, he also said she is struck with Penis Envy. The female wishes she had a penis, ostensibly because it seems to symbolize the male's strength and dominance. Since no woman will ever grow a penis on her body, although a transsexual change may hold out some possibility, she may satisfy the penis envy urge by "catching a man" and belonging to him. While the feminists would not likely agree, this line of thinking would suggest that female jealousy is rooted in the notion "this penis is mine."[20]

The feminists were making a case that if women were seen as socially belonging to men this imputed certain weaknesses in their character. They were, in poetic terms, to be seen as passive, fragile flowers in need of the physical strength, guidance, protection, and even idolization of men. Whether the women knew it or not, they needed men to hold them up, or to put it more properly in its pejorative description, women need men to cling to. They were too weak, emotionally and physically, to stand up to the adversities, the rigors of life and living alone. They did not have the mind; the ability to reason pragmatically and rationally that would permit them to be rugged individualists. In fact, their basic personality was not innately prepared for an individualist expression of self, or an individual way of life. Biologically, their bodies were suited for having babies, and they could not have these babies alone. They were, like it or not, destined to be a supporting player in male-female relationships. From this point of view, the feminists said that innately men were oppressors of women. And, if engaging in sexual relations could be taken as the example, nature confirms the fact that women should be on the bottom. This was one hell of a view that the feminists conjured up about the way they thought men saw them.

From this negative perspective, yes indeed, women had the weight of the men, physically and socially, pressing down on them, and if that wasn't enough, said the feminists, women were socially made to feel that this situation was for their own good. Indeed, they were expected to be thankful to men for giving them their names in wedlock, and they would also be in their husbands' debt. He had allowed them the chance to fulfill their social destiny as wife, mother, and *Hausfrau*. Any man that would be so giving of himself deserved respect and obedience. A good wife should always be humble before her husband. Without him, she would have little social status in society. Even courtesans of old and call girls today get more respect than an "old maid," or so the feminists said when they were evaluating the view they thought men had of them.[21]

Being seen as weak by men was something that women began to believe, and they began to assume a passive mode to the male's more aggressive posture. They learned to be submissive to men in attitude and demeanor, and they learned to yield to the male's ego because it conferred social recognition upon them. In their one-to-one personal relationships, women nurtured the male's egoistic sense of aggression by being inactive in the face of it. Women withdrew the totality of themselves from active participation in their relationships with men because the "total woman," a woman who expressed needs that could not be fulfilled by her male owner, was likely to be interpreted as a threat to the male ego. As the feminists were always quick to point out, the male seemed practically interested in only one aspect of a woman's character.

Primarily expressing themselves in the one way they thought the men wanted from them, women placed constraints upon their total development. They concentrated on being alluring and sexy. That was to be their primary modus operandi. Women believed that this was the way they had to be to "catch and hold a man." They would deny they're other talents if it would allow them to be more sexually pleasing to men. This kind of behavior was very detrimental to the total well being of women. This concentration on themselves as sexual objects lowered their sense of self-esteem as a fully mature and developed human being. At the same time, women learned how to use sex appeal in a cat and mouse fashion to move men in ways that they desired. And in hindsight, it is interesting to note that the feminists were admitting that women did use sex to achieve certain ends. As we know, because of the sexual harassment phenomenon today, women are now playing down this behavioral practice.

The Women's Liberation movement pointed out that women were unhappy with their roles as wife and mother for some very good reasons. To begin with, the roles were weighted down with ambiguity and contradiction. It was believed that a woman's place was in the home, raising the children and tending the hearth. She was taught that this was her sacred duty because the family was endowed with religious sainthood and cultural primacy as a social institution. The responsibilities of homemaking had to be assumed by women for the good of the human species, and women had no right to have feelings to the contrary. In many respects, this constituted a call to martyrdom.

It was a cruel joke, said the feminists that a woman's place was to be in the home whether her husband was a taxi driver or President of the United States. Homemaking was to be her career. But, while her natural place was thought to be in the home, she was not to be its master. It was the male's castle, and in more ways than one, the woman felt like she was just renting space in the place. And yes, the children, they were to be the crowning glory of every woman. Nothing was more exemplary of a woman's social status than her children. Next to her husband, or was it because of him, she belonged to them. They had the right to monopolize her time, her energies, and her life. Unfortunately, this may be necessary in the normal, procreative, human process. However, when it is coupled with male dominance and control, a woman could easily be reduced to little more than a servant in the home, and this was not to be acceptable to the new liberated woman.

Women were not to think of their own needs when it came to their families, in particular as it related to their children. Any sincere, loving mother should deny herself, to whatever degree necessary, if it would benefit the well being of her children. In fact, according to the edicts of society, motherhood meant denial, sacrifice, and martyrdom, and since children were inextricably bound to the woman's role, this was trumpeted as a woman's social, if not biological fate. This idea that women should deny themselves for the betterment of their children seems to have reached its greatest influence with the spread of the child-rearing philosophy of people like Dr. Benjamin Spock, who preached the glorification of children. It was the Spockian notion that every child has a unique potential, and it was the mother's most important mission to nurture this potential to total fulfillment. The mother was being asked to live by the will and dictates of the child, at any cost to her own personality or sense of fulfillment. Interestingly enough, the father was not expected to expend himself similarly, we are told.

And the women were no longer buying into the idea that they were rewarded for their sacrifice by being placed on a pedestal, said the feminists. This was a shabby way of intoning the woman's image with a supposedly certain purity of spirit, respect for life, undaunting faithfulness in love, a pension for being beautiful and happy, and possessed with an all around humanism. Men supposedly put women on a pedestal because women exemplified those human qualities they lacked. And, too, men said they put women on a pedestal to show admiration for them. However, Betty Friedan suggested that it was another way men put women down.[22] Her point being that women were no more possessed with a purity of spirit than men. This male attitude was unreal, and served to cause women to relate to themselves in fantasizing, unhealthy ways. In fact, it was not possible for a real woman to reach the heights of the pedestal.

The new feminists saw themselves as having been damaged in early childhood. For instance, one of the most unreal aspects of being on a pedestal was its myth or "fairy tale" component about the savior prince on the great white horse. As the tale goes, because a woman is possessed with innate goodness, if not saintly qualities, there are evil forces lurking in the environment that naturally want to subvert such goodness and pull the woman down from her pedestal. Remember how the devil coerced Eve. But when the danger strikes, the bonny prince on the great white horse would come galloping over the horizon, destroy the evil creature and save the princess. The two then ride off into the sunset to "live happily ever after."

Women have been taught to believe that there is a bonny prince out there on a white horse willing and able to save a woman on a pedestal. Therefore, a woman, who accepts her status and conducts herself accordingly, had nothing to fear in the environment because her prince was always available to save her from any danger. This little "fairy tale" could be understood in more realistic terms. It goes like this: for every woman there is a man who would save her from the suffering of social anonymity and obscurity by making her his wife. She would be saved from the outcast role of "old maid," and the shame of having lived to be a barren woman.

The feminist thinkers did make a very telling point with their analysis of the woman on the pedestal, and it related very much to the behavior of compulsive masculinity. Interestingly enough, the "southern belle" is still to be found in the Deep South, an area of the country where rugged individualism is a cherished ideal. The reality of the woman on a pedestal is complementary to that dominant male character; which is to say that Betty Friedan's comment on situation is very well taken.

Any true feminist today could, and without much urging would, give you this traditional image of a woman as mentioned above. But there is a much deeper dimension to the old image that was not being talked about, and that dimension is more subliminal than liminal because it is a function of the unconscious mind. This underlying characteristic has often plagued women in their fantasies, their dreams, and their nightmares. And, it is not the kind of thing that a woman would talk to her lover or husband about. A man just wouldn't understand. It is not even easy for one woman to articulate it to another female, perhaps out of fear of being misunderstood or appearing as a neurotic, if not a psychotic person.[23] Behind their traditional roles as housewife and mother, the description women were giving of themselves was that of an exploited, alienated, enslaved, puppet person who was totally manipulated by men. And most importantly, they apparently felt like they did not belong to themselves. This is a picture of severely emotionally deprived individuals, and it tells us how this phenomenon causes women to get caught up in a process of self-delusion, distortion, and introjections.

To begin with, in the existential sense, no human being can stop belonging to her or himself. The sense of existential belonging to the self is a matter of self-realization. It is a fact of the senses and not an idea of the mind. Self-realization can only be relinquished by death. Individuals can be made, through social imperatives, to think, believe, and accept the attitude that they do not belong to themselves. Enslaved Africans in the South prior to the Civil War, the Jews in the concentration camps of Dachau and Treblinka are such examples. The sense of belonging to oneself tells the person that she is in possession of the will and the power to determine her own identity and life chances. The feminist description of themselves, as seen through the eyes of men, implied that they had no such power, and they did not have it because they had no sense of self.

Because women believed that they belonged to men, they also thought that men determined their existence, actually their social existence, but it was not being perceived that way because women were seemingly taking a religious view of the situation. From their Christian upbringing, they have been taught to believe that they are one of Adam's ribs. This makes them nothing more than an extension of men, and therefore susceptible to male dominance and control. Surely, this was not a rational opinion women had of themselves. It was a function of faith and belief, a matter of feeling. For without women accepting the right of men to own them, in the first instance, they would not be able to believe that men were determining their identities and life chances.

But the more devastating aspect of this syndrome set women against themselves. It made them the chief causal instruments for their social and personal alienation. Their sense of person, self-esteem, and relational viability in the social sphere was accepted as coming through men, in actual and symbolic terms. It was a negation of personality and being. Women had to put themselves down to accept the belief that they should belong to a man. And, if men were only interested in women for sexual reasons, there was a sound basis for them to feel alienated and denied.

Unfortunately, over time, the situation with women was sure to worsen. Alienation is progressive, and it brings forth self-rejection and self-hatred for the entire self, the sexual character of women notwithstanding.[24] Within this syndrome, natural innate urges become threats to women. Desires for love, companionship, and children become realized through alienating and demeaning processes. In any case, fulfillment of these ends required a male, and this meant recognizing his ownership of them.

Because of self-rejection and self-hatred, the feminists saw women as feigning and disassembling themselves before the ego-dominating needs of men. They subordinated themselves to the men while their insides wretch from self-diminution. The pain of pretending, the pain of impersonating, the pain of denial was choking and stifling them, often bringing on headaches, constipation, diarrhea, blurred vision, hallucinations, sexual frigidity, child abuse, non-conversations, non-communications, tactics to emasculate the male, and a sundry of psychosomatic illnesses. Bouts of depression were frequent, and women tried to escape it by pumpkin eating, alcoholism, sexual promiscuity, volunteerism, separation or divorce from owner-husbands, or even suicide if the pressure became too intense.[25]

It was not new for women to see themselves as puppet people. What was new with Women's Liberation was the attitude they brought to it. In the past, when most women believed that to fulfill their destiny they had to belong to a man, they went through a symbolic act of disembodiment. In "catching a man," women turned their bodies over to them. As recognition of that fact, the men stamped their brand on the body, the brand that was their name. The act told all men that this specific body belonged to Mister So and so; but all too frequently, the spirit of womanhood was withheld from the body snatcher, and Mister So and so received only a shell. This was a protest by women for having to give their bodies to men in the first place. But the truth was that women were using their bodies as negotiable items. As payment for the opportunity of fulfilling their destiny, they would give men sex, but they would withhold the essence of themselves, their love, from the men. And no matter what name society wanted to give to it, this was a form of prostitution.

In psychological and emotional terms, this was the nature of the subliminal infrastructure that underlay the traditional image of women in American society. As housewives and mothers, the feminists saw themselves as being no better than whores, hiding behind the morally sanctioned and socially acceptable practice of marriage and mating. These *Hausfraus* did not stand on the street corner hawking their wares. Instead, they stood in the doorways of the family home kissing their husbands when they left for work and kissing them when they returned. Imagine the feminists seeing themselves as dispirited, disembodied whores.

If the founders of the Women's Liberation movement saw themselves this way, then they were indeed in a world of emotional trouble, and they certainly should have risen up to do something about it. But did they do the right thing by focusing on men as being responsible for their unhappiness? No. They did the wrong thing. The basis for their personal problems had to do with themselves, their dissatisfaction and discontent with their inability to achieve a fulfilling life. This can be easily recognized because at the core of their problems was alienation. It is something one person cannot force on another, but rather it is self-induced. Alienation is a response to the suppression of the innate self, and that bespeaks of emotional deprivation.

Throughout the negative description of themselves as a woman, a housewife and mother, the feminists use terms and imagery that suggest they are struggling with the symptoms of emotional deprivation. The first clue of this is in the fact that the women are describing themselves as they think men see them. It is not that men have told them that they are to be *Hausfraus*, martyrs, and disembodied whores, but these are terms women have come to use in trying to explain how they feel about the way they see themselves. It shows that they have a very low sense of self-esteem, and they lack a strong sense of individuality. In fact, there is too much talk about themselves as collectives, which is a sure sign that the innate self has been suppressed.

The view was also offered that women were innately unprepared for an individualistic expression of the self. It is interesting that women should think that men would know about their person even before they were born. So much of their description of themselves seems to impute God-like insight and mystical powers to men. This is not to say that men do not think of themselves as being better, even superior, to women. By and large, they do, and they are arrogant in this regard. But it is really the ego talking and nothing more. On the other hand, women think they are superior to men, too. They will often talk about the little boy that is inside of every man who needs a woman to take care of him. Clearly, this is the female's maternal instinct talking. This would seem to suggest that it was never the power men had over women that caused them so much unhappiness, but rather it was the female's need to be needed that caused them to acquiesce to the male ego. The biological imperative strikes again.

By the 1960s, women had become dissatisfied with their lives as home-makers. If this situation were to improve, they would have to get out into the larger world of jobs and professions. To do so, they had to enter the occupational system that had been traditionally male oriented. They were willing to do it because they believed that men were better off than them-selves. The men had more options and opportunities to acquire positions, as doctors, lawyers, and Indian Chiefs that allowed them to have rewarding and self-fulfilling lives. That is what the women wanted, too. Fair enough. But the feminists not only wanted the same opportunities as men, they wanted to be like men, and if men were so God-like and mystical, why not? If nothing else, it would make it easier for women to compete with the men in the occupational system.

But the feminists did not just want to be like men. They wanted to be men. Indeed, it was an old story taking on a new wrinkle. Freud saw it as penis envy. For the female, the penis was the symbol of the male's power. The occupational system was a repository of male power. To function like a man in the system, women could vicariously experience a sense of that power. Is this a stretch? I don't think so. As one representative of NOW said, "Women are now getting balls."[26]

Liberated women have taken great delight in mocking and rejecting the notion that they are motivated, at any time, by a maternal instinct. Yet, so much of their self-description has undertones of such an inborn tendency. They described themselves as being subordinate to men because of their biology, a biology that has them suited for having babies. In speaking of "getting balls," it alludes to procreation, and Freud said that a woman's desire for a penis becomes a desire for marriage and children. When she is giving birth, and the baby is coming from between her legs, this is a penis substitute.[27] Similarly, with women now engaging themselves fully in the occupational system, and acting like men, they can feel penis possessed.

It is very strange for women to be talking about getting balls, even when it is being used as a metaphor. The image of women with such objects dangling between their legs is totally antithetical to any notion of womanhood. Indeed, the idea is grotesque in and of itself. Unknown to women, there seems to be a form of introjections taking place here. They are projecting a monster from their collective id based on the belief in the power of the male sex organ. If they can vicariously take the male's balls, then they can usurp his power, but they don't seem to recognize that in the process they must surrealistically disembody themselves. When they do, by their own description, can some kind of whoring be far behind?

The feminists accuse men of treating them like weaklings, and they say it is unjustified. Yet, there was a time, when the world was much more hostile to humans, and women were quite willing to allow the men to protect them from threatening and dangerous animals, and the ravages of an uncontrollable, natural environment. Because women wanted to bear children and fulfill themselves as females, they also capitulated to the male's aggressive sexual behavior. This went on for centuries, and women developed a passive state of mind because it served their interest to do so. Therefore, it is wrong for women to now say that men are responsible for that sense of weakness they feel in their character. In this regard, women have created a self-fulfilling prophecy for themselves.

The self-fulfilling prophecy issue is very telling about the description overall that women have of themselves. The classic idea of self-fulfilling prophecy is that of a person who has a wrongheaded belief about others or oneself, and he or she would then behave in a manner that would support and confirm the belief. For example, women may believe that men see them as weaklings and unable to take care of themselves, but at the same time they say this is not true. However, there was a time when women catered to this image, and we know it because of the Madonna complex, the rise of chivalry, and Victorian values. Women acted the part of being a weakling because they wanted to be treated like Mary the sainted one, the princess before her knight, and the martyred wife and homemaker.

Liberated women complain about men treating them as sex objects, but in one fashion or another women are constantly enticing, titillating, and exposing themselves sexually. They do this in the tight, form fitting clothing they wear, the short skirts that practically exposes themselves all the way up to their crotch, the sheer blouses that are meant to show cleavage and the outline of their breasts, the bikini and thong bathing suits that let them approach being naked in public, the topless beaches and bars they frequent, and the thousands and thousands of women who are engaged in pornographic film-making. And in regular films, there are always the obligatory sex scenes of women getting off and enjoying it. On network TV, there are similar kinds of sex scenes, but toned down. On cable TV, HBO and Showtime for example, it is quite common to see women parading around in the nude, leaving nothing to the imagination. And yet, women complain about men treating them as sex objects. I wonder how men came upon such an idea?

Like Freud, Dr. Benjamin Spock became a philosophical enemy of the Women's Liberation movement. Why? Because he said that it was a mother's responsibility to fully nurture her child, and bring out his unique potential. Which simply means that a mother should give her child all the love and affection she can so that he might develop a strong, healthy sense of self. Why should the feminists take issue with this? They say that Dr. Spock told women to deny themselves for the betterment of their children, and the feminists are not about putting their children before themselves. Their attitude in this matter demonstrates once again that the core of their unhappiness is caused by emotional deprivation. The fact that women would question devoting their lives fully to their children, especially when they are defenseless, in the first few years of their lives, smacks of emotional immaturity. If the mother does not play the role as the chief significant other for her child, then it is a once in a lifetime-missed opportunity. The feminist do not seemed to be concerned with this. They are more concerned with their own opportunities and children will not be allowed to stand in the way. If children were going to be treated as adjunct persons in their lives, then one would wonder why feminists have children at all?

There is a profound immature character to the description liberated women seem to have of themselves. They complained about being put on a pedestal, but they obviously want men to give them more respect. At the same time, they attack men for being chauvinist pigs, and they feel justified in doing so because they say men are the cause of their unhappiness. When men objected to their hostilities and fight back, the women called them reactionary Neanderthals who want to keep them homebound, barefoot and pregnant. By attacking men, women provoke the males into reacting negatively and disrespectfully towards the opposite sex. Women used the male's behavior as the reason for calling them chauvinist pigs. But like immature people tend to do, they figuratively bite off their own noses to spite their face. Or, you could also say, they engaged in another form self-fulfilling prophecy.

In their treatise against men, the feminists tended to be intellectually and emotionally dishonest. They complained about myth of the savior prince on the great white horse who rescues endangered maidens and bring them happiness ever after. This is indeed nothing but a fairy tale, they say, to keep women on a pedestal and dependent. But what is the real basis for this myth? Practically, every woman knows what it is. Women are born to be progenitors. All of them may not perform in this task, but the ability is there. To fulfill this innate promise, a woman needs a man. Physically, psychically, and emotionally, a woman will yearn for a man. Being endowed with the responsibility of perpetuating the species, they will want the best man they can imagine, someone who is big, strong, and handsome. The bonny prince is a symbol of each woman's ideal man.

The feminists know exactly what the myth of the bonny prince stands for. It is the fantasy love interest that girls have when they are growing up. It is the same interest that causes them to fall in love with movie stars, TV entertainers, crooners, rock stars, and fictional characters in romance stories. But, all this aside, the use of this myth, women say, is just another way men put them down. However, the dishonesty here is quite glaring. The symbolism of the bonny prince is just as unreal as the woman on a pedestal. If women cannot live up to the image of a saintly person, then men should not have to be the bonny prince. In any case, by any account, the two images are mutually exclusive.

Why should the feminists be dishonest when promulgating their interpretation of the bonny prince myth? Because their thinking, perhaps not intentionally, is being guided by emotional deprivation. And speaking of symbolism, how striking it is that women should talk about evil forces lurking in the environment, and what does the bonny prince do when he comes galloping over the horizon? He destroys the evil creatures that threaten the well-being and happiness of the female. These creatures are likely to be a projection from the collective unconsciousness of women, monsters from their ids. Actually, there is not much of a surprise in this. Like all of us, the feminists have repressed their innate beings, and they are projecting monsters to take the blame for it. And because the women have become somewhat fixated on the males as the overall cause of their unhappiness and problems, they can come to see men as incarnates of these monsters.

I do not think it is too much of a stretch to give some thought to the image of the chauvinist pig. It is certainly not a term of endearment. Indeed, it is an objectionable, revolting term that is meant to conjurer up the picture of a gluttonous, vicious, selfish, contemptible person, and a thoroughly disgusting character. Men were swine creatures lurking in the environment, threatening and subverting women. They were shameless sexist beasts that worked hard at denying women the same equal rights as men. Perhaps the chauvinist pig was not a Wolfman or Frankenstein type creature, but he was a social monster all the same.

From the description that women have of themselves, there is no doubt that they feel frustrated. Like Freud's comment on society generating frustration, men seem to be playing the same role in respect to women. The frustration can lead to aggression, and the aggression can become violent. In attacking men, identifying them as chauvinist pigs, women were dehumanizing males, and that was an act of violence. They felt righteous in doing so because they felt men had done as much to them. They were just giving the men some of their own medicine. Inside of every liberated woman there is a Thelma or Louise ready to jump out, and she was targeting the chauvinist pig.

As the feminists put men in their gun sights, Hollywood quickly emulate the new stalwart woman. Female actors began to play more hardboiled, angry, fearless, aggressive, and extremely violent characters. Female, movie characters were portrayed as greedy, vengeful broads, gangsters, murderers, and serial killers. Whatever beastly things men were known to have done, such actions were now being done by women in motion pictures. The feminists applauded these new images of themselves that were being shown on the big screen. The traditional difference of behaviors between men and women were being altered in the collective consciousness of society. The male term "guy" became a description of any person. The so-called female passivity was bolstered into male aggressiveness. There was always that reservoir of free-floating aggression they could tap into, and as go the big screen, the little screen was sure to follow.

As the Women's movement evolved through the '70's and '80's, cries of the chauvinist pig died down. The women's organizations like NOW backed away from male bashing, and focused their attention on equal rights and economic parity for women. Specifically, the movement supported an Equal Rights Amendment to the US Constitution that would end sex discrimination in employment, education, and generally in every facet of American social life. There was even a push for paid maternity leaves and publicly supported day care facilities, and in all these areas, the movement has had some success. At the same time, there was that radical side to the women's movement. The radicals setup women's centers, childcare centers, rape clinics, legal counseling services, self-defense classes, and free feminists philosophy classes. These radical feminists were reacting to the fact that much of the interaction between a man and a woman happens in the home far from the public arena. Equal rights legislation would not do much to change that dynamic.

While members of the NOW organization criticized the radical feminists for being too far to the left, the radicals were simply recognizing a truth about the Women's Liberation movement. The movement had been founded on the belief that men were innately oppressors of women, and therefore any accommodations with them would be injurious to the cause. For as long as men seek sexual favors from women, there can be no equality between them, or so the radical feminists believed. Indeed, the radical feminists were only half wrong. Sex was at the core of the unhappiness women were feeling. Emotional deprivation had set them at war with their own bodies and kept them psycho-sexually immature. By their own admission, most of these women had never had an orgasm, or did not have them on a consistent basis. Generally, sex left them feeling frustrated. But men were constantly pressuring them to have sex, and as a wife they felt some obligation to do so. But, when they did submit to their husbands, it often left them feeling like streetwalking whores.

According to the radical feminists, there had always been a dispirited, disembodied whore behind the face of the contented *Hausfrau*; and she, unwillingly or not, invited exploitation and abuse. This is the way men have always treated whores, and it is a clear expression of the sexist attitude among men. This is to say that the male behavior towards women is very much influenced by the sexual stereotyping of women, and as it was pointed out, this is very distressing and depressing to females. If women have to be whores to live with men, then this clearly states the case of male dominance and control over the female. Therefore, if women were going to turn their image around, they certainly, symbolically speaking, needed some balls.

Passivity, the falling back before the male ego, had to be confronted and challenged. Men had to be "taken on" if real headway with the women's right movement was to be made. The war cry of "male chauvinist pig" had to be used to expose sexism. Women had to make that distinction in order to establish the right to be themselves. It wasn't something that men could give them, but it was something they had to take. There had to be that period of struggle for power, the power that would give women the right to determine their destinies. The struggle would extend from the bedroom to the White House, and across all institutional fronts. It would truly be the "battle of the sexes," and machismo would be met with chichismo.[28]

At the outset, the struggle would be more philosophical than physical, more symbolic than empirical. The movement had to wrestle with the ideas of Freud, stand nose to nose with Benjamin Spock and make him eat his foolish words. There would have to be discussion and lugubrious debate with men like Norman Mailer. Men had to understand said Kate Millett, "that the whole structure of male and female personality is entirely imposed by social conditioning."[29] Women were not born with a psyche that would naturally cause them to become dispirited, disembodied whores. It was the male dominated culture that produced this result. Our society was just one great, big house of prostitution, so say the feminists.

This level of struggle was good up to a point, but winning-debating points was not enough. Specifically, control over the female's body was at issue, and the battle for the body was not likely to be won with words alone. The control of the female's body was integrally tied to male domination. To state the case succinctly, women were treated as sex objects to please the male ego. To most men, women were nothing but a body, with no spirit and no mind. Women, as the dominated group, were just cunts. But, in a perverse way, this was a compliment to women living as dispirited, disembodied whores. Being seen as a cunt meant that they had some material substance.

The radical feminists felt they had to respond to this kind of sexist perversity. Philosophy aside, it was time to get more serious. They said that women had the right to use whatever physical means necessary to gain control of their bodies. To make the point, they gave their support to two high profile murder cases. Two women were on trial for killing men who had abused them. The husband of Francine Hughes beat her for many years. They were divorced, but they continued to have a relationship. And he continued to abuse her. Finally, one night, as he lay sleeping, she poured gasoline around his bed and set it afire. Mr. Hughes perished in the flames. In the other case, Inez Garcia used a rifle to shoot a man to death. She said the man had raped her twenty minutes earlier.[30]

The cases of both these women became a rallying cry for the feminists. It was maintained that both women were driven to their violent acts by the "unwritten law" which states that women belong to men. Therefore, men had the right to treat the female's body in whatever cavalier fashion they so desired. It was the "unwritten law" that helped to maintain the old double standard of sexual behavior between men and women. It was the "unwritten law" which caused women to be silent in the past when their husbands beat them and when they were raped. It was the "unwritten law" that allowed a policeman, in 1977, to say on an ABC-TV movie drama on battered wives, that "a good punching around is what some of these women need to turn 'em on."[31] This type of attitude manifest itself among the police and in the courts, and for a long time it made them unresponsive to a woman's cry of rape.

The feminists said Francine Hughes and Inez Garcia had taken steps to reclaim the integrity of their bodies, and in the process refused to accept the infamous "unwritten law." The point was made that women would never have control of their lives until they had control of their bodies, and even murder could not be ruled out as a legitimate means towards this end. While murder was not being advocated, when justified it was defensible. Why, that male cognate, the old "unwritten law," allowed men to kill their wives if they found them in bed with a lover. If male domination of the female, specifically in the sexual sense, could be understood as a function of machismo, then the feminists, with Francine Hughes and Inez Garcia, were advocating chichismo. Get your balls, girls!

Clearly, the battle for women's rights was to occur on all social fronts, but it was the male ego that was to be the object of siege no matter what the institutional setting. Expressions of physical power, in the abstract and the concrete that led to domination and control seemed to form the basis for the male ego. Therefore, aggressive behavior was valued in the male, while it was discouraged in the female. However, the feminists began to turn this aperture around. They put their sights on some of the main bastions of male institutionalized aggression: contact sports like football, hockey, and boxing; and they focused on the military establishment. They demanded that girls be allowed to participate in any sport of their choosing and that the military academies open their doors on an equal bases to female applicants. Moreover, they sought the full participation of women in all the combat areas of the armed forces.

The radical feminists must have thought that if women assumed the same roles as men in aggressive pursuits then females would develop the same sense of ego as males. This would make the females feel stronger and be more dominating in their relationships with men. As Kate Millett said, the "female personality is entirely imposed by social conditioning." If it can happen in the negative, just flip it over and turn it into something positive, as if social conditioning is really that simple. When speaking of the male ego, there are powerful forces involved that the conscious mind does not control. Through social conditioning, we may be able to influence the ego, but society can't create one. Women would not get very far assuming these male roles as a form of mental and emotional transformation.

However, the male ego is very fragile, and men were beginning to feel the pressure in trying to contend with the demands of the feminists. In particular, they were very upset with the idea that women should be allowed to fight in combat the same as men. War had always been the arena of men. It was where they proved their masculinity, bravery, and sustained their honor. Above all else, it was as a warrior that men demonstrated the superior differences between themselves and women. Men believed that the battlefield was no place for women. They did not have the strength, the attitude, or the will to be killers. Women were meant to create life and not to destroy it. But if women did prove themselves on the battlefield, what did that say about the so-called superiority of men?

In a1978 newspaper column, William F. Buckley, the reigning conservative, intellectual dilettante, attacked the idea of women being used in war, but in the process he exposed the hurt flanks of the male ego. The main point of Buckley's column was this: the feminists were trying to repeal the natural distinction that exists between men and women. He goes on to say that a sanctity and wisdom resides in women's breasts that makes them more than human. If women became gamboling warriors they would no longer have the right to claim the male's admiration, and indeed they would no longer be lovely nor very susceptible to love. It is the softness of women that is their charm. Women lack the vices of men, like that of war making, and for all these reasons they should be idealized. Of course, the feminists were saying that they did not want to be idealized. It was another way to lift the women up on a pedestal.

Buckley concluded his column by saying that any society that permits or encourages women to assume more aggressive postures, like developing the killer instinct, is endangering the venerable distinctions between men and women. This can only forecast illness for women, men, and society. Our society would be relinquishing sacred traditions in the process, and in effect functioning without its necessary, if not natural controls.[32] Buckley's column is instructive because his argument touches upon the generalized fears that many American men were having about the feminist movement. Men were worried that the movement would somehow turn women into men. This was a very silly notion. Women could no more become men than men could become women. However, such fears indicate the impact the Women's Liberation movement was having on men. Also, it was very interesting that Buckley should refer to aggression as being debilitating for men, women, and society. He seems to have come to the same realization as Freud about its negativity in the social construct, and Buckley is no Freudian intellectual. Moreover, if the truth were known, the radical feminists were not only interested in gaining control over their own bodies. They wanted control over men, too. They wanted to take the reigns of power away from them, crush their spirit, and deflate their egos. They were truly ball-busters.

Some of the radical feminists had a particular animus towards men. Susan Brownmiller and Professor Catherine MacKinnon expressed such feelings. They said men were only interested in women for sexual purposes. Indeed, they use women as objects for their aggression, and they are by their nature rapist, chauvinist pigs. To these two women, men were raging beasts, monsters from the id. How sad it is that some women should have reached that conclusion. Fortunately for the movement, there were some dissenting voices among them. The dissenters were telling the radical feminists that they may be becoming too aggressive, and it was making men feel like they had to fight back. This was exampled by the fact that many men opposed affirmative action for women in employment and education, the Equal Rights Amendment to the Constitution, government supported day care centers, and changes in the divorce laws, to mention just a few areas in dispute. And more men began filing for divorce and even asking for child support. They were on the defensive, and they did indeed circle the wagons to defend their prerogatives and their egos.

Harriet Van Horne, the newspaper columnist, said that the sweeping changes in the women's roles in society had produced an identity crisis for men. She said that it was sad to think of what lesbians with banners and buxom wenches demanding "equal orgasms" could do to the healthy male id. She said she did not want to be around when the men chuck it all in and decide to go off to a hunting lodge with the guys.[33] Opposition to the feminists also came from the religious fundamentalists groups of the Midwest and the South, the Catholic Church, and women's groups like the W.W.W.W. (Women Who Want to be Women). The W.W.W. W. was sending out the following message. "Ladies! Have you heard? God created you and gave you a beautiful and exalted place to fill. No women in history have every enjoyed such privileges, luxuries, and freedom as American women. Yet, a tiny majority of dissatisfied, highly vocal, militant women insist that you are being exploited as a 'domestic drudge' and 'pretty toy.' And they are determined to liberate you, whether you want it or not!"[34]

It would seem that all American women were not unhappy campers. To be sure, there were very few black and minority women who became involved in the movement, and their absence constituted somewhat of a rejection of the movement. They said that the movement was for white middle class women, and those women had their own agenda. But, if the core of a woman's problems is emotional deprivation, then this phenomenon surely cuts across class and ethnic lines. Therefore, it would seem that all women should be able to coalesce around some generic solution to this dilemma. But the fact that they did not come together as a unified group underscores the very individual and personal nature of their situation. Emotional deprivation is not a group problem, and forming a liberation movement is not the way to deal with it. Each person has to deal with her own demons that are conjured up from the id. Also, social movements like organizations suffer from the influence of The Iron Law of Oligarchy.[35] Over time, the movement itself becomes more important than the people and purposes it came into being to serve.

As it turned out, for many women some of the issues of the movement, like the need for day care centers, a woman's right to an abortion, and sexual harassment laws, became more important than achieving the ultimate goal of overall liberation through parity with men. This situation was not unique. American women, like all women around the world, have been socialized in a stratified social structure. There are many classes and ethnicities vying for social recognition. As well, because of emotional deprivation, class and ethnicity take on even more importance to Americans, and within this environment, radical feminists aside, women also have to compete with one another to "catch a man." In the midst of these many social currents, it cannot be expected that all these women will have the same social and political mind.

Karl Marx said it a long time ago, that class-consciousness, which was a false consciousness, could be an impediment to revolution. Also, Franz Fanon said that the first obstacle oppressed people have to climb over is themselves. And so, the feminist movement finds resistance among those it claims it wants to liberate. But many women, in the face of feminist proselytizing, find themselves in the proverbial posture of being between "a rock and a hard place." There are demands of the body and the spirit that run counter to the goals of the feminist movement. After four decades, some women are still not sure what the feminist movement wants, and they are saying, "In our eagerness to exact equal treatment, we women seem to be forgetting who we are: We are not men. Men cannot bear children. And for a woman, the birth of a child is a transforming experience." And, to be sure, birth by its nature brings forth social change, the next generation.

Women are members of an oppressed group, but men are not the oppressors. It is society, by its very nature, that suppresses basic impulses and restricts individual freedoms. This is the measure of the complaints that feminists have been talking about. They include problems of alien-ation and introjections, and men are not responsible for these emotional estrangements. Because emotional deprivation causes individuals to suppress their innate self, it is easy to become misguided and psychologi-cally confused. If we cannot be ourselves, we surely do not want to believe that we are our own oppressors. And if you are a woman and you feel oppressed, there is no one else to blame but men.

The Women's Liberation movement has put American women in a very odd position. The movement has turned many men into emotional adversaries. Women have declared men to be oppressors, and men feel they can no longer trust women as a consequence. A male-female divide has developed that has widened and deepened with the passage of time. The unhappiness that produced the feminist movement has now dissolved into social chaos between the sexes. Relationships have come to be more about rights, equality, sharing and fairness rather than love. Men and women are entering partnerships as takers and not givers. This is such a typical attitude of immature individuals, people who are suffering from emotional deprivation.

How very interesting that the Women's Liberation movement should get its impetus from the rejection of the roles of housewife and mother. Like it or not, women cannot deny that they are our human progenitors. Home and family, the province of wife and mother, would seem to be a logical extension of this process. If there is anything innate about a woman, it is her ability to procreate. When women suppress their innate beings, they are taking issue with this unique female function, and they are also, perhaps inadvertently, challenging the right of the species to survive. This is a self-eliminating emotion, and no person would want to acknowledge it. Certainly, this is all happening unconsciously, and this is the psychological and emotional stuff that creates monsters from the id.

Yes indeed, women are "between a rock and a hard place." They have turned men into emotional adversaries, and they have defamed them as chauvinist pigs and rapist monsters. However, women are still out there trying to "catch a man." If men are such terrible creatures, why do women want to be with them? The reason is they can't help themselves. Feminist rhetoric and philosophy aside, women need men, and men need women. Neither can survive without the other. Women complain that they are not free social agents. The truth of the matter is, as progenitors, they were never intended to be. If being a free social agent means not being beholden to men, then that can never be so. As long as women need men to deposit sperm in them for procreation they will be dependent upon the male, and their biological imperative will never let them forget it. But, by the same token, men are beholden to women. A man may give sperm to a woman, but it is the woman who gives a man his life.

Therefore, because women are beholden to men, it does not mean that they belong to men or that the male ego confers recognition upon them. It is simply a recognition that a procreative interdependency exists between the sexes. This is what men and women should focus on, and not their petty social differences. And it is sad that socialization has turned us into role players, and imagined gamboling warriors on one hand and chauvinist pigs on the other. Emotional deprivation has stolen our sense of individuality. So, Americans need causes to believe in and categories to belong to. When you feel vacuous inside, you look for your identity and fulfillment elsewhere. Almost anything will do, race, ethnicity, religion, a political ideology, a social movement.

After four decades, the dust has not completely settled over the Women's Liberation movement. But there have been successes. It has brought many significant changes to society in the corporate world, politics, government, and all the major professions. We now have women generals and admirals. There are female fighter pilots flying off the decks of aircraft carriers and women astronauts are flying in space. A woman is now running for President of the United States as I speak. The strides women have made are great, but, in the overall, with all this success women have not found the social and self-satisfaction they sought. They have gotten the educational and job opportunities they wanted, but they have had to sacrifice that traditional family life they once treasured. However, many women are beginning to wonder if the trade-off was worth it? Trying to be a super mom is wearing them down, and they are beginning to suspect that their children are being adversely affected by their routine, long periods away from home.

The feminist movement was about women trying to find themselves, but today women are still a long way from achieving that goal. Indeed, the movement seems to have lost its focus and splintered into many different causes, but that is not important. The movement would never have given women what they really wanted anyway. Sisterhood could only lead them in the wrong direction, and I think women are beginning to understand that. They thought the chauvinist pig was their enemy, but now they know that isn't so. It is not the men they should be worried about, but rather the stranger within them.

The Sexual Revolution

Almost forty years have past since the start of the Women's Liberation movement, and women are still wandering around in a fog. They have not yet found themselves. But then, how could they? They were looking in the wrong place, outside of themselves. They thought a movement, and sisterhood, would be the means for them to deal with their individual problems of alienation and frustration. But trying to collectivize their subjective feelings seems to have only succeeded in creating a greater void and estrangement within them. Nowhere is this more evident than in their efforts to gain sexual freedom from men. If they were ever going to be liberated from the traditional roles of wife, mother, and *Hausfrau*, women believed they had to achieve sexual parity with the fellows. They had been sexual prisoners long enough, and a new battle cry echoed across the land. Not only was it time for liberation, but also the situation called for revolution. Bastille Day was at hand.

When the sexual revolution began in the 1960s, no one could have imagined the tremendous impact it would have upon society and the social consciousness in general. To be sure, its effect went far beyond sexual behavior. This was due to the fact that it came about during a time when traditional, taken-for-granted social attitudes were being questioned and "the establishment" was under siege. Many groups, in particular young people, were demanding basic changes in the social system. They wanted a more equitable and just system for all citizens, the rich and the poor, black and white. Coincidently, the sexual revolution became a catalyst in this rebellious atmosphere. It helped to reduce people's inhibitions, and it opened up their social consciousness to all manner of new experiences, both good and bad.

On its own account, although not intended, the sexual revolution brought on many other changes in society, changes in motion pictures, television, sports, the youth culture, and the collective consciousness overall. Indeed, our social system is still rocking and reeling from these changes, and it is a good bet that this will continue well into the twenty-first century and perhaps even longer. For this important reason, we should try to gauge this phenomenon because it, too, is in large part a product of emotional deprivation.

The Women's Liberation movement exploded on the social scene at the same time as the sexual revolution. It was no accident that these two events should happen together. To be sure, they were independent phenomena, but each one helped to make the other possible. The sixties feminists were after new freedoms and a rediscovery of themselves, and integral to this effort was the attainment of sexual freedom. They believed that men were only interested in them for sexual reasons, and this was the basis for their domination and control of women. It was thought that liberation would never be achieved unless women gained control over their own bodies. To accomplish this, they had to free themselves from the egos and sexual appetites of men.

Betty Friedan spoke for a whole generation of women who said they were unhappy with their roles as wives and mothers. Family life was not rewarding enough for them. While the dissatisfaction of the women was real, they were casting blame in the wrong direction. The true source of their problems was not in homemaking itself. It was being caused by emotional deprivation and the suppression of their innate self. But not being consciously aware of this, women tried to use a movement to solve problems that were essentially individual and personal. Similarly, they tried to use the sexual revolution in the same way. Unfortunately, emotional deprivation had caused women to be at war with their own bodies, and this had kept them psycho-sexually immature. To be sure, the Liberation movement was populated with non-orgasmic, frustrated females who blamed men for their own coital ineptitude.

Also, the sexual revolution was indigenous to a period when beatniks, hippies, ethnic minorities, and welfare mothers were seeking social change. In 1961, the birth control pill was made available to American women, and in 1966, the students of the University of California at Berkeley began the Free Sex Movement. The student movement quickly spread to the Hippie neighborhood of Haight Asbury in San Francisco, and from there it crisscrossed the country as an element of the psychedelic, bohemian youth culture. All of these activities were a source of energy for the sexual revolution. It was the middle class kids who were leading the youth movement, and it was the middle class women who were leading the Liberation Movement. Suburban mothers and their children once again found themselves on common grounds as protesters, and inadvertently, they were forging a new set of middle class values.

The sexual revolution was characterized by libertarianism, the spontaneity of expression, and deliverance from the old Victorian values and their repressive sex laws. There were open challenges and objections to religious inhibitions and the restrictions of certain legal codes. The word was out that people should be allowed to do whatever they wanted, from homosexuality to sadomasochism. If the activities were between consenting adults, then it was okay. Pornography was even allowed to come out of the closet. Two movies in particular appeared in theaters and helped to establish pornography in the public's eye: *Deep Throat*, with Linda Lovelace, and *The Devil in Mrs. Jones*. They became classic porno films that opened the floodgates to once illicit sex movies. Now real sex was truly on the big screen, and things would never be the same in Hollywood again.

The impact of porno films on the sexual attitudes and behaviors of Americans have been enormous and cannot be under estimated. Motion pictures, with their music and drama, infused common events with a larger than life quality. In the same fashion, porno films raised sex to a surreal level of pretended pleasure that was entertaining to watch, but in reality unachievable. That was both its joy and its curse. The viewers who wanted to be as sexually vigorous as the people in the movies were much more likely to frustrate themselves, but the sexual activities in the motion pictures were used to create all kinds of exploitive, vicarious phantasmagoria, much of it for capitalist, profit-making purposes. And what followed was more form fitting, sexually suggestive clothing and underwear, sexually titillating aerobic exercises, sex clubs like Plato's Retreat, nude parties, wife-swapping, kinky sex soirees, sexually explicit magazines and weekly newspapers, advertised orgies, S & M bars, and sex shops with all kinds of accessories and adult sex toys. There was open public acceptance to any kind of sexual experimentation. And cable television was soon to make its appearance with its Real Sex programs and frankly speaking raunchy comedians.

Porno films also changed the language of the movies, and the everyday language in public life. Language that was once thought to be obscene and used mostly by men, words like screw, shit, asshole, cocksucker, cunt, fuck, and motherfucker, became common to public discourse. These are hot words, and the motion pictures began to live off of them. As well, porno movies are usually films with little or no story to tell. They are all about the visual content of sexual action, doing "it." In fact, sex, the American way, is mindless action, and this is what porno films portray. These movies also make it very clear that their stories are not about love-making. The women in the motion pictures may well have been willing participants, but nonetheless they were being exploited. The men treat them like sex objects, with disrespect for their humanity. This was violence incognito, and the porno films were delivering a clandestine message to men on how they should treat the new liberated woman.

Second only to the television, it was porno films that help to make electronic entertainment a part of the middle class home. The man of the house wanted to see porno movies in the privacy of his own bedroom. As a consequence, men popularized videocassette recorders, VCRs.

Unintentionally, the adults led the way for their children to become interested, and later hooked on video games. The VCR brought a new visceral reality to the television, a stimulus that was attractive to young people, and it was suited very well to the new mode of consciousness that McLuhan forecasted.

Beginning in the 1960s, many sexual attitudes and behaviors were changing, but the reason for the sexual revolution, as was the case with Women's Liberation, was not being addressed. Women were seeking sexual redemption with their newfound freedoms, and men reveled in the opportunities it presented them. But both sexes were playing the roles that were being dictated by emotional deprivation. Women were struggling with their non-orgasmic bodies and men were laboring under the aegis of compulsive masculinity. Both were also suffering from alienation and attempting to rediscover themselves through promiscuous, and even bizarre, sexual behavior.

To be sure, their efforts were not without foundation. Due to a new generation of young readers, the beatniks and hippies, authors like De Sade, James Joyce, D.H. Laurence, Aldous Huxley, and Henry Miller were in vogue. These writers championed the idea of sexual freedom and free sex. They argued that sex was the fundamental means by which a person expresses the totality of his existence. To really be yourself, you had to have sexual freedom. And from Eric Fromm and R. D. Laing, the word was that sexual freedom was to be a means by which the individual could overcome his alienation. All these writers were generally opposed to what some of them called the disease of rationality, and they vehemently objected to the intellectualization and the rationalization of sex. This is to say, they rejected the western social model for sexual behavior. It was destructive to the human being's spiritual development.

What was being talked about here was emotional deprivation by another name. These authors in their own way were trumpeting Freud's thesis about society suppressing basic impulses and restricting freedoms, and like Freud they believed that the sex drive was the principal, human motivating force. Because the feminists opposed most of Freud's ideas about sex, his theories were hotly debated and discussed during this period, and if one took the time to review them, by extension, these arguments inadvertently exposed the core of the problems behind the sexual revolution and the Women's Liberation movement.

Freud thought three forces influenced the human sex drive: the libido (sexual instinct flowing from psychic energy), the id (instinctual drive that is governed by the pleasure principle or hedonism), and Eros (sexual love or desire). When society causes the individual to suppress his innate self, it interferes with normal sexual desires and the general wish for bodily pleasures. This will stimulate reaction from the id as this unconscious force tries to find ways to express itself and achieve the pleasure the body wants. The response will be a reaction to the societal suppression, and it brings another factor into play. Freud pointed out that all human beings are innately polymorphously perverse.[36] Therefore, individuals can experience sexual pleasure from all kinds of strange and bizarre acts. This is to say, in seeking pleasure, the id can cause enjoyable pain, and as such monsters can arise from the id ready to inflict emotional and physical damage to the self and others. Like Morbius, we send out our monsters to do evil, to do good.

When the sexual revolution emerged on the social scene, like a whirlwind, it seemed as though all segments of society were involved. This was unusual for any social movement to have such wide appeal. The reason lay in the basic cause of emotional deprivation, and that is socialization. As we have noted, socialization prevents us from expressing our innate selves. We are pressured to conform to social norms and not to function according to the dictates of our individual desires. Consequently, we grow up with a weak sense of self-esteem, self-confidence, and self-actualization. As a result, we are robbed of our impulsiveness, spontaneity, and a clear, honest awareness of our personhood.

In this state of consciousness, there is emptiness inside the self that cries out to us "take away this alienation and feelings of unhappiness." This was the cry that caused women to form the Liberation Movement. But normally, society steps in and says, through socialization, "conform to the norms of social behavior and your ill-begotten feelings will be arrested." Sex is always one of those norms. Of course, we have to play social roles when we conform and that will help to bring on a conscious state of alienation, but since we have such a low level of self-esteem, we fall into the pattern with ease. Because of emotional deprivation, we are all open to suggestions of conformity. If a secondary type of socialization is being used to teach us new modes of sexuality, we are quite ready to jump aboard the new bandwagon. To be like everyone else in the herd feels very natural under the circumstances.

To meet our unfulfilled emotional needs society directs us to chase after wealth, power, love, and sex. Traditionally, men and women were expected to meet their love and sexual needs through marriage, but the sexual revolution changed all that. Sexual freedom was at hand and recreational sex ruled the day. Love and marriage became after thoughts, and sex was about finding oneself, so-called spiritual harmony, and pure, unadulterated hedonism. In the spirit of the times, both men and women de-emphasized their needs for family and children in favor of achieving sexual satisfaction. This point was clearly made when women began to push for legalized abortions. In effect, the pleasure principle had taken over the collective consciousness of America, and it was the instinctual power from the id that was the overriding influence of the new sexual morality. This resulted in promiscuity becoming a social monster that was taking control of the relationship between men and women.

Obviously, the behavior of compulsive masculinity feeds the social monster of promiscuity. At the same time, promiscuity feeds the male libido and ego, and it gives the individual a sense that he is proving his manhood. The more women a guy seduces, the more a he feels like a man. Therefore, men seek out women for their own sexual gratification, and not because they are looking for love. They allow the power of the id to possess them, and in the name of unrestrained hedonistic pleasure, they feel righteous in sexually exploiting women. And, their attitude towards women was seemingly confirmed by the mass media of the day, which projected a social image of females as liberal, freewheeling, multi-orgasmic persons who were sexually as venturesome as men. But clearly this was an erroneous image of women.

The sexual revolution had a distinct impact on the male consciousness and his perception of the female. With love out of the equation, women were being treated as vessels of flesh that lacked spiritual content. Indeed, this is what women seem to want. They quickly adopted the behavior of recreational sex. This was, however, a contradictory move on their part. The feminists had accused men of treating them as sex objects, but with their new sexual freedom that was how women were treating themselves. And to be sure, the men were quite willing to follow their lead in this matter. As a result, today men have lost a great deal of respect for women as wives, mothers, and ultimately as the progenitors of the species. If men ever put women on a pedestal, there is little desire to do that now. Of course, the women say they don't want it anyway. But something has been lost in this process.

The relationship between men and women has always been a matter of aesthetics and the physical. Love encompasses all of this, and sexual activity allows us to realize it in an extraordinary sensual manner. But when sex becomes only recreational, it obviously becomes less meaningful aesthetically. It is the aesthetics that leads a couple to form a permanent bond, but if beauty is taken out of sex, then things like marriage and children will become less important than serving ones own hedonistic desires. In terms of the family, sex itself would be debased and turned into a decadent exercise. For instance, in their traditional family roles, women had come to see themselves as *Hausfraus*, but in the worse of times they could still relate to the idea that they were the handmaidens of God. This meant they could always think of themselves as having spiritual value. But now women were rejecting any claims to such notions. It was strange that they would take such a position. They had chastised the men for marrying and treating them like whores, but now they were treating themselves like whores without the marriage.

The sexual revolution occurred because emotionally deprived people, men and women, were looking for a solution to their problems of alienation and a low sense of self-esteem, but in fact the problems brought on by emotional deprivation are not, in the usual sense, solvable. The situation arose during the first few years of our lives, and the solution in this case can take place only at the beginning of the process. If the child did not get the love and affection he needed originally, he cannot go back to that period and recover it. That would be a physical and emotional impossibility. An adult can never become a child again and sit in his mother's lap. The conscious mind cannot transform itself back to a state of non-consciousness.

Therefore, even with the sexual revolution, with plenty of action available, men who were being driven by compulsive masculinity were still unable to eliminate the negative feelings associated with their alienation. The more sex they got, the less they seem to get out of it. For many men, promiscuity became an exercise in futility. They were driven to prove their manhood, but a series of seductions left them still wanting. For all too many of them, frustration became a companion to their sexual engagements, and satisfaction was not to be had. So, men began to turn on women. Because of their egos, they could easily convince themselves that the women were responsible for the lack of sexual fulfillment they felt. Once they reached that conclusion, their frustration would often turn to anger, and it could lead to aggressive behavior. The reservoir of free-floating aggression was always at hand for individual and collective use.

The sexual revolution brought a new level of physical abuse by men towards women. And as it evolved, there was an increasing stream of news reports of girl bashing, stalking, wife-beating, date rape, predatory rape, spousal murder, and serial killing of women. These were distinctly, sexually motivated behaviors and crimes, and such occurrences became more concentrated and common. And to no one's surprise, these negative sexual behaviors began to manifest themselves in Hollywood motion pictures and in television programs. However, in films, these sexual manifestations tended to take on a more sinister and mysterious form. Women were seen as being under attack by unnatural forces, and being possessed and impregnated by demons, the devil, or aliens. These motion pictures were seemingly reaching into the collective unconsciousness of Americans. Movies like *Rosemary's Baby*, *The Devil in Mrs. Jones*, and *The Exorcist* became classic audience pleasers. And the most highly rated TV motion picture of the period was *The Night Stalker*. It was the story of a vampire who was preying on the beautiful women of Las Vegas, Nevada.

In response to the male's aggressive tendencies, women characters in films also began to take on a new and stronger image. They were more assertive, aggressive, confrontational, brave, bitchy, and often vicious. When men treated them badly, they knew how to return the favor. Female actors were allowed to show a ruthless side. In films, at least, women seem to have gotten the balls the radical feminists thought they should have. Women moviegoers were inspired by these images on the big screen, and they copied the behavior of the celluloid personalities. Invigorated by the motion picture characters, women became more willing to get into a man's face, be defiant, and express their sexual independence. Much of it was a pure put on, an acting job, and many of the women didn't even take themselves seriously when they tried to act tough. But being assertive was in the in-thing to do. This set off more active, open struggles between men and women. Relationships became more physically and emotionally combative. Men and women became sparring partners, and the bedroom practically became a fighting ring. Women wanted their sexual rights. They wanted to experience an orgasm when they had intercourse, and if the man did not deliver, he was going to hear about it.

The youth culture of the period was in the forefront of the sexual revolution, and they were into all kinds of drugs as they tried to enhance their sexual experiences. Young people used marijuana, hashish, mescaline, and LSD. Alcohol consumption was also a part of the enhancement mix. Young people were after that psychedelic, sexual experience. It was turn on, tune in, and drop out. The middle class mainstream also began to combine drugs and alcohol with their sexual dalliances. But unlike the hippies and beatniks, they tended to get involved with more hard drugs like cocaine and heroin. These chemical inputs brought a volatile element to the sexual revolution, and it certainly exacerbated the battle that was going on between the sexes.

In particular, the hippies were experimenting with new mental pathways. Having adopted the idea that rationality was a disease exposed by writers like Joyce, Huxley, and Miller, they took drugs to try and escape their consciousness. They specifically took LSD and other hallucinogens to take a trip through their own minds. We can only guess where these journeys took them, but from some of the descriptions of those who did take an LSD trip, it seemed they went to a surreal world that tended to be inhabited by monsters of all sorts. These trippers probably visited the land of the id, and for many of them, it was an overwhelming mind-bending experience.

Many young trippers never returned from the journey through their subconscious mind, and there may be residual effects of this that is still occurring today. In turning on, the psychedelic children of the 1960s were using mind-altering drugs, and for a time, the drugs changed the chemical balance of their brains. As the human mind is made up of electrical impulses, this status was altered, too. There is a good possibility that this phenomenon set the stage for the wedding of the next generation of children to the electronics that has now become so prevalent in out time. Many of their parents had their minds blown on psychedelic drugs, and perhaps this helped to establish the new social consciousness that Marshall McLuhan told us about.

During the 1960s, there was a lot of talk about consciousness-raising. This was a reference to a greater sense of self-awareness that was being sought by the youth culture, the feminist movement, and all who were involved in the new sexual freedoms. A part of this consciousness raising was the acceptance of sex as recreation. Having sex was all about satisfying oneself by engaging in a pleasurable exercise. Love, caring, and respect for the other person was thought to be a quaint idea that was left over from the Victorian Era. And with sexual partners becoming adversaries, "a roll in the hay" was being treated as a sport. This was consistent with the fun seeking times of the era. "Make love, not war." Indeed, the desire for fun proliferated through society in three main ways: the sexual revolution, professional sports, and motion pictures. They were also all encompassed in television programming that was beamed directly into the homes of Americans. The Pepsi generation had arrived.

The desire for fun and sexual freedom was being stimulated by calls for greater social freedoms throughout society, freedom from segregation, from sexism and male domination, from oppressive government, and from poverty. This yearning to be free also hit professional sports, baseball in particular. Since the early days of professional baseball, players were bound to the teams they signed contracts with throughout their careers unless the player was traded or management terminated their services. This was known as the reserve clause. In 1969, Curt Flood, a black out-fielder for the St. Louis Cardinals, challenged the legality of the reserve clause, claiming it constituted involuntary servitude. Flood lost the case in court, but he put the immoral, exploitive nature of the reserve clause on public display. The news media watched the case closely, and it became an event that even the feminist movement became interested in.

Six years would past before the power of the infamous reserve clause would be broken. Two pitchers were responsible, Andy Messersmith of the Los Angles Dodgers and Dave McNally of the Baltimore Orioles. They played the 1975 season without signing contracts with their respective teams, and they then declared themselves free agents. Management dis-agreed, and the case was turned over to an arbitrator. The players won in arbitration, and that effectively put an end to the reserve clause. Messersmith and McNally had become historical figures, and the media, largely television, turned them into folk heroes. Because of these two men, ball players strengthened their position when negotiating salaries, and soon they were signing contracts for millions of dollars. Once the income of ball players went up, so did their social standing, and this brought even more media attention to the game and the players.

In the past, with few exceptions, baseball players had never earned much money, but now with salaries in the six figures, they became media icons to be watched and studied more closely. And nothing sells better than success. TV advertisers latched on to these baseball stars and turned them into pitchmen, and as TV is want to do, these players were not only selling cars, underwear, and deodorant, but they were also selling sex. With television in practically every home in America, sexy baseball players, and figures from other sports, matched up very well with the times.

There was nothing essentially new about women finding baseball players sexually attractive. Babe Ruth, Ted Williams, and Reggie Jackson, among others, all had a strong contingent of female fans. But in the sixties, sex was very much on the public's mind, and TV took this opportunity to turn the new millionaires into sexy, cult heroes. The games they played in were given an enormous amount of television exposure. But more importantly, for marketing purposes, advertisers wanted to make these hucksters marquee standouts. So, the media also, across the boards, gave a lot of individual attention to certain ballplayers. It led to their performance in games being analyzed minutely. Television was selling the players to the public, which then gave the players creditability when they were selling products. And as they were selling products, they were being sold as role models to be emulated. When they were not huckstering, sports figure became part of the broadcast team on television and radio. This was a further inducement for fans to form vicarious relationships with the ballplayers. And, because of TV bringing the games into the home, many sports personalities became like members of the family.

The television industry also poured hundreds of millions of dollars into professional sports for the rights to show the games, and this was another source of money to help to escalate player's salary. But television also got involved with how the games were to be played. They were interested in fan appeal to increase their viewing audience. The games had to become more exciting and sexy to keep up with the times. Dancing girls and pompom girls became fixtures at basketball and football games, and the pace of games became influenced by television commercials. In basketball, there was even a recognized television timeout. But the games took on even more sex appeal when the players, often with sexy female pitchwomen, began advertising intimate body products like soaps, deodorants, and underwear, witness the pitcher Jim Palmer and Michael Jordan modeling briefs and Joe Namath modeling pantyhose. Nothing sells like sex and success.

In trying to bring more fun and excitement to sport's activities, TV programmers focused on record setting events. At the time of the sexual revolution, Henry Aaron was in pursuit of the most majestic record in baseball history: Babe Ruth's all time home run mark of 714 round trippers. The Babe had revolutionize the way baseball was played in the 1920's and '30s with his home run hitting, and he became one of the most recognized personalities in the world. This brought him a great deal of public attention, and the sportswriters turned him into a media phenomenon. He was so attractive that in his heyday, it was not uncommon to see women swoon over him. TV wanted to recreate that magic with Aaron.

In his time, the Babe had been a sex symbol, and his home run hitting prowess was considered to be a mark of his sexual virility. Television played on this past history. Interestingly enough, baseball is filled with sexual symbolism. For instance, like the skyscraper, a baseball bat is a phallic symbol. The ball can be seen as the male sperm, and the glove a woman's vagina. The big hit, the four-bagger or home run can be viewed as the explosion of an orgasm. This symbolism was not lost on TV programmers and advertisers. In a 1999 *Nike* sneaker commercial, Atlanta Braves pitchers Greg Maddux and Tom Glavine were featured taking extra batting practice because they said, "Chicks dig the long ball."[37] Of course, the symbolism is played out at the unconscious level of the mind, but that is the level where the game of emotional deprivation is played. And so it came to past that television and the sexual revolution turned up the hormone heat in baseball.

In response to the atmosphere of the time, and in the guiding hands of TV programmers, all professional sports followed the lead of baseball and acquired more sex appeal. The pattern was the same. TV advertisers sought out the millionaire players. They were perfect icons to be used as sexual hucksters, and as superstars they got a tremendous amount of media exposure that presented them as virtuous, ideal role models. This focus by the TV people caused the hormone heat to be turned up on all the players in all the major sports. But, whenever sex comes to play in male activities, the men involved are sure to become more aggressive, and inevitably aggression will lead to violence. One result of this sex-hype is that violence in professional sports has increased steadily over the last three decades.

In wanting to make professional sports more exciting and sexy, television programmers were trying to turn more women into interested and devoted fans, and they did have some success. Because of the feminist's movement, women made a concerted effort to become more involved in sports generally, but a much more peculiar relationship would come about between women in general and professional athletes that was a distinct outcome of the sexual revolution.

As the sexual revolution picked up steam, two distinct eating disorders developed among young women. They were anorexia nervosa and bulimia, two illnesses that hinged themselves to manic-depression. These disorders appeared almost entirely among white women of the upper classes, the same group of women who put the feminist movement in motion and who strongly backed the sexual revolution.[38] For these women, sex was going to be fun, the ultimate form of pleasure. On command, the orgasm would be there for them. And now with the pill, even pregnancy could be avoided. Since men were always willing, these women thought they would have no trouble achieving their sexual goals. But, as

Max Weber pointed out, human emotions variously sets in motion unanticipated consequences.

Love had gone packing. Sex was being used as a form of recreation, and men could now get it easier that ever. Women were anxious to put out and play musical beds, and the one-night stand was socially acceptable to both sexes. Things should have been beautiful for women. They were poised to take control of their bodies, or so they thought, but suddenly a new situation developed for them. With so much sex available, but without love and commitment, men found themselves in the driver's seat. Women soon discovered that men were quite willing to sleep with them, but it was difficult to get involved in a meaningful relationship, short term, or long.

As the sexual revolution rolled into its second decade, a cry could be heard reverberating through the singles bars across the land: "Where have all the good men gone?" As the book and movie, *Looking For Mr. Goodbar*, pointed out, women were seeking excitement and sex at gin joints and beer gardens in every major city. There was plenty of alcohol, drugs, and one-night stands to be had, but most of the women wanted more. The predicament they found themselves in was a reminder that a woman's sexual needs are different than that of men. And the men exploited the women who were looking for Mr. Goodbar, and they probably said to themselves, "Who wants to have a serious relationship with a woman who casually sleeps with every Tom, Dick, and Harry."

In effect, because of the new sexual freedom, women were finding it even more difficult to "catch a man." It would seem that every girl at the bar or on the block was putting out, and the situation was exacerbated by the fact that in the vanguard, the youth culture was calling for free love. The competition for a good man was fierce. Free love making was blurring the distinctions between most women, and they began feeling pressure to make themselves more attractive, body-beautiful and sexy. This caused an old nemesis to rise up and haunt women with new vigor. It was their bodies that were betraying them again, preventing them from getting the sexual satisfaction they deserved. That illusive orgasm and that meaningful relationship were surely waiting for them if they could transform themselves into the current ideal of beauty.

The liberated, sexy woman of the day was thought to be thin, even skinny, like the British model Twiggy, who had an absolutely, abnormally small body, but women were led to believe, by fashion designers, that she had a blessed, beautiful figure. It was an unrealistic standard, but it threw women into a panic to achieve that thinness look. Thinness was also equated with healthiness, and women turned to dieting, exercising, and eating health foods to become more slender. And, with propaganda from the media, an exercising, dieting industry emerged based on a cult of becoming healthy and staying that way. Actually, once again, women were taking out their emotional deprivation problems on their bodies.

Anorexia and bulimia became byproducts of this new sex dieting, health industry, and, too, legions of women allowed themselves to be regimented in dieting and health programs in the hopes that it would lead to a new, more pleasing self-image. The desire to be thin reached a compulsive level, and like athletes, women found themselves in competition with their own bodies. As well, all too many dieters let their efforts become all-consuming. They sacrificed a multi-dimensional life, through a devotion to exercising and dieting, in attempting to reach their goal.[39] And, like athletes they became dedicated to the idea of becoming winners. Therefore, the new sexy, liberated woman could identify more readily with professional athletes, and this form of identity had a vicarious mode to it. A result was that women began to become more involved with professional sports.

To all Americans, baseball has always been a likeable sport, but throughout its history, there was a common criticism that women made of the game. They said it was too slow. But, during the period of the sexual revolution, two interesting developments came about that was to help make the game more exciting. In the American League, the designated hitter was put into the lineup to bat for the pitcher, and a new pitching role came into being in both leagues, the closer. The TV producers liked the changes. With the closer, there was another opportunity to bring excitement and drama to the games in the late innings, but it also caused players to be more antagonistic and confrontational. And with the designated hitter, more offense would surely help to liven up the game and perk up female interest.

In making TV stars and sexy icons out of sports figures, and in attempting to make professional sports more exciting, TV programmers may have unwittingly given support to an atmosphere that was more conducive to the commission of violence. In sports, violence is a form of showing off, and the announcers and commentators encouraged such behavior from the players in the way they described the games to the listeners and viewers. It is that "in your face" style of broadcasting that comes from Marv Albert, the long time basketball announcer for the New York Knicks. Oddly enough, liberated, sexy women seem to like the present level of violence in professional sports. They cheer for it just like the men, and my how do they love to see those backboard rocking, slam dunks. It seems to thrill them to death. Now what is the sexual symbolism of having that ball jammed forcefully through that small, round basketball hole?

A woman's sexuality was central to the Women's Liberation movement, and a women's sexuality was a driving force to the sexual revolution. Women were out to reclaim their bodies and achieve that illusive orgasm. They were willing to push the envelope and experiment in every which way they could to accomplish those ends. But to some degree, women were also being driven by their own brand of compulsion that was linked to their biological imperative. In suppressing their innate selves, women can come to doubt their role as progenitors, but their maternal instinct will still bring pressure to bear on them to fulfill this innate promise. As such, they can experience a forceful desire to have sex. This desire is likely to begin at an earlier age, and it can be correlated to the degree of the emotional deprivation of the female. In fact, the greater the emotional deprivation, the greater the likelihood of the female urge to be sexually active.

This function is clearly noted if you relate this occurrence to the stratification in our society. Sexual activity is more common among young females in the lower socio-economic brackets. Even though minority women did not participate, to any significant degree, in the Women's Liberation movement, they became very comfortable with the new sexual freedoms, and this attitude tended to sanction youthful sexual activity in their communities. As a result, a monstrous number of young, poor and minority girls began to have babies out of wedlock, and it quickly became a social epidemic, thanks in part to the sexual revolution.

Unlike girls of the upper classes, unwed minority mothers tended to keep their babies. It was a badge of recognition for them, a statement of their womanhood, of their human purposefulness in an otherwise meaningless life. Having a baby gave these girls a feeling of self-worth, something they craved dearly because their backgrounds had left them severely emotionally deprived. But at the same time, these girls were emotionally immature and unprepared to be mothers; and as well, having a child was an economic burden to them and/or their families. Given the circumstances, their motherhood constituted self-defeating, if not self-destructive behavior. While politicians bemoaned the status of these minority women on welfare, the feminist movement generally gave the girls a pass, and they worked for government programs to support the needs of these youthful mothers. In effect, the movement gave tacit approval to their sexual behavior, but then what other choice did they have? These young women should have control over their own bodies, too.

However, there is the question of emotional immaturity. All emotionally deprived persons experience it to a lesser or greater degree. Again, because of their socio-economic situation, poor and minority individuals tend to be on the higher end of the immaturity scale, and they tend to reach pubescence earlier, while being emotionally regressive. This means that they can function physically like a sexually mature person, but emotionally they will function as pre-pubescent children. When young girls from this group have babies, they can create a most unwelcome situation for themselves and their children. In fact, this situation will be a functional problem for any severely emotionally deprived mother and her child no matter what socio-economic class they may be from.Emotionally regressive individuals have the emotions of a child. When they are sexually active, they are trying to use sex to relieve themselves of their feelings of being unwanted and unloved that was caused by emotional deprivation. But, raw sex is no solution to this problem. The love and affection they want to get from sex is the love and affection they should have gotten from their mothers during that period of their lives, 0-3 years old. And when these females give birth, it is equivalent to a pre-pubescent child having a baby. Now the emotionally regressive person has a child who is in need of the same love, affection, and nurturing that she is looking for. Conflict is sure to develop between the child-mother and her youngster as they compete for love and affection between themselves and from other significant others. This situation can get dire and ugly, and it is one that the baby of the child-mother is destined to lose. Child-mothers are incapable of giving unconditional love and nurturing to their offspring, and this helps to keep the cycle of emotional deprivation going from generation to generation. Unfortunately, the child-mother has become a common figure in American society since the beginning of the sexual revolution.

If nothing else, the cycle of emotional deprivation gets passed on because young girls want to be like their mothers. They readily take the role of their mothers in learning how to become a member of society. This is particularly true when it comes to their mothers' sexual behavior. Traditionally, prior to the sexual revolution, mothers prepared their daughters for marriage and motherhood, but with Women's Liberation, mothers began telling their daughters to think of other options for their life's pursuit. And homemaking did not have to be on their list. Indeed, daughters were counseled to think of their wants, their desires, their needs, and themselves first. On the face of it, this would seem to be a call to regenerate innateness, but it was not. The newest crop of young women were being told that marriage and motherhood was just one of many alternatives for them. Of course, in a logical, rational sense this is true, but in a bio-emotional sense, for a woman, this was nonsense.

As a human entity, women are constituted to procreate as fact of their life cycle. To be sure, men are adjunct participants to this function also. But the burden of species regeneration is with the female. Bearing a child and being a mother is the manner in which a woman fulfills the promise of her sex. She can do nothing else in life as important as this because all human activities, no matter how simple or complex, begins with the birth of a child. All our human rationalizations and society building cannot change this basic fact. We can try to fool ourselves about it, but we cannot fool Mother Nature. Therefore, the most realistic, significant thing that any woman can do for herself, for society, and for her species, is to have a sexual relationship with a man. As I have said before, this does not mean that every woman has to get married, have children and be a *Hausfrau*. But if enough women around the world begin to accept the idea that having a child and being a mother is just another occupational option, then the human species would find itself in jeopardy. That is just simple logic.

In fact, without saying so, the new liberated mothers were teaching their daughters a new sexual morality. In the pre-1960s days, proper sexual relations was conducted in marriage, but if marriage was no longer to be the gateway for a woman's self-fulfillment in life, then premarital sex and promiscuity was sure to increase. However, the new sexual morality was ignoring a basic truth about women. Female sexuality cannot be separated from procreation. The failure of Americans to accept this reality is producing nothing less than a social calamity, i.e., the abortion rights struggle and all the enormous psychological, emotional, and physical problems women are having with their bodies. As Freud concluded more than a hundred years ago, the human sex drive, probably because of the need to procreate, is the strongest motivating force we have; and when we begin to tamper with it, we are bound to create trouble for ourselves. For instance, the use of various methods of birth control, especially the pill, gives women a false sense of security that is constantly being shaken by monsters from the id. As Freud discovered, such creatures haunt women in their dreams.

Because of emotional deprivation, both men and women have become societal minions, but the species agenda of procreation must go on. Whether the new liberated, sexually free woman is aware of it or not, it is the spirit of motherhood that is behind her sexual behavior. Trying to be macho and promiscuous about sex like a man will only cause a female to doubt herself as a woman. Unlike a man, the desire for hedonistic pleasure aside, the quest for motherhood is the female's reason for being sexual. If it were not for the maternal instinct, most women can get along quite nicely without sex. Invariably, for most women, they will become less interested in sex once they become mothers. Nature wants them to concentrate fully on their nurturing functions. At the same time, the male sex drive does not diminish when he becomes a father, and the sexual revolution has not altered this dynamic one bit.

Once again, some individuals will surely say that what I am stressing here is nothing more than biological determinism. That be as it may, it cannot be denied that the human body has its demands and needs such as hunger, sex and survival. And they will be met or our species will cease to exist. In this context, to put it simply, a woman will have sex because she has to. A man will have sex because he wants to. The distinction lies in the fact that a woman, according to her life cycle, is not fully a woman until she has sex and bears a child. For her, motherhood defines the essences of womanhood, contrary to what the feminist would say. It may pain women to acknowledge it, but fatherhood does not define the essence of a man.

I am really saying nothing here that women have not suspected about themselves even if they have trouble admitting it. The sexual revolution notwithstanding, girls still grow up believing that they must look pretty and be sexy and alluring to attract the attention of the males. Why? Because it is the males who can fulfill their need to be progenitors. Since they also suffer from emotional deprivation, and because America has gone through a sexual revolution, this makes the desire, if not need, for a male and sex even more urgent for females. This may well bring about the onset of puberty at an earlier age than what would have otherwise been the case for many young girls. The earlier the age that girls reach puberty, the sooner they will become sexually active. This is one of the reasons why we have an epidemic of children having children.

Television and motion pictures have taken advantage of this general lowering of female pubescence. They are continuously presenting stories about young girls who are obsessed with sex and who are constantly trying to become involved in sexual escapades. It is the sex as recreation theme wrapped in the aura of the Pepsi generation, and within this theme there is another underlying message that is also being given to the young people of America. Along with the image of females being presented as sex objects, youths are being told that there is nothing wrong or immoral about girls having sex with a number of different fellows. Whoring around is equated with liberation, maturity, emotional stability, and realism. Youngsters are being led to believe that only a frigid, socially backward young woman would put any value and virtue in maintaining her virginity until marriage.

As members of the new electronic age, young girls identify very strongly with TV and motion picture characters. They grew up being stimulated and nurtured by electronic devices. They vicariously and fervently adopt the beliefs and the behaviors of these make-believe characters. From them, they are learning that sex is but a perfunctory exercise that is performed as recreational hedonism, and that females should not think of themselves as being moral entities put here on earth to fulfill the unique physical and spiritual function of procreation. The feminists have demanded that no special respect be shown to women, respect that used to be thought of as being God given and virtuous. Why? If women think of themselves as being special, then they are less likely to go whoring around. And, as Wendy Shalit pointed out in her book *A Return To Modesty*,[40] to make sure that the sexual revolutionary beat goes on, millions of young women are overmedicated with drugs like Prozac, Zoloft, and Demerol. It makes it easier for them to submit to the blows of promiscuity and one night stands.

Women have always used sex as a means for obtaining love. For them, sex is never an end in itself as is the case for men. But women were led to believe that the sexual revolution would bring them better sex and ipso facto love. It has not turned out that way. As women began to treat themselves with less respect, so did the men. The nightmare of the feminine mystique came to excruciating reality. It was not a Women's Liberation fantasy. Men did begin to treat women purely like sex objects, and another dynamic arose. Men accelerated an old male standard: find them, fuck them, and forget them (the 3Fs). Some women began reacting to the coldness of being treated as sex objects, and men began to turn them off. These women began to look for other means to get the sexual pleasure and the love they desired.

Possessed with the idea that there are very few good men out there anyway, more and more women are turning to lesbianism, machines, dildos, and other electronic devices for their sexual satisfaction. They are encouraged to do this by the images they see on TV and in motion pictures. It is obligatory to have a nude sex scene in practically every movie now whether it is suited to the story line or not. Audiences expected that kind of titillation for their money. And not infrequently, the sex scene is that of lesbians making out. What are women to think? If it is good for the beautiful people, then there must be something to it?

Nothing could be more natural for the young women of our day than to use electronic devices, stimulators of sorts, to seek sexual satisfaction. They have been wired up since childhood and raised on one form of electronic stimulation or another. They are emotionally suited for it, and this shows how libertarian young women have become. But it is causing a strange kind of role reversal. Consider this: Lesbianism is now seen as a statement of women's sexual freedom. Straight sex is thought to be limiting, old fashioned, and even neurotic. To be liberated and free is to sexually experiment. Women should be open to all avenues of sexual pleasure. What a turn around. The sexual tyranny of Victorianism has now been replaced with the tyranny of sexual freedom.

It should come as no surprise that the sexual revolution has led many women of the middle and upper classes to try lesbianism. These are the women who helped to get the revolutionary train rolling. They were on a journey to discover that illusive orgasm, but in the process they had declared men to be their enemy. All too many women agreed with Catherine McKinnon who said in effect that all men are beasts, and Susan Brownmiller who denounced all men as being rapists. It is not easy to find sexual satisfaction with your adversary. Therefore, for many women the failure of their heterosexual relationships was to a certain degree inevitable and a self-fulfilling prophecy. Also, for a liberated woman to go to bed with her feminist sister was yet another way to get back at men. Nothing cuts deeper into the male ego than sexual rejection, and when that rejection favors another woman, the cut is psychically that much more severe.

Moreover, as women are choosing, in ever-larger numbers, other careers than homemaking, they have put off having children; or in many cases, they have decided not to have children at all. If a woman does not want to have children in her life than it is easy to rationalize that one does not need a man just to obtain sexual pleasure. There are other options. And, as some radical feminists have offered, a woman lover might be better than a man because she would know more about the female body. The only thing at issue here is who can give the female body the most sexual pleasure? The gender of the lover is not important. Thus, this is a triumph of crass hedonism.

The sexual revolution has caused men and women to become more confused about their sexuality. This is not specifically due to the rejection of Victorian sexual values or sexual experimentation; but rather, both men and women, to compensate for their emotional deprivation, were using the sexual revolution. However, more than the confusion, the sexual revolution underscores the fact that men and women have grown up somewhat detached from their own emotions. Women attempted to be promiscuous like men, and the men took advantage of this situation and blatantly treated women as sexual objects. But they were both exploiting each other. There was no love lost because there was no love involved. Without a sense of innate self, it is difficult to sincerely love another person. This is detachment, and it becomes self-evident when a relationship is sexual between a man and a woman.

This detachment problem has its origins during the non-consciousness period of the person's life. The person represses his innate being and grows up feeling alienated from himself. At the same time, he will have a feeling of being rejected, and since the rejection seems to come from his mother, the feeling is inordinately one of self-rejection. To avoid the feeling, the person tries to shield himself from his own emotions, and thus the detachment. Detachment is a major emotional disorder among American men and women today. To participate in the kind of sexual life of our culture this would have to be the case. With the sex drive being the strongest motivating force within us, to consummate that drive brings us innate satisfaction. To deny it brings us the emotional dread of rejection. In loveless sexual relationships, it is better to withhold ones emotions rather than chance the latter.

From the start, the phenomenon of detachment was important to the sexual revolution. Indeed, without it the movement might never have gotten underway. It allowed women to become intimate in a carefree way, and it was the impetus to the male 3F standards. Detachment allowed persons freedom of action without commitment. Individuals could have sex and feel no moral responsibility for the emotional impact and outcomes it might have on the other person, or the self. All of this occurring within the possibility that whenever there is sexual intercourse between a healthy male and female, there is always the possibility that impregnation may happen. Unfortunately, all too many of these loveless liaisons and encounters do produce "unwanted babies." But women have the right to an abortion today, and the unwanted child can be dispatched in a detached fashion.

But some of these detached women have their unwanted babies before they realize that they don't want them, and they feel no sense of responsibility for their offspring's well being. So, in recent years, there have been increasing number news reports of mothers killing their own children. What a sickening testament to the depth of our inhumanity and the demonic nature of our violence prone culture. Whether we Americans want to believe it or not, motherhood is a sacred duty because species survival depends on it. If mothers are going to make a habit of killing their own children, then it brings into question the right of human beings to survive in the long term. In effect we are playing with the primal forces of nature. Perhaps, it is somewhat speculative to say this, but in the final analysis, it is possible for emotional deprivation to bring into jeopardy survival of the individual, the society, and ultimately the human species.

In a 1983 motion picture, *WarGames*, a character in the movie says that nature knows when to give up on a species. He was referring to the idea that when a species becomes so self-destructive that it endangers its own chances for long-term survival, nature allows the species to become extinct. The dinosaurs are the best-known examples. Because humans have developed nuclear weapons that could destroy the entire earth, the movie character thought that nature had reached the point when it was ready to give up on us. Suddenly in the 1980s, it seemed as though fiction had become fact. AIDS struck America as a mysterious, medical whirlpool, and our sexual practices were suddenly brought into question. Needless to say, the sexual revolution found itself faced with a roadblock, and to be sure, it almost came to a screeching halt.

AIDS (acquired immunodeficiency syndrome) is a disease caused by HIV (human immunodeficiency virus). Contaminated bodily fluids such as blood, semen, vaginal secretions, and breast milk transmit it. While there has been an enormous amount of speculation, the exact origins of AIDS are not yet known. However, it has been suggested that AIDS may have come from Africa or Haiti, black cultures outside of the United States. It has also been suggested that AIDS may have come from animals like monkeys, pigs, or mosquitoes.[41] But whatever its origin, we do know that the disease is largely transmitted by some type of genital intercourse, vaginal, anal, or oral. Therefore, the sexual practices of the seventies and eighties helped to spread the transmission of the disease. And the sexual revolution was undoubtedly instrumental in bringing about the AIDS epidemic.

When AIDS was first reported in the medical journals in 1981, it was thought to be a problem that only affected gay males. Some religious leaders in the Bible Belt of America's heartland thought that it was a sign of God's wrath. He had sent forth the pestilence to show His disapproval of homosexual relationships. But in a very short period of time, AIDS found it's way into the bedrooms of heterosexual couples, and fear began to shake the sexual confidence of all Americans. Moreover, the disease was appearing in other societies all around the world. Sexual intercourse, which had always been known for its pleasure and the ability to bring forth life, was now tagged as a harbinger of death. Sex had truly become an enemy, but the biological imperative and the orgasmic imperative would keep the girls and boys coming back for more in spite of the danger.

AIDS could be transmitted through infected hypodermic needles and blood transfusions, but essentially it was a sexually transmitted disease. The more the general public exposed itself sexually, the more the spread of the HIV infection. The public needed to alter its pattern of sexual behavior, but that was easier said then done. The sexual freedom genie had been let out of the bottle, and there was no way to put him back. The best public health authorities could do was to tell the people to have safe sex; that is, avoid engaging in unprotected sex of any kind. The public schools in many big cities tried to help by giving students free access to condoms. But these so-called prevention efforts truly missed the point. It was not the physical nature of the disease, the pneumocystic carini pneumonia, the shingles and cytomegalovirus, the encephalitis, the culosis, and other illnesses, that people should have been most worried about. It was the coded message in the disease that should have been the main focus, a message that was saying something unusual was occurring to the human body, something that was probably akin to genetic drift, a process of mutation.

AIDS is the most serious health problem of our time, and it represents a definite threat to the long-term survival of the human species. For this reason, we need to try and understand precisely what this problem is really all about. Health officials have rightly concentrated on the physical nature of the disease, and we know that HIV is a retrovirus. It reverses the order of reproduction in the cells it infects, and it is constantly mutating and presenting multiple strains. This is the process, but we don't know what gets the process started. However, there are some clues that might help us get a better understanding of the origins of the disease. It is now a physical health problem, but who can say that it started out that way. Think of psychosomatic illnesses.

To begin with, AIDS is a process in which elements of the human body are made to turn on itself by the HIV virus. The virus destroys the white blood cells in the immune system, and this causes the body to be vulnerable to opportunistic diseases. But what sort of force could cause the body to compromise its own immune system? White blood cells protect us from alien elements that enter the body and other pathogens like worn-out body cells. They protect the body from agents that want to debilitate it. Without a normal, healthy immune system, no human being can survive for very long in this earthly environment. AIDS therefore causes the body to become self-destructive. It would seem that the body withdraws its defenses because it wants itself to die. But this is counter to everything we know about the human desire to live and the will to survive. Still, it is as though the body has given up, and the reason for it maybe that the body's psychic mechanism already thinks it is dead.

AIDS has its physical manifestations, but the root of the problem may be spiritual. Because of emotional deprivation, a person will suppress his innate self and feelings of alienation will follow. The alienation can cause him to have a sense of being an empty nobody, and soulless. In the severest cases, the person can feel as though there is a stranger inside of him, or even that he does not exist. Take this common refrain. "There is someone in my head, and it's not me!" Severely, emotionally deprived individuals live as aliens inside of themselves. If a person thinks there is an alien in his own body, then psychically he can experience himself as an invader, a foreign agent. The body's immune system will always do battle with a foreign agents, but in this case the alien element is the body itself. With a sense that it is aiding its survival, the body reverses its normal immune procedure and submits to the alien takeover.

It may be that after hundreds of years of socialization that causes us to suppress our innate selves and bring on alienation, the body is beginning to react strongly, even genetically, to the emotional deprivation that plays such a major role in our lives as Americans. For instance, there is indication today that pubescence arrives earlier for young people than it used to. This is an impetus for youths to become sexually active at an earlier age with all its negative ramifications. Modern health protocols have conquered most of the communicable diseases, like tuberculosis, small pox, bubonic plague, and yellow fever that once ravaged humankind, but today we find ourselves much more susceptible to many different kinds of cancers and similar new illnesses like Lupus. Most of the cancers are a function of our behavior and lifestyles. Needless to say, our social patterns of behavior are greatly influenced by emotional deprivation, and cancer and Lupus are self-destructive diseases like AIDS. Some psychics even say that Lupus is caused by a spiritual infraction.

Recent events may have caused the body's reaction to emotional deprivation to take a quantum leap right into the lap of AIDS. These developments were unique spiritual disturbances. In the 1960s, the youth culture turned itself on with mind-blowing drugs, and through altered states of consciousness, they transmogrified their cognition. Many of these young people never experienced the world the same again. Later, these individuals, along with their offspring, became hooked into the electronic systems of the age, and as McLuhan stated they had their consciousness rearranged yet again. And then there was the feminist movement and the sexual revolution that impacted on the intimate behavior of men and women. The battle of the sexes erupted loud and ugly. Men were chauvinist pigs, and the radical feminists were dyke bitches. Dehumanizing metaphors were the verbal weapons of choice for the adversaries. In their sexual relations, women wanted men to be orgasmic facilitators, and men wanted women to be whoring cunts. Where had love gone?

However, the most disturbing spiritual event of the sixties was the public acceptance, and the feminist promotion of legalized abortion. Like a tornado, it ripped into the collective consciousness of American women and tore it asunder. On one side, there was the group for a woman's right to chose. On the other, individuals wanted to protect the sanctity of human life and the human fetus. Legalized abortion was seen as being fundamental to the quest of Women's Liberation. It was something women needed if they were going to gain control of their bodies. The opponents of abortion tended to see the situation as one of a religious and moral issue. Only God had the right to give and take human life. One side was deterministic in its view, and the other was fatalistic. There was no way to compromise.

In any case, both sides were being political, and thereby they both missed the point. The core of the disagreement had nothing to do with women's rights or God and morality in the religious sense. By the action itself, the commission of a planned, wishful abortion is a challenge to the intended human procreative process. It is tampering with the primal forces of nature, forces that we have no control over. In effect, the abortion issue has opened up an emotional Pandora's box that torments the psyche of women on both sides of the question. For example, the argument has boiled down to the discussion as to when does life begin in the womb, something human beings may never be able to determine. It is not only the physical development of the fetus that brings forth life. Just as important, or perhaps even more so, when does the human spirit enter the body of the fetus? And, is it the spirit itself that allows the fetus to become a living organism? Even the almighty, god-like doctors cannot answer that question.

Our willingness to legitimize abortion indicates how insensitive and callous we have become to human life. What can be more violent and inhumane than to destroy a defenseless fetus/child simply because we find his presence inconvenient? The libertarianism of the 1960s, the feminist movement, and the sexual revolution made it almost inevitable that abortion would be legalized. But the overall acceptance of legalized abortion indicates a distinct change in our collective consciousness. And when one couples that with the youth culture experimenting with mind-expanding drugs, and the "me generation" that grew up psychologically wired to electronic machines, is there any wonder that we have produced a generation X in the nineties? But more to the point, what has been the accumulative effect of all this on our human psyche; and as a consequence, what kind of unknown forces have we possibly unleashed? Of course, monsters from the id are very active in our personal and social lives today. Could AIDS be one of those monsters, generated by our willingness to destroy our future while it is still gestating in the womb? Think about it.

ROMANTIC LOVE

So, is that what this is all about? Are we really in the process of destroying our future? Throughout this book, I have been saying that in a number of different ways, but it is still difficult to imagine. However, it is a very interesting thought; and if it is happening, one might wonder is it purposeful or is it the back end of some unanticipated consequences? Better yet, can it be what the Hollywood actor said in the motion picture *WarGames*, "Nature knows when to give up." And what about emotional deprivation? Is it really the initiator of the process or is it just one of its results? All these questions are quite entertaining, as were the previous chapters in this book, but we don't need to worry about any of it. Because, no matter how desperate our situation is, or it may become, we always have the solution to our social problems, and it is called love, love in general and romantic love in particular. It can save us, but will we let it do so? Let us explore the possibility.

One of the dominant features of our emotionally deprived personalities is this feeling of having been unloved by our parents as a child. We absolutely needed their love in the first few years of our lives because it was paramount to our early emotional development, and because we didn't get it, to the degree we may have needed it, we grew up pining for that love we were denied. But then, as we matured into adulthood, our attentions were strongly directed towards romantic love as the ultimate means of recovering the lost love of childhood. This was accomplished through a calculated effort of emotional brainwashing by significant others, authority figures, and representatives of the government and the mass media. In story and song, in myth and reality, we were told about the wonders of love.

However, parental love and romantic love are not the same. Indeed, there are two distinct and very important differences between them. To begin with, romantic love is always attractive and enticing because with it comes the promise of sexual pleasure and gratification. Therefore, using romantic love as a substitute for parental love is sure to cause conflict in an individual, and as Freud would have pointed out, it probably indicates that there are some unresolved Oedipal Complex issues involved. Secondly, romantic love has become the be-all and cure-all for practically every kind of emotional problem we can have, real or imagined. This is the belief is that love conquers all. It is a magic portion that will serve the needs of everyone, rich or poor, black or white. Love is an equal opportunity provider.

Hollywood is the chief dispenser of the belief of the utilitarianism of romantic love. It is a legacy of the men who ran the studio system back in the 1930s and '40s. They were in search of their own kind of American Shangri-La, and romantic love (hereafter referred to as just love) was the means by which a person could get himself there. In this sense, love was generally thought of as a product or a discovery, and under certain challenging situations, it was believed to be something you had to win. Love, in this context, was understood to be a functional variable of cause and effect. Long before we reached adulthood, we were enlisted as agents to be on the lookout for the person that would cause us to fall in love. Taking all this into consideration, we then believe love is not thought of as being innate. But then, could the poets be wrong? Who can be sure?

Love is a heartthrob that makes our bodies tingle, and our stomachs jump and twitch. It is a feeling of immense joy, anticipation, and anxiety. It is a sensual and sexual stimulant that excites our entire being and turns us into a roaring passionate flame. It blinds us, and we want to see only the one we love. As a consequence, that person tends to be on our minds constantly, and we want to be with them all the time. We believe that for each of us, there is only one true love, and when we find her or him, it will strike us like a lightning bolt. Falling in love is supposed to make us exuberantly happy because we have discovered that very special person of our dreams. And with our true love we will live happily ever after. How do we know all this? Well, because it is standard fare. Since childhood, we have been prepped and guided in subtle and blatant ways about what love is and how we should react to it. Our belief in love tells us that it will make life worthwhile in spite of any negativity that we can experience or imagine. It is supposedly a God given elixir.

Love can be used as a cure-all because the origins of the problems caused by emotional deprivation occur during the non-consciousness stage of our lives. With no sense of I, and no mind to contemplate the situation, the young child experiences life in general and amorphous terms. Consequently, the reason for feeling of emotional deprivation can be attributed to almost anything the individual wants to focus on. Similarly, love can be perceived as a cure for any kind of problem in the same amorphous way that the emotional deprivation is realized.

Human amorphism suggests a lack of self-definition. Therefore, if a small child has any sense of self-awareness during his non-consciousness stage of life, then it must be through some kind of spiritual process. It is the distortion of this process that causes us to experience alienation. Our yearning for love is an attempt to fill this spiritual void. As an alienated person, we suffer from a great deal of inner emotional turmoil because we suppress our innate selves in order to play our social roles. As Freud noted, there is constant conflict between the id and the ego. This conflict can be disturbing enough to produce monsters from the id. To avoid this conflict, we will seek love as a hedonistic reward, and we will play the necessary formulaic social roles to accomplish it. Unfortunately, this does not relieve us of our alienation, even though we do get a sense of wish fulfillment. And my goodness, Hollywood does know this formula very well. In almost every motion picture, with a man and a woman in it, there is some element of this dynamic.

Alienation is indigenous to the American culture, and our attempts to experience love tend to be emotionally regressive as a result. The greater our need for love, the more immature we will behave. This occurs in part because we fail to recognize that alienation is a spiritual rather than a material problem. For example, we associate physical sex with love, and by sex is meant coitus. We think that sexual gratification will relieve us of our alienation, and it does, at the instant of orgasm. But that is a fleeting moment, with no lasting effect. This brief period of self-realization is also another reason why we are so willing to play musical beds with strangers in the face of sexually transmitted diseases and AIDS. However, intermittent sexual intercourse cannot give us the ongoing spiritual relief we want.

Because of socialization, all societies engender emotional deprivation that leads to some degree of alienation for its members. In western cultures, we tend to play down, or even ignore, this truth. In Eastern cultures, like India, the reality of perpetual, societal alienation is recognized, if not embraced, but in western societies, because we rely upon material supremacy, we try to look through our societal alienation like it was glass. Capitalist societies like our own are particularly vulnerable to the processes of alienation because we reject the importance of the human spirit. In India, at least in their religious philosophy, the reverse is true. The Indians believe that the human spirit is important to social interaction. This is how the individual soul is to achieve spiritual self-realization and eventually reach *Moksha*.

Our thoughts of love are frequently, if not most often, stimulated by sexual desire. Indeed, the two feelings are interrelated. Attitudes about sex will affect our feelings of love, and our feelings of love will affect our attitudes about sex. Americans think of sex in material terms, and love, therefore, is sought after as a hedonistic reward. The people of Eastern cultures would see this as a folly. They believed that sexuality, as an expression of love, is akin to spirituality. For instance, the Taoist in China believed that sex is a sacred duty and a form of worship. It could lead the soul toward immortality. In India, sex is cultivated as a spiritual ideal, and Indians codified their sexual practices in book known as the Kama Sutra.[42] Compared to Easterners, our attitudes of sex and love seem so immature and emotionally regressive. Many Hindus think that Westerners suffer from a severe case of spiritual retardation.

From an Eastern perspective, sex and love concern themselves with much more than just hedonistic pleasure. In the first instance, there is the need for procreation, and this is why sexual intercourse was designed to occur between a man and a woman. And, if sexuality is akin to spirituality, then lovemaking begins the process of the transmigration of the soul. This speaks of a Godly function. Therefore, women may well be the hand-maidens of the Holy Spirit after all. Because of this probability, it is only through sexual intercourse, between a man and a woman, that the primal virtues of lovemaking can be realized. When a person has a material notion of sex, the orgasm becomes the focus of sexual relations. With this attitude, participants are more likely to treat one another as objects and be emotionally detached during their sexual involvement. And also, male-to-male and female-to-female sex is more easily rationalized.

Since we use love in a utilitarian manner, to that degree we are deper-sonalized by it. As agents looking for love, we have been programmed to seek it. Before we reached pubescence, we had an emotional map and mindset that was suppose to guide us to the love of our life. The elements of the programming are biological and societal, innate and learned. The needs of procreation and culture are the stimulants. But, because we are rational beings, we disdain the thought of being controlled by instinct. So, we feed propaganda to ourselves to elevate the nature of our mindset. The propaganda comes in the form of an unending stream of coercive emo-tional, dramatic and musical stories about the importance of love to the individual, to society, and even to God.

These love stories, presented on the Broadway stage, on weekly and daily TV series, and in Hollywood movies, or in romance novels, are usu-ally intellectually simple, but dramatically arched and emotionally com-plicated. While these stories make a big show of characters, in fact they are not about people at all. They are really about love and the power it has over our lives. The power is made out to be mystical and magical, and we are led to believe that it is out there to be found, and to be used to relieve us of our feelings of emotional deprivation. Indeed, these stories as scripted dramas, supported by the appropriate theme music, feeds off of our emotional deprivation, and through vicariousness and introjections, we can feel one with the characters in the stories. This is why we become so involved with the role-players, like the actors on the daily TV soap operas, and show such concern, sympathy and empathy, joy and sadness, with and for them. The experience is one of having such feelings for our selves.

The utilitarianism of love is amply exploited by our capitalist economy. To the enterprising entrepreneur, love is just another product to be sold in the form of clothes, cars, perfumes, or as anything that can be marketed as a consumer product or be focused on as a fad. In American society, material worth is very important, and everyone is caught up in the throes of conspicuous consumption. Love for another, particularly of the male for the female, is to be acknowledged by offerings to the same. This is usually in the form of purchased items from flowers to diamonds. If you really love her, show it with a gift, preferably an expensive one. My, my how Hollywood likes to play up this conspicuous consumption theme. Practically every young woman in this country has been clued into believing that real, true love is always accompanied by a package tied with a ribbon.

In giving a gift to someone we love, we would like to believe that it is just a show of appreciation, but if that were the simple case, then the importance, or lack of it, would not matter so much. But the material offerings in love have become a matter of great expectations because it would seem to demonstrate the power of love in concrete terms. However, love by its nature is spiritual and unexplainable; but if it can be objectified, then it can serve very well as conspicuous consumption items. This happens because of introjections, backed up by emotional deprivation.

Introjections instill an unrealistic sense of value in our psyche for love offerings. Because we receive them as gifts, they give us a feeling of self-worth. Since these offerings are usually purchased, they have a dollar value, and we can equate our sense of self-worth in money terms. If the item is expensive, our feeling of self-worth is magnified. This tells us that love is being bought and sold like any other supermarket product. Once you put a price tag on love, no one can claim it as his or her own. It goes to the highest bidder, and then it can be readily used to manipulate and exploit people. As a result, it is a common ploy used by Hollywood moviemakers and the hucksters in the business world.

To measure one's self-worth on the basis of gifts, money, or any other form of conspicuous consumption, is an inducement to alienation. And, under these circumstances, as Marx pointed out over a hundred years ago, false consciousness is a guaranteed phenomenon. This is the external package of the American notions of love. It is a bourgeois idea of love that is based on banal materialism and superficialities, and it underscores the lack spirituality involved with it. Our credo of love is founded upon wish fulfillment. We do not seek love to know beauty and truth. We want love to take away the general, unhappy feelings we have about ourselves that was engendered by emotional deprivation.

Obviously then, we seek love for a purpose. The purpose is to meet our needs. But, as those needs relate to the problems of emotional deprivation, love is no answer for them. Even if we find the one person we always dreamed about, the love he or she offers us cannot remove the negative effects of our primary socialization. The problems it has produced are not solvable in this stage of life, but both individuals are still likely to look to the other person to be his or her mother love; that is, to have their partner in the relationship interact with them as Mommy did during that non-consciousness period of their lives. Because of emotional deprivation, there is always that yearning inside of us for mother's nurturing and affection. However, the situation is further emotionally complicated by sexual feelings the two have for each other. This may lead to Oedipal, incestuous feelings haunting both the man and the woman. However, bringing up a psycho-emotional shield of detachment can block these feelings.

For a woman, love and sex go together. This is why women like to speak of sexual intercourse as making love. A woman seeks sexual relationships because essentially her body needs to reaffirm itself by engaging in the procreative process whether it leads to pregnancy or not. The fact that love and sex go together for a woman is important to the commitment she must give to an infant child if she becomes a mother. At the moment of its occurrence, the sexual orgasm does explode a feeling of innateness and self throughout the network of the human nervous system. It is a reaffirmation of personhood and the spirit of the human soul. This is the unconscious drive of a woman, to have these qualities pass through her to a baby; and because of this, she can feel obligated to nurture and defend that child's life as though it were her own.

At the same time, love and sex do not necessarily go together for a man. A man's desire for sex is not due to a biological desire to reproduce, as is the case for a woman. The man is driven sexually by the demands of an orgasmic imperative. For a man love is never an end in itself. It is always a means to an end, sexual gratification. Men never go out looking for love as women do. They go out looking for sex. It is probably safe to say that sex leads to love for men, and it is the other way around for women. Therefore, men and women seek love for individually different purposes; and make no mistake about it, we are talking about two different kinds of love. To a woman, love is the notion of that deep, tender feeling that calls for attachment, commitment, and responsibility in a long- term relation-ship. For a man, love, in the first instance, is about self-satisfaction, self-gratification, self-aggrandizement, and self-realization. Yes, it is all about himself. It is about the excitement of his accomplishment, about scoring sexually, about the power of his sexual energy, about being a good fucks-man, about getting his reward for rending services, about reaching climax while bringing the woman to orgasm, and about a feeling of the complete fulfillment of his ego. In a word, it is all about machismo.

When they speak of love, men and women come at it from two entirely different starting points. And if sex is the focus, then women have sex to be loved, while men have sex out of pure uninhibited lust. For women love and sex are like the poet Keats' proclamation of truth and beauty. In essence, they are the same thing, and to truly experience and enjoy one, or the other, you must have both. The desire of men to satisfy their lust is male normalcy. It is through lust that they reach the plateau of love, as women know it. The process that gets them there is more aptly expressed as *Luv* as was displayed in a 1967 Hollywood motion picture by the same name. As it indicated, when men are in luv, they are in an orgasmic imperative frenzy. This tells us that the sexual drive of men and women not only begin from different starting points, but they also seem to be trying to achieve different purposes. However, if we think of sex and love in the spiritual context, as do Eastern cultures, we can see that the male luv and the female love match up well to the Chinese philosophical concepts of yang and yin. They are primal, complementary forces of the universe.

In America, we have strong beliefs in individualism. It is a basic idea in our social philosophy. As such, individualism helped to inspire the civil rights movement, feminism, the sexual revolution, and gay rights, but at the same time it is also a view that places the emphasis on the needs of one person above that of a couple or the group.[43] Consequently, Americans do tend to have a "me first attitude" in their social relationships; and as a result, men and women tend not to give recognition and respect to their differences. This attitude has caused a lot of problems in our love lives, and it may be one of the root causes for the battle between the sexes that is ongoing in this society.

The feminist movement and the sexual revolution were both infected with this "me first attitude." The situation was exacerbated further by women's attempt to behave like macho fucksmen, and it became a source of emotional confusion for them. They did not have the innate constitution to perform sexually like a man. Given their female status, they were actually telling themselves to settle for less than what their needs for love required, and their behavior has played right into the luv hands of men. In answering the call of nature, and keep in mind that females always outnumber males, men will invariably take up the challenge to seek new conquests unless a woman can demonstrate to him the complementariness of her yin to his yang; and by doing so, help him lift himself sexually from the material plane to the spiritual one. For Westerners, this is not easy to do. Our rational, cultural philosophy tends to oppose it.

The need we all have for love may well be a need for mother love. It may be a call back to our non-consciousness days. From within our subconsciousness, an infant child may be crying out for Mommy and the nurturing he never got in the past. The cry is eternal because our mothers are largely responsible for shaping our individual, emotional response to the world we live in. As to the good or bad of it, they initially shaped our emotional sense of self from the womb through that 0-3 year period. For this reason, we have a lifelong, unique emotional tie to our mothers, and when we grow to adulthood, the females tend to behave like their mothers. And the males tend to marry women who are like their mothers in ways that are most significant to them. More importantly, the female will tend to have her mother's attitudes and moral judgments about love and sex, even when she is in disagreement with them. The male will tend to oppose his mother's moral judgments about love and sex, as it relates to himself, but he will want his wife/sex partner to be of the *marianismo* character because that is how he thinks of his mother.[44] To that infant child inside of him, mother is always seen in ideal terms.

Given the complex, emotional connections mothers can have with their adult children, it is no surprise that their relationship to a son or daughter can often be quite contentious. One might think that there would be a healthy, loving relationship between a mother and her offspring; but all too often today, the relationship can be so volatile it is fraught with ugly, emotional conflicts and violence. Matricide is not even out of the question. Thinking about all that we have said here, it would not be a stretch to say that emotional deprivation is probably intimate to the contentiousness that can exist between a mother and her adult offspring. Think about this: if there is an infant inside of us crying for mother love, then we know that mother holds the keys to the kingdom. We cannot go back to the non-consciousness stage of our lives, but we have wish fulfillment and the power of hope, that springs eternal. It binds us in a neurotic knot to mother love. We are trapped in a situation that cannot be resolved, and to that degree we are emotional hostages. When this feeling comes over us, we can become very angry and aggressive towards our mothers.

A feeling of being an emotional hostage may also be connected to the neurosis known as a mother-fixation, which is excessive attachment to ones mother to the extent that inhibits maturation. This sounds like another take on an aspect of emotional deprivation, and it is a problem that is more readily exhibited by male offspring. Mother-fixated men may select women who emotionally remind them of their mothers; but by the same token, women who are using love to fulfill their sense of emptiness because of deprivation may also look for men that have the same attitudes and moral judgments as their mothers. Imagine the strain such a situation would put on a couple's relationship. For example, incestuous guilt feelings would overshadow their sexual relations. And to make it more peculiar for them, the feeling would be coming from their unconscious mind.

The search for love is a search for emotional security. Through that infant in our unconsciousness, we know there was a time when we had such security, a time when we were safe, protected from cold, hunger, and strife. It was that time when we were in our mother's womb. We will never know the pleasure, and pure joy of being that safe again, as we knew it during our gestation period. It has left an impression in our psyche that we will carry for all our days throughout our mortal lives. If we can find a woman, or a man, who is like our mothers, then maybe we can know that security again. The need for mother love indicates a strong desire to feel secure within our own psyche. That sense of security was interfered with by emotional deprivation.

Because we may seek mother love from the woman or man of our choice, all our relationships are likely to be emotionally triangular in nature. In emotional spirit, if not substance, our mothers will be with us as we make a life with a partner. Such a third party presence can either help or hurt the relationship. It is probably the X-factor of the individuals involved that will tilt the relationship in one direction or the other, but feelings of being an emotional hostage can also play a role. This triangular connection is a function of the person's unconscious mind. So, we are not cognitively aware of it, but in Hollywood motion pictures and television shows, we see various forms of triangular relationships being played out over and over again. And we never seem to tire of it. There is something about such displays that appeals to us. Could they be tuning into our unconscious mind?

It may well be that the emotional presence of our mothers in our love relationships is meant to be a stimulus, a reminder that we must fulfill, as the Eastern philosophers say, our sacred, spiritual duty. That is, to lead our soul to immortality. Since this is accomplished through sexual intercourse, procreation must be a part of it. Therefore, sexual intercourse, albeit between a man and a woman, is one of the most venerated functions that any two human beings can perform. Following this logic, sexual intercourse starts the process that leads to the Hindu notion of the transmigration of the soul. This would mean that when a woman has a baby, it is indeed the most creative act that any human being can perform, and to think that the feminist movement put women down who were satisfied with just being mothers.

Our attitudes about love and sex are entwined, and I have said that sexual intercourse reaffirms our individuality. Is this the same for love? If we are all distinct human beings, and no two of us are alike, then does each one of us have our own sense of, and capacity for, love? Yes, that would seem to be the case. But, can we give our love to whomever we chose? No. The other person, who is the object of our affection and sexual desires, initiates our feelings of love. We know that there is a natural attraction between a man and a woman. Love helps to bring them together for procreative purposes. But how do we explain homosexual attraction and declarations of love for the same?

What of the spiritual quality of sex? Is it the same for homosexuals? Are they involved in the transmigration of souls? If love making, between a man and a woman, is a sacred duty then the answer to all these questions has to be no. There can be no two ways about the matter. There is but one Holy Spirit, and one sexual path to God and nirvana. However, this is not to say that homosexuals do not know of love. They do, but it is an odd kind of love. According to many social scientists, homosexuality is a form of narcissism. Narcissism is a compulsive behavior of self-love, and all humans seem to have some aspect of it in their character. But gay individuals can be obsessive about it.

Narcissism results from arrested libidinal development, and we can infer from this that such individuals have regressive personalities. And, immaturity of this type is an indication of severe emotional deprivation. If there is a natural sexual attraction between a man and a woman, then the force of it must be innate. Or, to put it differently, it is biologically based. What does this say about homosexuality? It may very well be sociologically based. As part of the effort to reclaim their bodies, many women have physically retreated from men, and these women have been increasingly seeking the fulfillment of love in lesbian relationships. But, if lesbianism is a form of narcissism, then these new recruits to the island of Lesbos are exhibiting regressive behavior. How strange that so many women have come to the acceptance of lesbianism as a viable love option in the wake of the feminist movement. Women started their liberation movement to find themselves and be free, but now they seem more lost than ever.

Homosexual relations is delimiting by its very nature. It cannot lead to procreation and the transmigration of souls. Its purpose is that of self-pleasure, and self-pleasure only. It is a form of mutual masturbation. Lesbianism prevents a female from reaching her full potential as a woman, and this is what the feminist movement was supposed to be all about. Homosexuals specifically treat sex relations as a form of recreation, and this mode of behavior was fostered upon the general public with the sexual revolution. When homosexuals speak of love, more than likely they are referring to lust.

To distinguish the importance of coitus, love making between a male and a female, a woman is invested with the Grafenberg spot or the "G-spot." This is a small area within in the anterior wall of the vagina. The G-spot is located at the top of the vagina, one to two inches from the entrance, and penile thrusting in rear entry or female-superior sexual positions best stimulate it. Stimulation of this spot produces erotic sensations and a prolonged, distinct kind of sensual ecstasy for a woman that is more spiritual in nature than physical.[45] The presence of the G-spot gives some credence to Eastern notion of spirituality and sexuality being interwoven as one. This is very much realized in the Tantric sex tradition.

Tantric sex is largely unknown to Westerners, and its purpose is to bring spiritual unity to a male and female couple through sexual relations by playing down orgasmic release. In Tantric sex, the male controls and delays his own orgasm, and he redirects his sexual energy throughout his and his partner's body.[46] This is how a man can sexually lift himself from the material plane to a spiritual one. The G-spot may be an important element in this process, and as love is interwoven with sex, the Tantric tradition is as much about love as it is about sex. And, too, since the purpose of Tantric sex is to produce spiritual unity, then love making also concerns itself with spiritual development or in the words of enlightenment, a self-realization of the spirit. There is no more intimate, subjective feeling than an orgasm, and to receive its full spiritual benefits, sexual intercourse should be experienced as nature intended it, without condoms, pills, or any other contraceptives devices or agents.

I know it sounds foolish and irresponsible to speak of having sex without any consideration of contraceptive devices today, but that is only because we Americans look at sex in such a limited material way. Lovemaking was never intended to be just orgasmic recreation. It has always had a higher purpose, a more spiritual purpose, and that truth has always been a part of Western history as the Greeks philosophized about it and the poets have written about it for at least two millenniums. That purpose is procreation and the transmigration of the soul. But as Max Weber has pointed out, over the centuries Western societies have developed a rational way of thinking that relies upon logic and reasoning,[47] and we have become dependent upon the scientific method that is based on materiality. To our own satisfaction, we have demystified the world, and we have come to reject the relevance and meaningfulness of spirituality in our lives. But that does not change the reality of the situation.

If lovemaking is a scared duty, then it is a responsibility that all humans share, and it cannot be denied. That sacred duty is based upon the larger spiritual purpose of the continuation of the human soul, through transmigration in the new life of a child. This is the road the Taoist spoke of that leads to immortality. To fulfill this sacred duty, and for sexual intercourse to be all that it can be to the participants, a man and a woman must accept the responsibility that they can, and may, create a new life. In doing this, they are giving recognition to the fact that they are essentially spirit, and not just physical beings that are satisfying a material, lustful urge. As this gives recognition to the true nature of the self, this is a matter of self-realization, and it brings the person closer to his repressed innate self. Thus, being responsible during sexual intercourse poses a challenge to our spiritual retardation, and it can allow us to disengage ourselves from the impact of emotional deprivation for a short while. And in so doing, it can offer us some relief from our sense of alienation.

Tantric sex brings about spiritual unity between a man and a woman by creating the Infinite Cycle. This occurs when a man and a woman join together sexually, penis in vagina. The two are in a sitting position, the woman straddling the man with her legs about his waist. They embrace and kiss. Thrusting is kept to a minimum, and they generate energy between them by flexing their genital muscles. The couple harmonizes their breathing, finding a common rhythm of inhaling and exhaling.[48] This creates a flow of energy from the genitalia up through the body of the participants, and there is a spiritual unity. It is important that flesh touch flesh in the genital area, and that there be no contraceptive inhibitors or agents involved. The two bodies must be in natural sexual contact.

Tantric sex would allow us to fill our souls with passionate energy, and it is just that kind of fulfillment that is needed to fight off the ravages of emotional deprivation. But we have become our own worse enemy in this matter. Our rationalizing consciousness prevents us from seeking the spiritual way of lovemaking. We find meaning only in the superficial, materialistic sense of it. Verily when Americans speak of love they address the sex and passion of it. And for individuals like John Allen Lee[49] and Gordon & Snyder[50] who have attempted to discover what love is, they might say that we seem to be stuck in the infatuation stage of love. This also tells us about our immaturity, and gives us another reason why we so eagerly identify with the fictional love characters in motion pictures and on television. And, since we received our introduction to the program of love through fairy tales like Sleeping Beauty and Snow White, we are easily attracted to similar romantic dramas. Because of the various forms of vicarious lifestyles that are generalized in our time, it is easy for us to fall in love with celluloid and TV thespians as they have come to represent the characters from our childhood fantasies.

As fairy tales would suggest, love used to be thought of as being magical, mysterious, and ethereal. Sexual desires, and certainly not lust, were never in the forefront. Prince Charming loved his Princess not because he wanted to sleep with her, but because she was saintly, angelic, pure, and a wonder of God. The Princess was by all accounts spiritual in nature, deserving to be worshipped and placed on a pedestal. And, she could sleep for an eternity until the Prince's kiss awakens her. But since the sexual revolution, this view has been turned around. Now sex leads the way. Sleeping Beauty has become Linda Lovelace, the cocksucker of the classic movie "Deep Throat," and the focus of love is on sex. Romance is an afterthought.

Americans still talk about love as their supreme desire, but we are now, more than ever, uninhibited in saying that we must have sexual fulfillment with our love. Indeed, today love is thought to be contingent upon sexual satisfaction. Like truth and beauty, you can't have one without the other.

So, we have come to place extraordinary emphasis upon sexual performance. The good or bad of our relationships is strictly measured along these
lines, and in large part we must thank the feminist movement and the sexual revolution for this. Women were so anxiety ridden and rabid about
discovering that illusive orgasm, they have allowed their efforts to become
the sin qua non of their romantic involvements. Because of their ego and
attempts to cope with compulsive masculinity, men were easily drawn into
this pattern of behavior as they tried to give the women what they wanted.

This emphasis on performance has produced a strange situation for
men and women. They find themselves evaluating their male or female
partners on the basis of the narrow issue of sexual ability, and it reduces
the person down to being less than one-dimensional. Everything about
the person is seen through the magnifying glass of sexual satisfaction; and
there is an enormous amount of pressure placed on individuals to be very
good in bed. Since this is now the most important criterion in determining what the status of the relationship will be, there is the added pressure
on the two to get to the bed as soon as possible. If he or she is not very
good in bed, then you don't want to waste too much time with the person.
With sex leading the way to love, if you are getting bad sex, then there can
be no "true love" in the relationship.

With such pressure to prove you are good in the sack, a couple can find
themselves competing with each other to see who is better. Or, out of fear
of failure, one or both persons might withhold their full participation.
And, unconsciously, either one or both of them might purposefully sabo-
tage the efforts of their partner. Neither one wants to take responsibility if
the relationship doesn't work out. Once again, it is quite interesting to
note how the behavior of so-called adults can be so immature and regressive. Emotional deprivation has a way of causing us to turn the good we
try to do into something negative. In this case, in the name of love, we
nurture self-defeating behavior, and what can be more personally cruel. It
is a Jekyll and Hyde syndrome that is difficult to stop once it gets started.

Sex is supposed to lead us to love. Therefore, the more we know about sex, the better our understanding of love, or so the logic would seem to go. We have then, in our time, gone about the business of demystifying sex just like we demystified the rest of the world. Our scientific methods tell us that we can explain any unknown if we study it long enough and collect the data. We think of sex as being material. Then it follows that we should be able to deal with it empirically. As a result, there have been hundreds of books and a variety of sex projects that have studied human sexuality from every conceivable angle. And, consistent with our present interest, many of these books have focused on performance in bed. There are manuals and guides that supposedly tell us how to get the best results between the sheets. But they can only be generalized instructions that are less than appropriate for individual behavior. Even so, the public has taken these types of instructions to heart, and love making for many has come to be rationalized, goal-oriented activity.

We have also allowed our sexual behavior to become influenced by sexual researchers and therapists like Kinsey[51] and Masters and Johnson.[52] They have given a veneer of scientism to their research findings and therapies, and the public is asked to let their observations and conclusions be the means by which we understand our own individual behavior. The effect of all this is to bring another avenue of depersonalization into our lives. And since the purpose of these instructions and therapies is to help us get the most out of our sex lives, they tend to re-enforce our materialistic, hedonistic approach to love making. As well, we are now being offered objective standards for sexual achievement, and our performance can be compared to others generally throughout society. For better or worse, our bedroom performance can be located on some kind of national scale, and the judgment about the good or bad of it is taken out of our hands.

All this information about lovemaking has had another unanticipated effect. Prior to the sexual revolution, there was Victorian moral standards about the right and wrong of our sexual behavior. As a society, we did not always abide by these standards, but they were there to be referred to and be a matter of each individual's conscience. Now the old moral standards have been rejected, but there has been nothing to replace them. Instead, there are guidelines and instructions on how to get the most out of coitus by achieving an orgasm. Given this situation, we find ourselves depersonalizing our lovers and identifying them as sex partners. Such relationships can easily become superficial and mechanical, something akin to a one-night-stand, and/or an act of mutual masturbation.

Love has always been a mystery, but now we find ourselves caught in a love maze. We can feel stupefied and confused about love because we have come to equate it to sex. We no longer seek to love a person for who they are, but rather what they do. Our partner must please us or we will not be able to love him or her. This is precisely the type of relationship we had early in our lives with our parents, principally our mothers. They wanted us to behave and perform in such a way as to please them. We were rewarded with love and affection when we did, and it was not as forthcoming if we did not. This pattern of behavior can now comes back to haunt us as adults in our sex relations.

The focus of our sense of love is on our selves. It is a function of the "me first attitude." This is a selfish and anti-love way of thinking and feeling, but we cannot help ourselves. It is that emptiness inside of us that make us feel this way, the emptiness that was deposited there by emotional deprivation. Like the inner child that we are, we want our way in the matter. Our needs must come first. That is the only way we can feel loved. What we want is unconditional love, the kind of love we should have gotten from our significant others. But such love is not healthy among adults. Still, that is the way we want it. Consider the problems that are sure to arise when both individuals in the relationship feel this way. There would be little cooperation, understanding, and sharing that is needed to make a good relationship.

Indeed, when it comes to love, Americans do seem to be stuck at the infatuation stage of it, and this is very consistent with our regressive personalities. But even more sadly, the elements that tend to make for a good love relationship are turned into negatives as a consequence. Consider the following. Most people would agree with the psychologist Zick Rubin. He said that love probably has three main components: attachment, caring, and intimacy.[53] However, with our selfish, "me first attitude" toward love, it is not true attachment we feel for the person who is the object of our affections, but rather it is detachment. We don't want to give love as much as receive it, and we can fear that it will not be forthcoming since we are acting out the same pattern of behavior we experienced with our mothers when we were a small child. Therefore, we anticipate rejection, and we withdraw our feelings, remaining emotionally detached.

But, we do want to care for someone else, because we want that someone to care for us. This attitude can only be superficial and shallow at best when the relationship is based on infatuation. If nothing else, the situation would raise conflict issues as to whether we should give unconditional love to another person and place their well being above our own. We could interpret such actions as subverting our own needs. And it would fracture the basis for our involvement with the individual. To be sure, caring for someone is a responsibility, but as regressive personalities we are not emotionally prepared to assume such a role. And, being in a so-called love relationship can bring undue pressure on us to do so, and this can cause us to develop neurotic, avoidance mechanisms to defend ourselves against it.

Without intimacy, there can be no love. Being physically close to another person, having sexual relations with them, and being overall emotionally involved is the wish fulfillment we have for the ultimate satisfaction that love can bring. But to achieve this requires a certain kind of commitment, an honest giving of oneself, a sharing openness of feelings, mutual respect, and above all else trust. For someone to present himself to another in such a fashion, he or she would have to be very confident and secure within himself. And this is precisely what an emotional deprived person is not. He will have a fear of true intimacy because it requires exposure of the innate self, which has been repressed. To call upon it is to conjure up old guilt and anxiety feelings from the unconscious mind, the realm of the id. These feelings may very well emerge as monsters of one sort or another, and they are likely to attack the person who we say we have fallen in love with. Is this why we always seem to hurt the one we love?

Whatever love is, it's a powerful emotion. It can make us feel happy, sad, wonderful, or depressed. Love can emotionally blind us, and it can seem to drive us crazy. When love arouses our passions, it can even drive us to commit murder. This is to say that there is a thin line between love and hate. To be sure, love can be a strong stimulus to hate. Nothing can make us angrier, frustrated, and violent than when we are ignored, denied, or rejected by someone we have declared our love for. Given the fact that we fantasize about love being the cure-all for our emotional ills, and with our long years of being burdened with feelings of low self-esteem, alienation and emptiness, it would be asking too much of us to give up the person who could change all that. To keep our one and only true love, we would do just about anything.

As Freud has spoken of society suppressing our basic instincts, so it has suppressed our ability to love freely, and this generates frustration, anger, hate, and aggressive behavior. Once again, our human actions have produced dire, unintended consequences. Through socialization, we have taken one of the most endearing, spiritual qualities of humanity and turned into something that produces hate and violence. Love has even become a justification for murder, and who suffers the most from this, women, and the reason is quite obvious. As a child, men were emotionally battered, and now they feel justified in doing the same to their mother substitutes. And to be sure, in this instance, one woman is as good as another.

How strange. Love has become one of the chief contributors to the reservoir of free-floating aggression in our society. Because of emotional deprivation, the overwhelming majority of us have spent the greater part of our adult lives, seeking, and trying to maintain a good love relationship. Most of us have loved and lost many times. And in the post sexual revolutionary years, love has become even harder to find. Both men and women are complaining that love "isn't what it used to be." Both sexes are frustrated, uptight, and angry about it, and each group is apt to blame the other.

Unfortunately, this has added fuel to the fire in the battle between the sexes, and with women today feeling that they must contest the authority of the male chauvinist pig, as matter of their feminist rights, these situations are exacerbated even more.

Imagine all those Hollywood motion pictures and television dramas about the heartache and heartbreak of love. The fighting and violence that is shown to us that occurs between individuals who once declared undying love for one another. Those dramas help to suck up our emotions and feed it into the reservoir of free-floating aggression, and there are millions and millions of Americans who are pouring their emotions into that reservoir on a daily basis. Undoubtedly, it brings pressures on most of us, in our collective consciousness, to partake of it. Or, at least it presents us with an atmosphere, a justification for the use of aggression when we do want to tap into it. Is there any wonder that America is a violent society? And what is the most common symbol of violence in this country: the handgun. As a society, we may tolerate the gun because it is the arch symbol of the free-floating aggression that is rooted in the psyche of our collective consciousness.

If love is so emotionally injurious and physically threatening to us, why do we, almost to every man and woman, search for it, wish for, and some get down on their knees and pray for it? Surely sex has a lot to do with it, and too the propagation of the species has to be considered also. But that still does not seem to give us the complete answer to the question. We consider ourselves rational, intelligent beings, but yet we drive ourselves unmercifully, to the point in many cases of being neurotic about it, to find that one true love that is waiting for us over the next horizon, or at the next party, or among the crowd at the bar during the next happy hour. And we do this with the knowledge that a good relationship is becoming increasingly more difficult to find and maintain. As well, if love is to fulfill our desire for a permanent relationship, we know that today marriage is a crapshoot, and just as uncertain as the weather. Yet, we forge on driven by some inner desperate need that won't let us stop, even though we know that today's love has many faces, and it can transform itself, like Dr. Jekyll, into a monster from the id.

Why are we so desperate for love? It may be because the child from our non-consciousness days is still within us. He or she never fully grew up because the need for mother love was never satisfied, and now as adults we seek its fulfillment from our mother substitutes. But the situation has become much more complicated. Good sex, satisfying orgasmic sex, is equated with love. Indeed, in the mind of the so-called liberated woman there is the fantasy that satisfying sex makes women equal to men, and this is another twist on the utilitarianism of sex in our time. In the past, we believed that love conquers all, but now we believe that sex has that power. Consequently, we have come to focus on the materiality of sex, coitus and the orgasm, to the negation of its spiritual purposes. This attitude alone has given our sexual behavior a Jekyll and Hyde character.

Just a few short years ago, Americans used to yearn for romance and love, but now they cross their fingers and hope they can have a good sex life. We used to be afraid that we would not fall in love, but now we are afraid that we might not be virile enough for our sex partner. And we are inundated with propaganda from the media, in words, symbols, and images that good sex brings happiness. We are made to feel that if we are not getting satisfying sex then there is something, physically, emotionally, or psychologically wrong with us. Or, that we are unattractive, unappealing, or just down right ugly. We have been told that to be sexy is to be beautiful. They are one in the same thing. So, men and women do everything they can with fad and fashion to make themselves look sexy as the media would dictate. As a result, sex has made a fetish of beauty.

Unmarried Americans are engaging in sexual activities now more than ever, and the term of premarital sex is hardly ever spoken of anymore because it is not appropriate in this era of recreational sex. The assumption is that all couples are doing it on a regular basis, in and out of wedlock. That is the only way they can be happy with themselves, with each other, with the world. If a person is not in a relationship, he or she can still go bed hopping. Even in the face of AIDS, causal sex is still rampant. Men who are driven by compulsive masculinity have been measuring their self-worth by the number of women they have slept with for a long time, and now women are measuring their self-worth by the number of men they have been sleeping with. What's good for the gander is good for the goose.

Undoubtedly, we Americans are sleeping around a lot with many different individuals as we seek maximum gratification and the ultimate sex partner. But if sex by the numbers is suppose to bring us love and happiness, the process seems to be failing a great many people. We know that a good relationship is difficult to come by, and that a long-term marriage is less than a fifty-fifty proposition. But there is an even more damning indictment of our sexual discontent. As Wendy Shalit pointed out in her book, *A Return To Modesty*, there are today too many young women who are overmedicated and emotionally dysfunctional precisely because they are having too much sex. Depression is a rapidly growing mental disorder among young people, along with rising numbers of acts of self-mutilation and suicide. Many of them are so psychologically and emotionally debilitated, they cannot function as a normal person without Prozac, Lithium Carbonate, or some other such antidepressant drug.

Individual Americans are generally having more sex with many different partners, but they seem to be getting less from it. The poor mental health that is so widespread in the nation would suggest that today many people are as frustrated as ever with their sex lives. And it doesn't help to have all the media instructions, the national surveys, the sex therapists, and the guidebooks telling us how to get to sexual nirvana. This just deepens our sense of frustration, and it makes us feel stupid and dumb. The experts are telling us what to do, and we still can't get it right. What kind of misfits are we? Or is it that we were never meant to be sexy, beautiful, and happy like most people? So, we begin to doubt our selves and not the instructions that are given to us, and we fall deeper into our well of emotional emptiness.

No wonder we are frustrated. Our rights to personal love and sex have been taken away from us. We do not engage in these activities to please ourselves, per se anymore. We do it to vicariously please society. There is fad and fashion to make us beautiful, and we have expert instructions on how to achieve sexual gratification. But this is not subjective validation for us as individuals. Our most intimate behavior has been transformed into a style, like a type of clothing, hairdo, or pair of shoes. Sexiness comes off the production line as lipstick, perfume, and deodorant. It is packaged, marketed, and sold just like toilet paper. We have, by all accounts become sex consumers, and the capitalist economic system has turned us all into prostitutes.

We have allowed society to take our need for love and sex and turn it against us, and to this extent we are alienated from society. However, this process is not new. Our alienation from society began with our primary socialization, and it matured with us like the muscles in our bodies and the thoughts in our heads. It has been with us for so long, it has become embedded in our psyche, and we now know it as self-alienation. After all, in the final analysis, society and we, are one. What society does to us is simply to say what we do to ourselves. And what is it that we have done to ourselves? Collectively, we have become a very self-defeating, self-destructive force that threatens our own long-term survival. Because of our rationalizing minds, our total faith in materialism, and our dedication to hedonistic pursuits, we have come to disregard our simple, everyday, ordinary common sense. In the process, we have forgotten what our basic, human purpose is all about.

And to be sure, that purpose is not about anything grandiose or extraordinary. It is about that which is fundamental to human life, spiritual development and the transmigration of the soul. Most cultures around the world acknowledge a belief that humans have an immortal soul or spirit, and it is thought to survive the death of the physical body. Many philosophers and religious thinkers from the ancient Greeks to the present day Hindus have maintained that it is our essential life force. Hindus also believe that each individual soul was created at the beginning of time and imprisoned in an earthly body at birth. Christians and Moslems believe that the soul comes into being during the gestation period of the child before birth, and it has a life of its own.

All of these explanations of the soul tell us that it is fundamental to our existence, and it is generally understood that birth is necessary for there to be a presences of the soul in the human body. And if one accepts the religious philosophy of the billions of people who believe in Hinduism, Janism, Buddhism, and Sikhism, then transmigration is the path that the soul must take until it achieves salvation. This requires the individual soul to undergo birth and rebirths, or reincarnation, until it realizes that the individual soul and the absolute soul are one, and then there is a reunion with God. This is the context of human spiritual development.

However, there can be no spiritual development without transmigration, and there can be no transmigration without procreation. This brings us right back to love and sex because ultimately it is about human propagation. Therefore, emotional deprivation may cause us to be compulsive and excessive about love and sex, but in the final analysis, we are going to be out there trying to do it because our biology demands it. Nature, God, the absolute soul, call it what you will, realized that species survival, through transmigration, was too important to allow humans, as individuals or a collective, to have power over it. As a distinct animal species, we want to survive, and it is through species survival that we are able to perpetuate our progeny and save our souls.

So, the desire to perpetuate our selves is a function of our being. We may try to control this behavior, but we can never stop it. There are potent forces within us that won't let that happen. For the female, there is the maternal instinct, that is a biological imperative, and for the male there is the orgasmic imperative. These two forces will drive a man and a woman together. The X-factor will keep it all individually relative, but one thing will be kept constant. Our passions will burn the hottest when we are young at heart. We should always remember the time of our pubescence.

It charged our bodies with energy that fueled our desire for romance, love, and sex.

Freud has pointed out that society tries to control our instinctual, sex drives. Specifically, society wants to define the meaning and methods of our reproductive behavior as it tries to ensure its survival from one generation to the next. Indeed, this is the main purpose of socialization. However, our reproductive behavior has been changing rapidly in recent decades, and this has led to a chain reaction of negative, unanticipated consequences that we now rationalize as a social good. For example, free love, recreational and promiscuous sex, equating sex with love, and using sexual performance as the basis for a good or bad relationship, these attitudes and behaviors are all thought to be good for society today. But the worse outcome of all from these unanticipated consequences has to be the denigration of parenthood, children, and the use of abortion as a form of birth control.

The defamation of parenthood became so viral in the 1970s; an organization was formed known as the National Organization for Non-Parents (NON). It was based in Baltimore, Maryland and it had only a few thousand members, but the significance of the organization was in the fact that it was in the vanguard of the fight to put self and sexual pleasure ahead of procreation. This is generally the attitude the children of the baby boomers have today. Some of the members of NON-included Steward Mott, the philanthropist, Shirley MacLaine, the actress, and John Simon, the art critic. The proponents of the organization said they stood for positive parenthood and the childfree life. The group also had some eminent supporters like Stefanie Mills, Dan Wakefield, population control activist, writer-scientist Isaac Asimov, and Alvin Toffler, author of Future Shock.[54]

It is interesting, if not frightening, to take note of how NON-members, and some of their supporters, felt about parenthood. Toffler justified nonparenthood by citing the upheaval and experimentation in the family system, along with the ongoing industrial and economic crisis in the world. John Simon argued that having children, who are demanding and often in the way, interfered with a happy sex life. Dr. Robert Gould, a Manhattan psychiatrist, put it this way, "It's really time to demythologize and deromanticize the process of having children. People do not deserve honor and respect simply for having a baby. Children are not that perfect, or likeable either."[55] How fascinating. We hear these same attitudes among increasing numbers of young people today. They want to be a part of the action and live in the fast lane. Children would get in the way and slow them down, and it is not uncommon to hear them say, "Who needs the little bastards."

However, if there is one indicator that can show us how far we have fallen from grace, it has to be abortion. It shows the height of selfishness, irresponsibility, immaturity, and disrespect for human life. As a society, we have taken to abortion because it reassures us that we will not have to take care of unwanted babies and that sex is really for fun and not procreation. Listen to the words of a prominent theologian and professor of medical ethics, Joseph Fletcher. He said that sex ought to be strictly for making whoopee. Baby making ought to be left to the assembly line, where a planner can control human defects. "From now on we ought to use sexual intercourse for love-making, and artificial methods for baby-making. Modern medicine has decisively separated love-making from baby-making."[56] Imagined how emotionally deprived the children would be in his Aldous Huxley-like *Brave New World*.

Abortion is a social policy that is supported by the majority of America's men and women, and it takes us far beyond spiritual retardation. We are so ignorant of the purpose of our lives, we aren't even aware that we are playing Russia Roulette with our future. How many Einsteins, Beethovens, and Pushkins have we already destroyed, all for the sake of a few moments of hedonistic pleasure? Indeed, we have become so involved trying to meet our own needs, we have little true affection or love to give to another person, especially a child. And all too many of us are so emotionally deprived, we think that only egotism, that "me first attitude," can offer us the social salvation we seek; but in particular, this solution is fraught with peril.

Witness history. The ancient Greeks and Romans cultivated societies that relied on the romance of egotism, and inevitably they became narcissistical societies; which is to say, they became more and more interested in only their own way of life, well being, importance, and abilities. We also know that as social narcissism increased, so did the level of violence and sexual promiscuity, both heterosexual and homosexual. The ancient Greeks and Romans are long gone, but could narcissism have been instrumental in their demise? And is there a lesson for us to learn from it? Self-love does not further the ends of transmigration. Indeed, like the surrealist painting, it leaves one stationary in time.

Given what has just been said, the following question needs to be asked. At the dawn of the new millennium, is America becoming a narcissistical society? There is much to indicate that this is happening. Professor Fletcher wants us to replace God as the Creator because he thinks we can do a better job. He wants to turn society into a Dr. Frankenstein laboratory and manufacture babies on the assembly line. But Professor Fletcher is overlooking a very significant point. Assembly line babies are sure to be without souls, and as Dr. Frankenstein discovered, a human facsimile without a soul is a monster. And unless we forget, the monster destroyed the Doctor. Would our manufactured babies eventually do the same to us? At the rate we are going, we won't have to wait too long to find out. If the soul is our essential life force, then we had better rediscover it before our monsters from the id meet the monsters from the assembly line. At that point, neither love nor sex will be able to save us.

CONCLUSION

Well then, are we going to replace the Creator, as Professor Fletcher opines? I don't think so. And the reason is this: to our unholy detriment we have allowed emotional deprivation to play a deadly game with us, and that game has led us back to a more primal state of consciousness. It is strange and ambiguous that at the start of the twenty-first century, in spite of all our technological progress, we Americans have become unenlightened, regressive personalities; and as such, emotionally we are going backwards. This is to say, that in a very real sense, the psychology of the primordial world seems to be with us again. And to be sure, our social environment is very well suited for it. The violence and alienation in society, along with the insensitivity to human life, especially fetal life, is causing us to behave like primitive people; and as a consequence, we have become our own worst enemy.

How did we get in this situation? Well, first we should credit socialization, but we can also believe Marshall McLuhan, who said that because of the electronic media, the people in the modern world would return to tribal society. Tribal society was a primitive society, and it was a time when people lived under a siege mentality. The primal instincts of the id were the guiding force for their emotions, and much of their behavior was motivated by fear. In the primordial world, wild beasts threatened humans. In our social world today, we have become the beasts. Americans are stalking Americans as prey to feed their hate, their licentiousness, and their hubris. Barbaric acts like murder, rape, kidnap, racism and other forms of vile, aggressive behavior, are common occurrences in our society. Because our social environment is so dangerous and there are random

223

threats to the individual, we have had to fall back on our primal instincts to better our individual chances for survival.

McLuhan also said that people would stop depending on the written word for information. We see that this has come to past, and it is indicative of a primitive culture. Today, we get most of our information pictorially; and to certain extent, it is even done in a perverse manner. For example, even though crime and violence are major social problems in our society, we also use them as forms of communications and entertainment on TV, in motion pictures, and in the sports arenas. At the same time, the energy and excitement that accompanies deviant behavior feeds into the prevailing action mode, and this, too, can give us a feeling very much like the siege mentality humans must have experienced in the primordial world.

During primordial times, the face of danger was everywhere, and humans lived with the threat of death hanging over them constantly. People had to be vigilant and on guard constantly. Many Americans in our big cities feel the same way today. There are bad guys and criminals roaming the streets, and there are scary motion pictures and violent sports activities that keep us wound up in an action mode. Moreover, motion pictures and sports activities have come to be used in another very unique way.

Movies and sports give us vicarious feelings that there is more excitement in our lives than is the reality, and it makes us feel that our lives are filled with adventures and challenges when they are not. This is to offset the fact that all too many of us have become only copycat caricatures of movie actors and sports figures. We have willingly surrendered our individuality to them because they are role models and sports icons. Our real selves are hidden behind costumes, uniforms, and logos, and this is encouraged as normal behavior in a society that cultivates mass media heroes. But, we seem to be unaware that a caricature is not a real person, and to surrender one's individuality is to surrender one's soul, which then causes one to function as a conscienceless primitive. Make no mistake about it; at issue here has always been the human spirit. Therefore, we need to take notice and realize that submitting to the devil is not the only way we can lose our souls.

But then, perhaps our image of the devil is wrong. Maybe he comes in many different shapes and forms. Our Hollywood motion pictures seem to tell us this story, and where do those celluloid images come from? They are projected from our unconscious mind. And you recall, at the beginning of this book, it was said that society, by its nature, generates frustrations in people since it suppresses basic impulses and restrict individual freedoms. This produces the phenomenon that causes us to surrender our individuality and lose our souls. Now we can understand why our situation is an unholy one. Society is turning us into soulless monsters. Well, that statement is not entirely true because we have to remember that society is made up of nothing more than the people who are in it. Therefore, it is not what society is doing to us, but rather what we are doing to ourselves. Of course, we do not acknowledge this truth. Like Morbius, we are too close to the problem.

Morbius refused to believe that he was the creator of the monster that was stalking his planet. He could not accept the idea that it was a projection from his id. He was a modern, scientific, sophisticated man. The conscienceless primitive could not be a part of him, even at the level of his unconscious mind. But still he always felt that the monster was nearby, sly and irresistible, and somehow in contact with him. The truth was, he had to do battle with himself. And the more he refused to believe what the monster was, the stronger it became. Eventually, the creature threatened him. It was then that he realized that his naiveté and ignorance gave inspiration and strength to the monster, and he could stop it only by killing himself. For the sake of his progeny, Morbius was trying to save his immortal soul. Today, we Americans find ourselves in the same kind of struggle that Morbuis had to face.

Because our innate being has been suppressed, we are in constant tension with the society. Indeed, we are a nation of monsters fighting the system to try and save our souls, and our behavior is beset with contradiction. To begin with, our egos push us to express our individuality. While at the same time, the primal forces of the id demand that we seek out the pleasure our body desires, and our overall sense of self cries out for us to reject the alienation that has such a strong influence on our social behavior. As a result, we find ourselves in a situation where society seems to control our consciousness and body, and we contest this control with our unconsciousness and spirit. This is the classic case of *I* versus *Me*.

Emotional deprivation causes us to fight with our selves. Will we express our *I* or will we live by the dictates of the *Me*? It is an unending struggle. And we function under a constant shadow of ambivalence because we have become conformist minions pretending to live the life of an individual, but we have no real sense of it. We watch ourselves performing social roles and routines on a daily basis, but we feel subjectively separated from most of what we do. The problem is, we don't feel spiritually connected to our activities. Therefore, we can be alienated by our social behavior. And who, or what, is responsible for this? In our adversary state of mine, we can come to blame our bodies.

Casting blame upon ourselves confuses us. But, we are not totally unmindful of what needs to be done. We sense that we must reclaim our spirituality and connect it once again to our general, everyday behavior, but we find ourselves in a crazy situation. We play social roles, and a role by definition is false. So, as a spirit we can feel imprisoned in our own bodies. For women, this is particularly true because they are more intuitive, sensitive, and aesthetic than men. In either case, this underscores what Rosseau said. We are born free, but we find ourselves in chains. However, the human spirit will always fight to break its chains. It is society with its socialization that has enchained us; but when we perceive the problem up close and personal, we can feel that our bodies are keeping us from being self-realized and spiritually free. Like Morbuis then, we may come to the conclusion that our bodies must die before our spirit can escape.

This attitude has become a part of the reservoir of free-floating aggression that helps to make up our culture, and it is available in our collective consciousness for any one to tap into. And because we have reverted to a primal state of mind, we are once again practically living under a siege mentality. This is to say; we have cause to believe that the law of the jungle reigns. This situation becomes very clear when we allow our social roles to possess us. It is then we know that society, in the final analysis, is the destroyer of the human spirit, and that it is the jungle by another name. It is kill or be killed; and if we are going to save our souls, we must dispatch our bodies.

So, we attack our bodies in one monster form or another, and we encourage others to join into the mayhem. At the same time, our behavior is made even more peculiar because it is wrapped in subterfuge. With the intent of making ourselves feel good, as we seek hedonistic pleasures, we smoke, drink alcoholic beverages, abuse drugs, and we are sexually promiscuous. These are deadly activities that can slowly debilitate us and eventually cause our death, and we know this. As such, we are willfully destroying our bodies, and we are doing it with a smile. We think we are vanquishing an enemy, defeating the guards, breaking out of prison, and setting our spirit free. What do you think "getting high," means? We say it is a pleasure, and we are using that pleasure to kill ourselves. How strange. How extraordinary. And just think of the millions of people who are engaging in these activities. What does this tell us? It says that Americans have developed a death wish, and this wish is a function of a culture of suicide.

Self-defeating, self-destructive, violent, and suicidal behavior is a hallmark of our times, and it is being exhibited in many different ways. At the start of the twenty-first century, America is riding the crest of an unprecedented economic boom. People have more wealth in money, houses, cars, and clothes than ever before. We undoubtedly have the highest standard of living than any nation in history, but still we are a very troubled population. We seem to have too much wealth and too little humanity; and in a world where most of the people still live in poverty, we cannot morally and emotionally justify either of the two extremes. This is a dichotomy that puts a strain on our culture, and we have to keep coming up with rationalizations and lies to explain it. More and more people are finding it difficult to put up with the charade, and they are turning to violence as a form of communications to express their frustrations and to send out a cry for help. They are also suffering from a myriad of mental problems. "There is something terribly wrong with society, and it is not me."

In God's eyes, the worse kind of violence is self-murder, suicide. In 1999, the Surgeon General of the United States, David Satcher, said that suicide was a serious national threat to the nation, and it should be recognized as a major health problem. It was also said that millions of Americans suffer from mental illness, and this was often the reason for the suicide attempt. It is also known that people with drug and alcohol problems are more likely to commit suicide. Someone ought to tell the Hollywood moviemakers this so that they can stop showing the beautiful people enjoying drugs and alcohol.

In any case, self-murder is the eighth leading cause of death, claiming about 30,000 lives a year. However, more than a half a million Americans attempt suicide each year but survive.[57] At the same time, it was reported over the national television media that suicide was rising specifically among young people, ages 10 to 14. And it seems that when people are not trying to kill themselves, they are killing others, and this is being done to strangers, friends, and relatives alike. There are about 23,000 homicides a year in this country.[58]

With so many people suffering from mental illness, from the poor to the rich, the possibility cannot be ignored that the cause is indigenous to our society. Could emotional deprivation be the reason? There are millions of Americans who suffer from depression; and if they can't function as their innate selves, then they are bound to become depressed over it. Moreover, their condition maybe worsened by the behavioral drugs that are being given to them by the medical community. This is particularly true for young people who fall into the age group that is prone to commit suicide. There is a long list of antidepressant drugs that are used to help mental illness suffers. Prozac, Zoloft, Demerol, and Lithium just to mention some of their names again. But there are two drugs in particular that are used to treat young people. They are Ritalin and Luvox.

There is evidence to suggest that dozens of violent crimes, including the massacre at Columbine High School in Littleton, Colorado in 1999, have been committed by young people taking psychotropic drugs. One of the teenage shooters at Columbine, Eric Harris, had been taking Luvox.[59] Psychotropic drugs are mind-altering drugs that are similar in hallucinogenic effect to LSD and mescaline. These are the kinds of drugs that were very popular with the psychedelic youths of the 1960s. As you recall, they went on hallucinogenic trips through their own minds. We don't know for certain where they went, but we can guess that they traveled to the surreal land of the id. On their mind trips, many of the psychedelic youths reported seeing monsters, and still others returned from their mind-bending excursions to become monsters themselves. They suffered from melancholy and paranoia, and they could go into a rage and become physically abusive to family and friends. Some even became killers, like the "Manson hippie family" that were convicted of the Tate-LaBianca murders in Los Angles in 1969.

We have known for a long time that psychotropic drugs changes the chemistry of the brain in ways that we do not fully understand. We also know that they can alter the personality of individuals in very extreme ways and produce sociopathic behavior. Why then are we giving it to children? Does it have something to do with a Death Wish? For some young people, psychotropic drugs may be the means by which they can transform themselves into monsters like Dr. Jeykll turned himself into Mr. Hyde. Surely, Eric Harris was transformed because he was not born a killer. It is also not so ironic that he should end up committing suicide. Now, I wonder what role emotional deprivation and Luvox might have played in all of this?

America is a drug culture, and the use of drugs has increased considerably in the last four decades. We use all kinds of drugs to fight common illnesses like colds, flu, viruses, and drugs are used to fight most major diseases. Drug therapy is institutionalized in American life, and we have a fluid habit of taking over the counter medications as we need them just like we feed ourselves when we are hungry. To this degree, the public has become drug dependent. This is a subtle form of addiction, but we don't recognize it as such. When we speak of addictive drugs, we think of such things as alcohol, cocaine, heroin, nicotine, and amphetamines. However, in either case, long-term drug use can change the brain in fundamental and lasting ways, and the consequences are not fully understood says Dr. Alan Leshner, director of the National Institute on Drug Abuse.[60]

What if changes in the brain were causing, or giving support to, changes in the basic, human nature of Americans. As a people, we have become callus, uncaring, and unsympathetic towards one another. The "me first attitude" and greed are now extolled as virtues, and we no longer think that we should be our brothers keeper. Indeed, we are more likely to believe that our brother is out to get us; and because of this, we are generally suspicious of others and uptight about it. All of this speaks to how selfish we have become and how important immediate self-gratification is to us. We tend to believe that we have a right to happiness and all the hedonistic pleasures the culture can provide, and we will not allow anything to stand in our way, not even unborn children.

Legalized abortion is public policy, and this shows that there has been a fundamental shift in the social nature of the majority of the American people. We do not feel the same responsibility for children as we did just a few years ago. But what is even more striking, the generation of young people who came after the social upheavals of the 1960s are truly of a different social consciousness than their parents, as McLuhan predicted. And this is not just the difference between age groups. These young people today, mainly middle class youths, think differently, see themselves differently, and they are emotionally different than their parents. But in particular, they relate to the electronic world around them like they are plugged into it. They seem to have an insatiable need for constant action in their lives, and they willingly give themselves up to vicarious lifestyles in an effort to satisfy it.

As well, to be like their movie and sports heroes, they will become dare-devils, and put their lives on the line with addictive drugs, quickie sex, fast cars, and other dangerous things like skydiving and bungee jumping. They are forever looking for that high you get from doing something that is exciting and dangerous. They seem to have a Death Wish. Or, are they so different than the generation of their parents that we can say they are mutants, a whole new human breed. The two young shooters of the Columbine High School massacre talked about mutants when they were preparing for their assault on their classmates. What an interesting thought; and if it is true, our society has one big threatening problem on its hands. The magnitude of the problem becomes clearer when we take into account the fact that it is estimated that 4 million Americans are drug addicts, including 2 to 3 million hooked on cocaine and 800,000 on heroin. There are millions more, though not addicted, who use illegal drugs, and 14 million are alcoholics.[61]

Is there a new breed of youngsters on the block? Of course there is. We can argue about whether they are true mutants or not, but every genera-tion produces a new breed. Well, at the beginning of twenty-first century, what kind of broad, sociological description can we give to the crop of youngsters who are going to lead us through the next century? First and foremost, they are truly social actors, obsessed with role-playing. That is to say, in their minds, they are constantly on stage performing, making "pre-sentations of themselves" to family, friends, and the general public, and they do this because they want to get noticed and win the attention of their elders.

These are youngsters who, by and large, have grown up severely emotion-ally deprived, and they have had, comparatively speaking, an abundance of material comforts, too much electronic stroking, and not enough uncondi-tional parental love. They also tend to be angry because they believe that their parents do not really care about them, and this attitude can be transferred to the entire adult world. Adults are seen as materialists, concerned with their jobs, their careers, their well being, and money. The young people want to expose this, so they do just the opposite of what the adult world and their parents expect of them, and they can see their parents as life-killers. Young people can believe that their parents destroyed their lives before they had a chance to live it. These kids can think of themselves as being the walking dead.

Secondly, these youngsters are extremely tribal in their peer group relationships. That is, they are cliquish, clannish, and exclusive. Individuals with a common outlook on life, or who have similar behavioral problems, or who are lumped together by some gross identity, will tend to hang out with each other for mutual support. They will use names, punk, techno, Goth, the Herbs; or use music, a dress code, makeup, or a hairstyle to form the basis for their tribe.[62] Like tribal people of the past, they tend not to be very literate, and they are anti-intellectual. They also have the same penchant for self-mutilation: tattoos, nose rings, tongue studs, pierce belly buttons, breasts, penises, and vaginas. As to their language, they are cryptic and metaphorical in their speech that is more realist than abstract. And every tribe will have its own God to worship and look up to. He or she could come from the movies, television, or sports; but whomever it is, the person is to be idolized and the model for a tribal, vicarious lifestyle.

Finally, the new breeds of youngsters are addicts. They are addicted to electronic stimulation and communications, and drug use. Electronics is something they have grown up with, and it supports their non-literate attitude and action mode of behavior. They use electronics to get information, for entertainment, and to stay in touch with members, and like members, of their tribes. The internet meets all these criteria for them and then some, and it has the added advantage of letting a person talk to strangers who can share their darkest secrets, their most nagging itches, their most violent inclinations.[63] Who knows? It might even be the God that you worship, the person you so fervently idolize.

The Internet gives a whole new dimension to role-playing and the "presentation of self," and being on the net can become a compulsion. Strangers on the net can be anything you want them to be, and they have all the advantages of imaginary friends. "Online, your imaginary friend really talks back. The realness, or potential realness, is part of the compulsion here: Whenever you want, you can take this unreal world and make it real. It is sci-fi in its dimensions. You have this fantasy; you've developed it, plotted it, played it out. Now you have the power to keep it a fantasy, or make it real." With this kind of interaction going on, is there any wonder that the Internet is changing kids in mysterious, potentially dangerous ways, as Michael Wolff says.[64]

Also, like tribal people, some of the new breeds are nomadic in a modern groupie sense. In recent years, a new counterculture has emerged that is being nourished by music and the Internet. A group of young people gets together in a van, and they follow rock bands around the country. "The 'jam band community' is a major underground force in pop (music), with thousands of fans meeting over the Internet, teaming up to tour with Phish or other bands like Moe and the Disco Biscuits, disseminating hundreds of bootleg tapes and supporting a myriad (of) local scenes." Some Phish performances can attract up to 70,000 people.[65] This shows that there is a great deal of substance to this developing counterculture; and with 35 million people expected to be on America Online by 2002, the possibility that this new breed of youngsters, with their tribalism and Internet morality, will be a major social force in our future is all but certain. And we are talking about a counterculture that could span the world.

The new breed has always been into rock band music, but they are now beginning to lend more and more of an ear to Hip-hop or rap music. Hip-hop hit the American youth scene in the 1970s. The music was a way for black minority kids to inform white suburban kids, and the rest of the world, about life in the inner city, and rappers mainly preached drug culture and violence. By the 1990s, Hip-hop had gone mainstream, and it was said that the hop had become the new rock and roll.[66] But its emergences into the mainstream came at a time when Hip-hop music had fallen under the spell of gangster rappers. These rap artist, like Tupac Shakur, Snoop Doggy Dogg, and Flavor Flav of the group Public Enemy, not only sang about the drug culture and violence, they openly lived that lifestyle. Shakur was indicted for a sexual attack on a woman. Snoop Doggy Dogg was indicted for murder, and Flavor Flav was arrested for attempted murder in a shooting. Many "of the rappers share a culture where education is discounted, poverty is the norm, mothers are the main parent and prison or early death is destiny."[67] Is this not a primal outlook on life? And, it sounds like a Death Wish to me.

Rappers like Ice Cube, Ice-t, and LL Cool J have become movie stars, and so did Tupac Shakur before he was gunned down and killed. Rappers are making commercials and doing advertising on TV. The mainstream media has sucked them up, with all the influence that entails. What will be the impact of gangster rap on this new breed of youngsters and their counterculture movement? The last time the inner city young people met with suburban youths, there was antiestablishment terrorism and revolution in the 1960s. If such a thing is to happen again, it will surely be of a different kind. Already there is talk of cyberterrorism; and to some extent, a new revolution may have already begun in the heads of the new breed. Being so wired up to electronics, the youths of today are thoroughly outer-directed.

The behavior of gangster rappers suggests that there is a nexus between mass media, violence, and youths. What is more primitive and self-destructive of a society than to encourage its children, by intent or by unintentional example, to solve their problems by selfishness and aggression? After the Columbine High School shootings in the spring of 1999, the federal government called for investigations into the effects of media violence on American youths. But most academic researchers were saying that the evidence was already available. "Hundreds of studies done at the nation's top universities in the last three decades have come to the same conclusion: that there is at least some demonstrable link between watching violent acts in movies or television shows and acting aggressively in life."[68]

The Surgeon General's office did two comprehensive overviews of existing studies, one in 1972, and the other in 1982. Both findings singled out television violence as a contributing factor to increases in violent crime and antisocial behavior. And, "from 1990 to 1996, major reviews of scientific studies on the subject were separately conducted by the American Medical Association, the American Psychological Association, the American Academy of Pediatrics, The American Academy of Child and Adolescent Psychiatry, and the National Institute of Mental Health." They all found that television violence contributes to real-world violence.[69] "The research does not demonstrate that watching violent acts in films or on television shows directly and immediately causes people to commit violent acts. The scholarly evidence . . . demonstrates the cumulative effects of violent entertainment or establishes it as a 'risk factor' that contributes to increasing a person's aggressiveness."[70]

Teenagers are particularly attracted to violence in the media when it is presented as entertainment. It offers something forbidden, and taboos are broken. It is also voyeuristic in nature.[71] It is a form of escapism that uses imagination to tap into the psyche. This would involve the unconscious minds of youngsters at the level of the id, and the id is the power source for aggression. By its nature then, violence as entertainment would be a stimulus to aggressive tendencies; and when young people consistently watch violence as entertainment, they may internalize what they see as an action mode of behavior. Aggression turned inward can lead to self-destructiveness, or suicide, and studies have shown that aggression towards one's self and aggression toward others are not contradictory. It is not surprising then that "rates of suicides and homicides committed by teenagers have risen sharply in the last three decades."[72]

The electronic media is not the cause of youth violence. It is only an influence that exacerbates a given situation; one that began with children being emotional deprived by their significant others. Young people, like the rest of us, have grown up suffering from alienation, and they tend to hold their parents responsible. They are angry about it, and at a conference on violence in the media, at the New School University, Dr. Alvin Pouissant of Harvard University said the media can not be blamed for the high levels of anger among young people.[73] Dr. Pouissant was right.

However, it is the anger that makes the young people vulnerable to the media violence; and in turn, the media violence reflects their anger.

At that same conference, Carol Wilder, a Dean at the New School, suggested that present day media storytelling moves audiences to incitement. Linda Ellerbe, a TV producer, added "you don't need 3,000 polls to tell you there's too much violence in media." She went on to say that kids themselves admit to becoming desensitized to violence from movies, television, video games and the most violent, "scariest" TV outlet of all, the news.[74] "Stanley Tucci, who co-directed, co-wrote and acted in the acclaimed film, *Big Night*, spoke of how difficult it is to get non-violent, non-spectacular movies produced. He also cited the lack of venues for them even if they are made. Mr. Tucci suggested that one reason for the proliferation of recent small-town and suburban (school) massacres is that in non-urban America, there are only mall screens, which present basically the same violent films, rather than providing the diversity of cultural perspectives one can find in larger cities."[75]

Small towns and suburban schools tend to be under the spell of a jock culture, and this is particularly true of high schools. It exists as an attempt to establish a sense of community in spite of the pervasive, competitive, bourgeois lifestyle of the students. The point about jock culture is not that you play sports, but you watch it, mostly on TV.[76] Also, the jock culture participants wear the shirts, the hats, the jackets with the team names and logos, and they have sports heroes, role models, and icons to copy and look up to. But what are these young students learning from jock culture? They are learning that the ethos of the jock says it is okay to beat up women, abuse drugs and alcohol, and to be involved in illegal gambling if one so desires. Athletes are routinely charged and convicted of these offenses. "In fact, beating up women seems to have become such a routine news event that there is even a Web site devoted to listing male athletes and coaches who have been accused of abusing women."[77] To male athletes, it would seem that women are the enemy.

Indeed, athletes train under a siege mentality. They are told that members of the opposing team are the enemy, and if they want to succeed in their chosen sport, they must be aggressive. When you stimulate aggression it is going to lead to violence. The question then is how do you contain it, and keep it in the game. Apparently, that is very difficult to do. In the 1990s, athletes are making more news with their off-field violence than their play in the games. This is particularly true in all of the major professional sports, but truer than ever in professional football. Indeed, football is the crown jewel of the jock culture, and it lives off the male ego and violence. It is a bastion of compulsive masculinity, and women are not welcomed within. Better yet, women are expected to service gridironers.

In the 1999 National Football League season, the most indelible image of professional football came from the police blotter. "A linebacker in Baltimore was arrested on a charge of punching a woman in a Maryland bar. A safety in Denver was arrested and charged with punching a topless dancer. Two Buffalo players were arrested in the sexual assault of an off-duty female police officers in a nightclub. On Long Island, two current and one former member of the (New York) Jets were charged with setting off a barroom brawl."[78] And it is interesting to note that the majority of these incidents occurred because women rejected the advances of the players. But the most astonishing report on the police blotter is that of Rae Carruth. He was a member of the Carolina football team, and he was accused of orchestrating the drive-by shooting of his pregnant girlfriend.[79] She later died from gunshot wounds. And let it be noted that this abusing, beating, brutalizing, and murdering of women is certainly uncivil, primal behavior.

In and of themselves, these violent incidents by players off the field are atrocious, but there is something else that makes them even more dangerous. The behavior is infectious. People connected to sports, the players, managers, coaches, sportswriters, and the fans are becoming disturbed by a trend endemic to the 1990s. There is a causal attitude regarding the decline of simple civility and sportsmanship in and around sports.[80] There have been a number of reasons given for this. Unruly fans who drink beer at sports events. A jock culture attitude that cannot tolerate losing without casting blame, and a bottom-line culture that almost revels in disrespect. And when Joe Torre, the manager of the New York Yankees was asked about what he thought of the deteriorating climate of sports, he said, "What's allowed (this) to happen, look at TV, go to the movies, listen to the radio. Everything 's down now; there's no barriers anymore."[81]

There is that trifecta: sports, the media, and aggressive behavior that leads to violence. And why is so much of the extracurricular violence by athletes directed at women? Historical coincidence may have something to do with it. Since the feminist movement began in the 1960s, women have been striving to reach social and sexual parity with men. Around the same time, because of television, sports were exploding into a megabucks business. Winning became the only thing that mattered. Players at all levels of sports were taught that you had to be aggressive if you were going to be winners. Males began to work harder to built up their bodies, even using illegal drugs like anabolic steroids to accelerate muscular development and to improve strength. However, at the same time all the exercise and bodybuilding stimulated the male sex hormone testosterone, and this stimulation can act like an aphrodisiac.[82]

The more aggressive the males became, the more their egos were in play, and the more desire they had to prove themselves sexually. But as women were seeking sexual parity, they in effect challenged the male's right to treat them as some kind of sex toy. For the male athlete, who relies upon his ego to have a respectable place in the jock culture, a female's challenge to his sexual needs cannot be tolerated. To let her get away with it would cause him to lose face with the boys. Also, players today tend to be bipolar personalities of a manic and depressive nature. It is all about winning and losing. You're up there when you win, and down there when you lose. And with a fifty-fifty chance of winning or losing in every contest, athletes are continually on edge and feeling frustrated, and they tend to take out their frustration on women if their sexual authority is challenged.

In recent years, it has not been only the jocks that have been feeling the pressure from the sexual demands of women and their call for complete social equality. The average guy is feeling uptight about it, too, and so are many women. The pressure has been on both genders since the feminist movement began, and the situation blew up in America's face in 1993 when Lorena Bobbitt cut her husband's penis off. This incident of male genital mutilation immediately became the subject of newspaper columns, editorial cartoons, and water-cooler conversations across the land. Men and women took sides, each supporting their sex. The real war that had been going on between the sexes was now fully exposed in the public's eye, and the Bobbitts had suddenly become symbols for their genders.[83]

Pro and anti-feminist debates spread quickly through the media. It seemed like every pundit and social commentator on the air or in the print media had something to say about this act of malicious wounding. The atmosphere was very similar to the start of the Women's Liberation movement when the women took on the likes of Freud, Spock, and Mailer. But this time the adversaries were even nastier to each other. The two perspectives could be summed up by the spokespersons for NOM, the National Organization For Men and NOW, the National Organization For Women. Sidney Stiller, the president of NOM said, "There's a very deep hatred of men in this country. When in the hell could you ever talk to a radical feminist? In this country, men have been put into a position where they're being blamed for every ill that society has."[84]

Patricia Ireland, the president of NOW, countered with the statement that in the past decade, violence against women had increased four times faster than any other crime. "There is not even a term for hatred of men. Does he, (Stiller), think the term 'misogyny', hatred of women, came from Fantasyland? I think it's a bum rap to say women, feminists in particular, hate men. On the contrary (it's the other way around)."[85]

Many women around the country sent letters of support to Lorena Bobbitt, and feminists were scuffling to find ways to justify her barbarous act. Some women even implied that it was payback time for all those slasher movies of the 1980s that filled Cineplexes with female blood. And still others suggested that Lorena Bobbitt was some kind of incarnate of "Thelma and Louise," come to life to strike a blow for womanhood in the battle between the sexes.[86] How strange. Women were justifying primitive cruelty in the name of feminism, women's sexual parity and liberation. They did not seem to understand that they were using the same kind of primal thinking that men used when they abused and brutalized women, and they did not realize it because they were blinded by their mania for sexual parity.

This mania for sexual equity, as the feminist Adele M. Stan calls it, has been driving women to distraction for over four decades now, and they are no closer to achieving it today than when they started. But, they still believe they will never be free of male dominance until they achieve it. Unfortunately, they are wrong. In a time of democracies and guaranteed political rights, women do not want their sense of free will compromised. These same women then mistakenly blame men for having power over them because they are dependent upon men to fulfill their needs for nesting, a relationship, and maternity. They find it difficult to admit that these needs are more biological than social because emotional deprivation has turned their heads around. The Lorena Bobbitt matter is a case in point. What is more ridiculously, primitive, and socially suicidal than to have men and women fighting one another over the bragging rights to an act that is unquestionably brutal and brutalizing?

This suggests that women are at a lost as to how they can reach their goal, and in seeking sexual parity, they have practically and philosophically disassembled themselves time and time again. When the Women's Liberation movement began, the activist women became attack dogs, going after the chauvinist pig with blood in their eyes. "The kingly male is growing pale; we're kicking the balls between his tail."[87] If they could humble men, then sexually they would ascend. It didn't happen. Next they became social debaters and pundits. They would explain away their sexual inequality, but that didn't work either. So, they organized and became political animals. They would fight for legislation that would give them social equality, and perhaps this would then lead to sexual equity. Uh, uh. It didn't come to past. The women then went back to a more aggressive posture. It was chichismo time. "Get your balls girls." There was the battered woman defense that justified the killing of a mate. But once again, this failed to get the women to where they wanted to go. Today the women's movement has splintered into factions: the moderates, the radical, the revisionists, and the protectionists' feminists. And none of them seem to know what to do to achieve their goal.

But the most disappointing move by women in their quest for sexual parity has to be their adoption of oral contraceptives: "the pill." Nothing says more about how badly women want sexual parity than their use of the pill. There is probably nothing on earth more sophisticated, beautiful, spiritual, and mysterious than a woman's body. The reproductive organs of the female are some of the most complex in the human body, and there is the important menstrual cycle that is delicately regulated by structures in the brain. We have a good idea how these elements work mechanically, but we don't fully understand how they influence emotions, or how emotions influence them. Innately, a woman's sexuality is what defines her, makes her the unique individual that she is. Therefore, it is beyond me to understand how women can take the pill and allow themselves to become pharmaceutical herd animals, kinship to a junkie. Why do they take drugs that interfere with the natural process of one of the most important functions of their body? Yes, I know what they say. It is all for the illusive sexual parity.

But what is even more difficult to understand, why would women take a drug that has serious health risks. Taking the pill can have the side effects of nausea, vomiting, retention of fluid, weight gain, increase vaginal discharge, headaches, tenderness of breasts, and dizziness. It may also increase blood pressure, cause blood clots, and cardiovascular problems in some women. The pill may cause psychological problems such as depression and irritability. Use of the pill is also linked to certain forms of cancer, especially breast cancer, and there is the possibility that use of the pill increases the risk of cervical cancer.[88] Why are women playing Russian roulette with their health? Once again, it would seem that they are searching for the illusive sexual parity.

Finally, it needs to be said that women should honestly face up to what they are doing. Taking a birth control pill is a wholly, unnatural act. It is an invasive action that prevents the female's body from functioning normally. Therefore, it is an action that is being taken against a woman's humanity. This is a form of violence. To be sure, all forms of contraceptive devices are subtle forms of violence against humanity. And be aware, the primal consciousness does work in covert, mysterious ways.

On the philosophical side, for decades now, the feminists have been doing an intellectual tap dance to prove their need and right to sexual equity; and most of the time, it is difficult to follow the music that accompanies the dance. In book after book, female writers and their commentators make extended arguments about subjects that relate only tangentially, if at all, to female sexual parity, but in the end the arguments tend to boil down to a call for just that. The reason: it is almost impossible for women to talk about their problems without talking about men; and once men are brought into the discussion, sex becomes the central issue. It is always the sexual relations, or the lack thereof, that establishes the basis for the relationship between a man and a woman. A few examples will suffice.

Betty Friedan is recognized as the mother and inspiration of the Women's Liberation movement. With her book, *The Feminine Mystique*, it is said that she comprehensively changed the world.[89] Friedan gave voice to the concerns of middle class women who had become unhappy with their lives as homemakers, but she was not out to change the world as such. She was much more circumspect than that. She was not a man-hating, radical feminist. Men did have a higher status in society, but they were not specifically responsible for the plight of women. Women should certainly have opportunities commensurate with all their talents, but she also thought that they should have good marriages, i.e. good sex, and loving families. This would make the lives of men and women happier and more fulfilling.[90] Now how is this going to happen? No doubt, only if there is sexual parity for women.

Germaine Greer, author of *The Female Eunuch*[91] in 1970, was hailed as a feminist revolutionary thinker, provocative, political, and daring. She used language to shock people and to question female sexual tradition. In her book she associates female passivity with castration. She said that this was authenticated by historical record, and that the behaviors of women themselves were partly responsible for the situation. Nevertheless, she championed women's sexual rights, and she openly aspired to male sexual freedom.[92] She said that sexual parity would require a change in social habits and attitudes, and she said this as an angry woman who disliked men. She thought of them as being cheats and parasites, but yet she wanted to be like them, in the sexual behavioral sense. Her personal struggles with her sexuality and parity, mirrors the feminist movement on this issue.

Natalie Angier wrote her book, *Woman*,[93] for the purpose of celebrating the female body, its anatomy, chemistry, evolution and laughter. She wants to explain what it means to be a woman, and she goes about doing it in a very lyrical, metaphorical fashion. With the eye of a medical professional, she makes a tour through the female body, starting with the primordial egg, leading up to the basis for biodiversity. The point is made that women are special because there is no maleness in their bodily or psychic structures. Moreover, there is a special kind of woman who has the androgen insensitivity syndrome, or A.I.S. These are superwomen who are self-possessed and self-defined, and they cannot be replicated. She chastises Darwin and his theory of evolution, and says that cultural evolution works better. "Culture has a way of becoming a habit, and habits have a way of getting physical, of feeding back on the loop and transforming the substrate." (This sounds very much like a formula for the mutation that may have occurred with AIDS.) In conclusion, if survival of the fittest is not good for us, then neither is man's sexual superiority from whence it comes. Parity is on the table again.

There is that long-standing question. What is more important in determining our sexuality? Is it culture or biology, nurture or nature? Helen Fisher tries to answer this question with her book, *The First Sex*.[94] She comes down on the side of nature, but then she goes on to say that evolution has produced different brain traits in men and women. Men maybe bigger and stronger, but women have the better brains. Women have many advantages over men. In particular, they are in closer touch with their emotions, and they are better performers in bed. Because of a woman's mental abilities, she sees them as more suited to the technological age of the twenty-first century. But her most important point is made on the feminization of sex. She brags that women can give themselves an organism by just thinking about sex. That is something that most men cannot do. This all leads her to say the following. "The 21st century may be the first in the modern era to see the sexes work and live as equals, the way men and women were designed to live."

In reviewing the book *Why Sex Matters*,[95] Colin McGinn, professor of philosophy at Rutgers University, made the following statement. "Bobbi S. Low, a professor of resource ecology at the University of Michigan, is interested in the differences between male and female animals, including humans, in the matter of sexual reproduction, what contributes to reproductive success in males and females? What reproductive strategies do males and females adopt, and why? Once again, the selfish gene is the puppeteer pulling the strings: we are all the Punch and Judy of our DNA, acting out our gene-transmitting roles. Both males and females act so as to maximize the number of their genes in later populations; the question is how differently they go about fulfilling this biological imperative."[96] If there is such a thing as a biological imperative, there can be no sexual parity as women speak of it. Professor McGinn goes on to say that the book is a sobering dip into the grim reality of sexual behavior, and it serves its disillusioning purpose. "Nature is indeed red in tooth and claw, and it is not much better where other organs are concerned." When it comes to survival, all things are primal.

The desire for sexual parity is not a primal force in women; nor is it indigenous in nature in anyway. Therefore, it is not important to human survival. The pressure women put on themselves, and men, to achieve it has caused more damage to our society than rampant violence, criminality, racism, or sexism. And the reason is, it brings into question what this society, and any society, is essentially all about, procreation and transmigration. We can play our social games of love and hate, compulsive masculinity and Women's Liberation. We can call ourselves Christians and Jews. But in the end, the spirit of life plays the same for all of us. We are born. We live. We die, and the spark that allowed us to live moves on. Against that continuum, all else is trivial.

Let it finally be said that there can never be sexual parity between a man and a woman. And to be sure, there has been too much gabbing about it already. All the talk has just caused the two sexes to become more psychically and emotionally separated. And this lack of parity has nothing to do with the fact that men are bigger, more aggressive, and cannot have babies. As well, it has nothing to do with evolutionary biology or culture either. The reason is simply this: one cannot have sexual parity with oneself.

At the very start of this book, I spoke of reincarnation. It is based on the idea that all human beings have souls, and that the soul is eternal. Souls are on earth for the purpose of spiritual development, and they come in two organic packages, male and female. Spiritual development of the soul is not complete until it has lived through the full human experience in both the male and female body. This means, in our reincarnating journey, all of us must live a life as a man and a life as a woman. Perhaps, we have had to live many lives as both sexes. Therefore the talk of inequalities between men and women is absolutely meaningless when seen from this spiritual point view. The so-called male superiority today will belong to the woman tomorrow, if she has not yet experienced it. As there is the belief that the soul has an existence, a life of its own independent of the body, then as such it is surely asexual. And as it was said, how does one have sexual parity with oneself?

Nevertheless, the question of sexual parity is nagging, divisive, and very disruptive to the relationships between men and women. From the bedroom to the boardroom, the temperature in one and the so-called harassment climate in the other, the question is driving an emotional wedge between the sexes. And what does this tell us? At the basic, primary level of their existence, women are not happy with themselves; and since they are the seeds of society, when they are unhappy it affects everything and everyone else in the system. They have not been living up to their spiritual promise as progenitors because they have betrothed themselves to a false God. We know where the fault lies, in socialization, and we know what it leads to, emotional deprivation. But, how do we correct this situation? The answer to that question is not absolutely clear; but in any case, the process may be already underway.

In his famous study of suicide, Emile Durkheim concluded that when a person feels he or she no longer fits in or belongs to their social group, the person would suffer anomie. Also, when society is going through a period of rapid change, this can produce a feeling of anomie in individuals. And too, the need to belong to the group, to someone, is so strong that a person, who is an outsider and lonely, might very well commit suicide. In particular, unmarried, lonely women are more likely to commit suicide than married women or those who are in a relationship. Since the start of the Women's Liberation Movement, women have been protesting and complaining that they did not have an equal place in society with the men. They saw themselves as exploited, alienated puppet people who were being totally manipulated by their male counterparts. It was a man's world, and they were just allowed to live in it.

In effect, women were saying they did not fit into the society, and it had to change. Then along came the sexual revolution, the various civil disobedience movements, the battle over legalized abortion, and the politics of sexual harassment. Social turmoil was everywhere, and women were at the center of it. Society was under great stress, and women had created a psychic storm for themselves. The social center of society was changing, and both men and women were experiencing a sense of anomie and increased pressure from feelings of alienation. It was difficult for people to keep up with the pace of the social change that was taking place, and when this was coupled with their need for fulfillment from society because of their emotional deprivation, it produced a hypnotic concentration and reliance on the secular world. There is a name for this kind of focus on the material world to the exclusion of aesthetic and non-corporeal reality. It is called dispiritualization,[97] and it occurs when people have a tendency to depreciate the spirit, or the sense of it, in order to meet societal obligations and expectations. This is the kind of social consciousness that helps to promote a narcissistical society.

Despiritualization can be understood as another name for socialization, and to speak of alienation is to speak of a lack of spiritual awareness and a lack of spiritual identity. Without a sense of spirit, we cannot live to our full potential, which means we are not allowing ourselves to be ourselves. Such a condition exacerbates our existing feelings of anomie, and that sense of imprisonment overwhelms us. This deepens our awareness that society is the destroyer of the human spirit, and it causes our minds to be engulfed in psychic pain. But society is not a separate entity. We are society. Therefore, we are our own tormentors, and it makes us feel like we do not belong to ourselves. Our innate being cries out for relief from the psychic pain and alienation that seems to be caused by our bodies. What can we do about it? We want to be free. We have to be free, and suicide seems the only answer.

However, our Judeo-Christian religion teaches us that life is sacred and precious, and God wants us to live it fully until He decides to call us to Heaven. But, we don't seem to believe that anymore because suicide is epidemic in our American society. Indeed, it has become essential to our way of life, and we are killing ourselves with pleasure, mental illness, anger, and fear. Count the ways. We are doing it with hedonism and promiscuity, depression and low spirits, aggression and violence, alienation and anomie. This tells us that individuals will kill themselves to escape the pain of living. Might they be heeding a call to return to the spirit world because society is not allowing them to be their innate selves? Self-murder would free the spirit. This is ultimately where emotional deprivation takes us, and how could it be otherwise. We are both the perpetrator and victim in this situation.

I have spoken of reincarnation that is based on the notion of the eternal spirit, the soul, but Americans in general do not believe in the soul. They believe in material reality, that people are their bodies, and that we are mortal, with one life to live. But, if that were so, why would we create a culture of suicide? Our belief in material reality suggests that we would want to live as long as we could, but we don't. We purposefully do many things that we know can shorten our lives. Why? It seems that we know the innate essence of ourselves can never die, and the awareness of it is embedded in our psyche. The truth of this idea can actually be seen in the kind of society we have. As the German philosopher Georg Hegel pointed out, we may create societies and call them objective realities, but intuitively, in our own unique way, we know that the human spirit is the cause of it all. This is to say, that in each one of us there is the awareness that we are spirit and the possessor of a soul. In fact, this is the only meaningful explanation for why we live such self-destructive, suicidal lives.

If we really believe that we are our bodies, and that the only existence we have had, or will ever have, is the life we are now living, then we would not have the power to commit suicide. We would not have the power to, in effect, completely destroy ourselves. Let us not forget that science, religion, and simply everything we know about the fundamental forces of the universe, from electromagnetism to gravity, tell us that matter, and this includes human beings, can not be destroyed. If this is true, how can we have the power to do the undoable? In fact, if this life were the only existence we will ever have, then we would have to live it forever. But, because we all eventually die, we have sufficient reason to believe that there is some kind of spirit reality waiting for us after physical death. The truth is our human essence will simply be transformed.

Because we tell ourselves that we are only our bodies and that we will only live once, we are in psychic pain. To think this way, we are in denial of the spirit, and that means we, as a matter of course, do harbor a death wish. When the widespread nature of the death wish becomes institutionalized, the psychic pain weighs heavy on the collective consciousness, and this gives unrestrained support to a culture of suicide. It means that our society does not function to sustain life, but it function to destroy it. And if this were not true, we would not be such aggressive, violent people who have lost respect for human life. And, as a nation, we would not live in a gun culture and be divided along racial, ethnic, religious, and class lines. And there would be no racism, prejudice and discrimination in America or war between the sexes. And, we would not have a capitalist economy that exists by exploiting the workers and consumers. And, we would not have a government that serves a rich, oligarchical elite instead of the people. And surely we would not have so many unresolved, resolvable social problems. All of this cannot be happenstance, and it isn't. Our society is one gigantic monster from the id, albeit one that functions from our collective unconsciousness.

To be sure, in modern times, the human condition, especially in America, is socially and psychically ambiguous. We created society to do well, but now it has turned against us. And the reason is obvious. Society, as we know it, has no soul. In the name of conformity, we used socialization to deny our innate selves, and this has left us without a sense of individuality and functioning as social minions. And yes, unfortunately, women are under the gun for this in large measure because nature has given them the responsibility to look after the emotional development of the child during that critical non-conscious period of his life. This is a job for each mother with her child, the baby she gave birth to. But the importance of mother has been replaced with the importance of society, and consequently, we must live with all the negativity that flows from emotional deprivation.

Is it any wonder then that we have returned to a primal state of consciousness? Contrary to what we have been told, we do not live in a civil society. Those armies of the night are leading us against ourselves, and we must struggle to survive in a hostile environment. It is a contest between the *I* and the *Me*, and we are losing the battle. Our innate selves have been forced to retreat to the unconscious, to the land of the id. In fact, like Jonah, we are living in the belly of the beast; but unlike Jonah, we cannot expect God to save us. We created the problem, and we have to come up with the solution. And time is running out. We live in a society that has nuclear weapons, an epidemic of AIDS, and a large population of people who have a death wish that is supported by a culture of suicide. Given this situation, it is not an exaggeration to say that the survival of our species may hang in the balance. We are rapidly reaching the point of no return, and I must remind the reader again. Nature knows when to give up. Let us hope that we have not reached that point just yet. Only time will tell.

INDEX

[1] John Dollar, Caste and Class in a Southern Town, 3rd ed. (Garden City, New York, Doubleday Anchor Books, 1957).

[2] Marshall McLuhan, *Understanding Media: The Extensions of Man*, (New York, McGraw-Hill, 1964).

[3] Philip Selznick, *TVA And The Grass Roots* (New York, Harper Torchbook, Harper & Row Publishers, 1966).

[4] George Herbert Mead, Mind, Self and Society (Chicago, University of Chicago Press, 1934).

[5] Stanford M. Lyman, *The Black American in Sociological Thought* (New York, G.P. Putnam's Sons, 1972).

[6] Gordon Allport, *The Nature of Prejudice* (Garden City, New York, Doubleday Anchor, 1958).

[7] Talcott Parsons, "Certain Primary Sources of Aggression in the Social Structure of the Essays in Sociological Theory (New York, Dell, 1963).

[8] Betty Friedan, *The Feminine Mystique* (New York, Free Press, 1964).

[9] Karl Marx and Friedrich Engels, *Communist Manifesto* (Baltimore: Penquin Books, 1969).

[10] Emile Durkheim, *The Division of Labor in Society* (New York, Free Press, 1964).

[11] Robert K. Merton, "The Self-Fulfilling Prophecy," *Antioch Review*, 8:2 (Summer, 1948).

[12] Erving Goffman, *The Presentation of Self in Everyday Life* (Garden City, New York, Doubleday, Anchor, 1959).

[13] Gregory Boyington, *BAA BAA Black Sheep* (New York, G.P. Putnam's Sons, 1958).

[14] Durkheim, *Suicide*, (New York, Free Press, 1951), pp.214-40.

[15] Emile Durkheim, *Suicide*, p.210.

[16] Durkheim, *Suicide*, pp.241-76.

[17] L. Alan Sroufe, Robert G. Cooper, G.B. DeHart, *Child Development* (New York, McGraw-Hill, 1992), pp.22-3.

[18] Films For The Humanities & Science, "Two Views on Feminism," (Princeton, NJ, CPC 244).

[19] John L. Cooper, *The Seventh Decade* (Dubuque, Iowa, Kendall/Hunt Co., 1980).

[20] Ibid., p,11.

[21] Ibid., p.12.

[22] *The New York Times*, "In a Changing Society, Manners Change Too," March 14, 1975, p.44.

[23] Cooper, p.14.

[24] R.D. Laing, *The Politics of Experience* (New York, Ballantine Books, 1968).

[25] *Science News*, Robert Trotter, "Sexism is Depressing," September 13, 1975.

[26] Cooper, p.9.

[27] S.A. Rathus, J.S. Nevid, L. Fichner-Rathus, *Essentials of Human Sexualiity* (Needham Heights, MA, Allyn & Bacon, 1998), p.190.

[28] Cooper, p.19.

[29] Kate Millett, *Bernard Alumanae*, Spring, 1970, p.28.

[30] *The New York Times*, "Hers," December 1, 1977, p.C2.

[31] Cooper, p.19.

[32] William F. Buckley, "Women in Combat? Its All Really Just A Bit Too Much," *New York Post*, March 14, 1978, p.31.

[33] *New York Post*, "Give Thought to The Poor Male Psyche," November 30, 1977, p.32.

[34] *The New York Times*, "The Equal Rights Amendment: Missouri is The Target Now," February 7, 1975, p.1.

[35] Robert Michels, *Political Parties* (New York: Free Press, 1966).

36 Rathus, Nevid, Fichner-Rathus, p.189.

37 A commercial advertisement for the Nike Sneaker Company that ran on network television and Cable TV, during the 1999 baseball season.

38 David N. Suggs & Andrew W. Miracle, *Culture And Human Sexuality* (Pacific Grove, CA, Brooks/Cole Publishing, Co., 1993).

39 Ibid., p.61.

40 Wendy A. Shalit, *A Return To Modesty* (New York, The Free Press, 1998).

41 Robert Crooks and Karla Baur, *Our Sexuality* (Pacific Grove, CA., Brooks/Cole Publishing Co., 1999), p.514.

42 Rathus, Nevid, Fichner-Rathus, P.7.

43 Crooks and Baur, pp.214-15.

44 Ibid., p.61.

45 Rathus, Nevid, Fichner-Rathus, p.90.

46 Crooks and Baur, p.267.

47 Max Weber, *The Theory of Social and Economic Organization* (New Yortk, Oxford University Press, 1947).

48 Crooks and Baur, p.267.

49 John Allen Lee, Love-styles, Sternberg & Barnes. *The Psychology of Love*, pp.38-67, New Haven: Yale University Press, 1988).

50 Gordon, S., & Snyder, C.W., *Personal issues in human sexuality: A guidebook for better sexual health* (Boston, Allyn & Bacon, 1989).

51 Alfred Kinsey, W. Pomeroy I P. Gebhard, *Sexual Behavior in the Human Male* (Philadelphia, Saunders, 1948).

52 William Masters & Virginia Johnson, *Human Sexual Reponse* (Boston, Little Brown, 1966).

53 Crooks and Baur, pp.181-2.

54 Cooper, p.115.

55 *New York Post*, "Procreation: For Them, I Rite Says Its Wrong," August 2, 1974, p.18.

56 *Daily News*, "Sex-play All The Way And No Kidding: Prof.," November 7, 1974, p.4.

57 *The Miami Herald*, "Surgeon General: Suicide a serious national threat," July 29, 1974, p.1.

58 *The Miami Herald*. "A Public Health Crisis," July 29, 1999, p.16A.

59 *The New York Times*, "Colorado Fuels U.S. Debate over Use of Behavioral Drugs," 1998, p,1.

60 *The New York Times*, "Hardes Habit to Break: Memories of the High," October 27, 1998, p.1.

61 Ibid., p.1.

62 *New York*, "Why New York Kids Say It Couldn't Happen Here," May 17, 1999, p.32.

63 *New York*, "Why Your Kids Know More About the Future Than You Do," May 17, 1999, p.30.

64 Ibid., p.30

65 *The New York Times*, "A New Variety of Flower Child In Full Bloom," July 21, 1999, p.E1.

66 *New York*, "The Mix Master," May 10, 1999, pp.20-29.

67 *The New York Times*, "Gangster Rappers: The Lives, The Lyrics," November 28, 1993, Section 4, p.3.

68 *The New York Times*, "Many Researchers Say Link Is Already Clear on Media and Youth Violence," May 9, 1999, p.27.

69 Ibid., p.27.

70 Ibid., p.27.

71 *New York*, "Why your Kids Know More About The Future Than You Do," p.30.

72 *The New York Times*, "Deeper Truths Sought in Violence by Youths," May 9, 1999.

73 *New School University Observer*, "Screen Violence is debated," October, 1999, p.5.

74 Ibid., p.5.

75 Ibid., p.5.

76 Wolff, p.85.

[77] *The New York Times*, "This Year, Sports Went Over The Edge," December 26, 1999, p.10.

[78] *The New York Times*, "Stains From The Police Blotter Leave N.F.L. Embarassed," January 9, 2000, p.1.

[79] Ibid., p.1.

[80] *The New York Times*, "Basic Civility Is The Loser Every Time," October 19, 1999, p.D1.

[81] Ibid., p.D1

[82] Rathus, Nevid, Fichner-Rathus, pp.235-38.

[83] *The Oregonian*, "Bobbitt Case Defines State of The Sexes," January 13, 1994, p.A3.

[84] Ibid., p.A3.

[85] Ibid., p.A3.

[86] *The Oregonian*, "War between the sexes a misnomer for women who fight past abuses," January 12, 1994, p.A3.

[87] Cooper, p.1.

[88] Rathus, Nevid, Fichner-Rathus, pp.235-38.

[89] *The New York Times Book Review*, "Outside Agitator," May 9, 1999, p.18.

[90] Daniel Horowitz, *Betty Friedan* (Amherst: University of Masachusetts Press, 1999).

[91] Germaine Greer, *The Female Eunuch* (New York, 1970).

[92] Christine Wallace, *Germaine Greer* (New York, Faber & Faber, 1999).

[93] Natalie Angier, *Woman* (New York, Houghton Mifflin Company, 1999).

[94] Helen Fisher, *The First Sex* (New York, Random House, 1999).

[95] Bobbi S. Low, *Why Sex Matters* (Princeton, NJ., Princeton University Press, 1999).

[96] Collin McGinn, "Some Guys Have All the Luck," *New York Times Book Review*, January 9, 2000, p.12.

[97] John L. Cooper, *Spiritlock* (New York, Unpublished manuscript, 1993), p.10.

CPSIA information can be obtained at www.ICGtesting.com
Printed in the USA
BVOW041928010812

296830BV00002B/3/A